Devolution
and the UK Economy

Devolution and the UK Economy

Edited by
David Bailey and Leslie Budd

ROWMAN &
LITTLEFIELD
INTERNATIONAL

London • New York

Published by Rowman & Littlefield International Ltd
Unit A, Whitacre Mews, 26-34 Stannary Street, London SE11 4AB
www.rowmaninternational.com

Rowman & Littlefield International Ltd. is an affiliate of Rowman & Littlefield
4501 Forbes Boulevard, Suite 200, Lanham, Maryland 20706, USA
With additional offices in Boulder, New York, Toronto (Canada), and Plymouth (UK)
www.rowman.com

British Library Cataloguing in Publication Data
A catalogue record for this book is available from the British Library

ISBN: HB 978-1-7834-8630-4
       PB 978-1-7834-8631-1

Library of Congress Cataloging-in-Publication Data
Names: Bailey, David, 1966- editor. | Budd, Leslie, 1949- editor.
Title: Devolution and the UK economy / edited by David Bailey and Leslie Budd.
Description: London ; New York : Rowman & Littlefield International, [2016] | Includes
    bibliographical references and index.
Identifiers: LCCN 2015037398| ISBN 9781783486304 (cloth : alk. paper) | ISBN
    9781783486311 (pbk. : alk. paper) | ISBN 9781783486328 (electronic)
Subjects: LCSH: Decentralization in government--Economic aspects--Great Britain. |
    Economic development--Great Britain. | Regional planning--Great Britain.
Classification: LCC JN329.D43 D475 2016 | DDC 330.941--dc23 LC record available at
    http://lccn.loc.gov/2015037398

♾™ The paper used in this publication meets the minimum requirements of American
National Standard for Information Sciences—Permanence of Paper for Printed Library
Materials, ANSI/NISO Z39.48-1992.

Printed in the United States of America

We are grateful to Ken Gibb and John Parr for proposing the Urban and Regional Economics Seminar Group (URESG) Workshop that was held at the Open University in Scotland in early 2015 on which this volume is based. Without the financial support of Policy Scotland and the Centre for Innovation Knowledge and Development (IKD), this workshop and hence volume would not have been possible.

We extend our thanks to the editorial directors Sarah Campbell and Sinead Murphy at Rowman and Littlefield International for their support and forbearance, as well as to the former editorial director Alison Howson.

The figures in the chapter by Bailey et al. were devised by Paul Hildreth and some originally appeared in HM Treasury et al. (2006).

Leslie Budd is also grateful to Glen Barklie at FDI Intelligence, Belfast Telegraph, Phillipa Briggs, Institute for Fiscal Studies, KPMG, Stephen Roper and Nichola Shaxson for permission in reproducing figures and tables in his chapter. Gratitude is also due to Siv Vangen and colleagues in the Department for Public Leadership and Social Enterprise (PuLSE) at the Open University for their collegiality.

Finally without the continuing support of Vanessa Davidson, and Mikey Bailey's patience, none of this would be possible.

Contents

Introduction

Devolution and the UK Economy

David Bailey and Leslie Budd

PREAMBLE

Charles Dickens and George Orwell wrote tales of two cities whose historical relationships have been the 'best of times and the worst of times'. In respect of their governmental systems, they have both been 'down and out' in the degree of exercising centralized power over the national territories they govern. In recent times, policy makers and commentators have looked enviously across the Channel as France introduced a comprehensive system of decentralization in the 1980s. The English journey seems to have started to reach a similar point, following the rise of nationalist sentiment in Scotland. This follows on from the Referendum held in September 2014 on independence for Scotland that resulted in a vote to remain within the United Kingdom. In the lead-up to this event, it was observed that increased political discourse and greater engagement within and among local communities had occurred. The result did not dampen pro- independence and nationalist spirits. Indeed, what can be called the 'Scottish question' has had a direct impact on the outcome of the UK General Election of May 2015 in the election of fifty Members of Parliament representing the Scottish Nationalist Party (SNP).

The ramifications for the rest of the United Kingdom are currently being played out but have stimulated formal and informal proposals for some form of a new constitutional settlement. In particular, the pressure for more fiscal devolution and other economic powers in the devolved nations has increased demands for greater economic decentralization in the cities and regions of England (*The Guardian*, 2014; *The Economist*, 2014a and 2014b). The support for a Northern Economic Powerhouse (centred on the Manchester metropolitan areas) by the Chancellor of the Exchequer is one such example. Furthermore, calls by the political leadership of the 'core cities' of England

1

outside of London for a more spatially balanced economy in the United Kingdom reinforce demands for change. Of course, debates around devolution in England go back many years, but the referendum debate over Scottish independence has re-energized them, and they have found fertile ground given the limited role and financial autonomy of local government in the United Kingdom in international comparison (Blöchliger and King, 2006; Chapain and Renney, 2011; Wilcox, 2016). Greater powers for the Scottish government and devolution to city regions in England was a major element of the Queen's Speech 2015, and at the time of writing, the Devolution Bill for England is being debated and amended in Parliament. On the one hand, this process so far has disappointed many proponents of stronger devolution, with conditions for combined authorities and elected mayors as conditions for devolving powers. Here, there are concerns that the process of devolution to city regions through city deals and combined authorities is top-down and heavily prescribed by Whitehall as to what can be included in each individual city deal, with the danger of fragmentation and 'divide and rule' (Hambleton, 2014) leading to a questioning of the actual process of city-region devolution (Diamond and Carr-West, 2015). On the other hand, others have argued more positively that once the 'genie is out of the bottle', the tide of change may not be easily staunched. What is apparent from the debate is that the United Kingdom lacks a coherent and developed system of centre–periphery governmental relations in which a more balanced economy can be sustained.

The structure of the book picks up on the expert testimony of the contributors addressing particular issues across devolution debates in all four countries of the United Kingdom. The authors of the collection are thus in a position to provide an informed, insightful and intelligent analysis of the components of a wider and deeper narrative for a larger audience. The disciplinary basis of this collection is that of urban and regional economics, but it draws upon political, social and territorial implications and analysis where appropriate. The theoretical framework draws upon a combination of fiscal federalism and agglomeration economies in order to investigate the restructuring and reorganization of economic territories. The dominance of these theoretical perspectives informed the debates about the consequences of an independent Scotland as they focused on economic benefits and costs. Most of these are framed in terms of fiscal reform, including tax revenues (particularly from North Sea oil); choice of currency; and, a more equitable and balanced economic development path. But as two chapters in this collection show, the implications for housing and welfare are just as profound. Balance in this instance is between both industrial sectors and spatial entities.

Evidence from federal governmental systems suggests that economic welfare (the term that economists use to encompass the creation and distribution of the social product) is enhanced within them. The International Monetary

Fund (IMF) and the Organisation for Economic Cooperation and Development (OECD, 2015) link this evidence to the contribution of equality to economic growth as set out in recent work by the OECD (Cingano, 2014). In the United Kingdom, inequality of income and wealth has a marked spatial dimension (Dorling and Ballas, 2008). This evidence forms part of a strengthening narrative of the increasing utility of devolved and federalized economic development powers. Following increased decentralization of some of these powers and new forms of economic governance in London, Northern Ireland, Scotland and Wales, the pressure for more devolution in England has strengthened.

Much of this pressure is based upon an assumption of the unalloyed economic benefits of agglomeration. Perhaps the most vocal supporter of this view is the City Growth Commission led by former Chief Economist of Goldman Sachs, Jim O'Neil. The Commission's uncritical assumption is expressed in its final report, *Unleashing Metro Growth*, as follows:

> Agglomeration effects are crucial; sustainable UK growth will rely increasingly on our major cities doing for the North West, North East, West Yorkshire and Midlands – for example – what London does for the South East – driving investment, productivity and growth.

The evidence for this assertion notwithstanding, agglomeration effects of urban areas also generate diseconomies. There is also the issue of what type of agglomeration economy is dominant and what constitutes the economic boundaries of any agglomeration. The latter is pertinent to the insider-outsider problem in respect of the rural hinterlands of urban economies: a universal problem.

What is apparent in the UK experience of asymmetrical devolution is that many of the complex issues surrounding decentralized economic governance are not going to be addressed through simple expedients. The pertinent question is what the appropriate institutional logics and formal policy bailiwicks underpinning a new constitutional settlement should be. In other words, what are the new governmental powers and accompanying forms of governance needed to achieve a more economically and spatially balanced economy?

THE CONTEXT OF REGIONALISM

We have so far concentrated on developing a narrative on economic decentralization; particularly the role of agglomeration economies in creating and sustaining devolved urban and regional economies. There is an important subtext to promoting these economies that is sometimes overlooked: the distribution of intra-regional devolved economic powers and responsibilities, as well as the important questions of what are the boundaries of any new territorial entities and spillovers between them. In the United Kingdom, the region is a geographical territory and the current regional divisions are partly a combination of the Standard Regions and the administrative distribution as represented by the former Government Offices for the Regions.

Many of the proposals for new city regions or what should constitute reformed Local Enterprise Partnerships (LEPs), for example, are based upon different conceptions, of which the three traditional ones are the following:

1. Functional regional economies;
2. Travel-to-work areas;
3. Labour market areas.

The role of possibly restructured and more empowered LEPs as the basis of re-energized regional devolution has tended to have been overlooked in debates about revived regional governance. But, as the chapter by David Bailey, Paul Hidreth and Lisa De Propris shows, this is an issue that is unlikely to go away (Bailey, Hidreth and De Propris 2016). Elsewhere in the world, growth poles have been created as new devolved and decentralized economic territories. China provides an example of this form of development. In examining the particular issues in the collection, readers will be able to draw their own conclusions on what is most appropriate in a UK setting and elsewhere.

In the rest of the European Union (EU), we have seen a revival of interest in Jaqcues Delors's concept of *A Europe of the Regions* and sustaining the principle of subsidiarity. The ten-year strategy *Europe2020* focuses on economic efficiency but has now been more strongly balanced by the 5th and 6th Cohesion Reports that promote economic and spatial equality. In developing economic strategies to manage the consequences of the Global Financial Crisis (GFC), this balance has become crucial in the EU's cities and regions. The EU's influence on recent regional developments in the United Kingdom was manifested in the signing of the Maastricht Treaty in 1992. This outcome encouraged the creation of regional boundaries for selection of members for the Committee of the Regions of the European Union: Wales, Scotland and Northern Ireland had each constituted a region, but England represents such a large proportion of the population of the United Kingdom that further division was thought necessary. This led to the creation of the nine devolved English regions from 1994 until 2011. The rejection of an elected assembly in the North-East in the 2004 referendum put paid to the project that became known as 'asymmetrical regionalism', referring to the Spanish experience.

Since the election of the Coalition government in 2010, the regions as centres of devolved power have been scrapped. The current regional landscape consists of the city regions, principally based upon the old metropolitan authorities, and greater, albeit variable, powers vested in local authorities. However, many of the policy levers to retain territorial balance within the United Kingdom have been removed or their effectiveness undermined. A particular challenge for British economic policy makers has been managing increased centralization against the backdrop of the economic and territorial impact of austerity in the wake of the Global Financial Crisis (GFC).

As the most centralized state in Europe, the United Kingdom clearly has a variable relationship with devolution and federalism. Devolution in London, Northern Ireland, Scotland and Wales has created demands for a revival of multilevel and multilateral forms of government in order to rebalance the sectoral and territorial composition of the economy. By focusing on a number of key issues in the light of a post-Referendum Scotland, the composition of this collection provides a means by which to read current debates in the context of the history of regionalism and its economic effects, many of which are currently uninformed. Despite the a-historical claims to overcentralization, these tensions go back centuries.

This book evolved from the joint *Devolution and Federalism in a post-Referendum UK* workshop held by the Urban and Regional Economic Seminar Group (URESG), Policy Scotland and the Centre for Innovation, Knowledge and Development (IKD) at the Open University in early 2015. Although regional and urban economics were central to the narrative of the workshop, it took a multidisciplinary approach to what lessons could be learned and applied from the Scottish model and its understanding in a wider European context. In doing so, the book seeks to reach out to a wider audience including final year undergraduates; post-graduates and academics in the social sciences and related area studies; policy makers in central and local government and associated agencies; learned societies; think tanks and campaign groups; as well as practitioners in different localities.

THE NARRATIVE OF 'FROM THE SCOTTISH QUESTION TO THE SCOTTISH MODEL FOR THE UK'

The book is divided into two parts. The first, *Lessons from a Post-Referendum Scotland*, sets out the context in which pressure for further devolution has intensified in the other nations of the United Kingdom. It begins with Jim Gallagher's chapter *Where Next for Scotland and the UK?* (chapter 1) in which he states that the Scottish people appear to express two contradictory wishes: first, voting to remain in the Union in the Referendum whilst electing the Scottish National Party (SNP) to overwhelmingly represent them in the General Election. As a consequence, there is a significant constitutional challenge for the relationship between Scotland and the rest of the United Kingdom. As Gallagher points out:

> The discussion on Scotland's constitutional position can no longer be construed merely as what concessions Scottish politicians can wrest from reluctant UK ministers: this will be a negotiation with a mobilized English opinion, which requires a serious look at the UK territorial constitution as a whole. (Gallagher, 2015)

The chapter reviews the constitutional and related issues in the lead-up to the Referendum, in particular the crucial issue of fiscal unions within a currency union and federal systems in general. In the former case, the role and future of the Barnett Formula for redistributing resources to the devolved nations is particularly relevant. As noted by Gallagher, the Smith Commission established to review these issues came up with more radical solutions than anticipated in the pre-Referendum environment. The crucial point is the scale and degree of financial responsibility between the possible rock of Devo-Max (maximum devolution) and independence. This provides the context in which Gallagher proposes a set of constitutional changes for the whole of the United Kingdom. It also provides the basis of the analytical narrative in David Bell's chapter *The Aftermath of the Scottish Referendum: A New Fiscal Settlement for the UK?*

Bell's chapter (chapter 2) starts by giving a critical insight into fiscal federalism, a subject that often seems far from debates in the United Kingdom, and is one many commentators are ignorant of. Bell does a service by providing an internationally comparative analysis of fiscally decentralized nations from which Scotland and the rest of the United Kingdom can learn. The main section of the chapter sets out the complex details of developments in Scotland, particularly the ability to set the Scottish Rate of Income Tax (SRIT). In spite of various claims, Scotland will not be able to create a more 'progressive' system of income tax as SRIT accounts for only 10 pence in the pound, with HM Treasury still controlling marginal rates of taxation in the United Kingdom. If the Scotland Bill of 2015–2016 is passed, the Scottish Government will control 41% of the revenues raised within its borders. Of more significance, as Bell points out, is the ending of the UK postwar consensus on the universalism of social welfare, with the devolution of associated expenditure. What is crucial in this regard is this:

> The issue of transfers between the Scottish and UK Governments is critical to understanding the incentives – risks and rewards – that follow from the substantial increase in revenue raising and spending powers for the Scottish Government that is currently in train. This argument further generalizes to the Welsh and Northern Irish cases. (Bell, 2015)

The question and ramifications of full fiscal autonomy are central to the debates about devolution in Scotland. Bell notes that it is rare in sub-national territories and draws on the cases of Basque Country and Navarra in Spain that are most frequently cited. He provides a comparison with Scotland and concludes that it would be premature for Scotland to be given this responsibility. The reliance on North Sea oil and gas revenues to underpin full fiscal autonomy is too uncertain a prospect. The chapter concludes that prospects for fiscal federalism in the United Kingdom are poor given the current inchoate and incoherent legal and institutional structures. For the devolved nations, the move towards symmetrical devolution of some taxation and spending powers is likely to make the whole UK system more complex with intra-territorial conflicts more difficult to resolve.

How changes in the environment in which devolving and federalizing pressures are increasing in particular, Scottish domains, is the subject of the next two chapters. In chapter 3, entitled *Local Tax Reform in Scotland: Fiscal Decentralisation or Political Solution?*, Kenneth Gibb and Linda Christie examine local government finance reforms following the establishment of the Commission on Local Taxation Reform (CLTR). The CLTR was established to ascertain and assess alternatives to the Council Tax in order to create a fairer system of local taxation. The main points for consideration are: the impacts on individuals, households and inequalities in income and wealth; wider impacts, including housing market and land use; administration & collection, including transition and subsequent operation; potential timetables for transition, given the 2017 Local Government elections; impacts on supporting local democracy, that is, financial accountability and, autonomy; and, the revenue raising capacity of alternatives.

This chapter addresses a number of issues in the context of CLTR's work, with firstly an overview of how council taxes works and the problems that arise. The authors also examine the role of council tax in a number of contexts in recent Scottish history. Secondly, it offers an assessment of the five types of local taxation that have been advanced as the basis of strategic reform, as well as their alternatives. The substantive section draws on a recent international evidence review of local taxation by the authors for the CLTR. In particular, it looks at experience of reform elsewhere. The final section asks whether given the limited remit of the CLTR what are the most conceivable or wanted outcomes. Moreover, what are likely consequences that may emerge and how these outcomes could become something more long-lasting. Gibb and Christie conclude that political stasis may overcome the CLTR's findings and the possibility of lasting reforms being implemented. They are clearly correct in issuing this warning, but one can only hope that the transformation in the political landscape and its future economic evolution provide a sufficient bulwark.

In his chapter David Bell points that greater control over welfare expenditure is just as important an element of devolution in Scotland. Gerry Mooney takes up this issue in his chapter 4, *Questions of Social Justice and Social Welfare in Post-Independence Referendum Scotland.* His premise is that the conventional wisdom about the Referendum and the implications of the 2015 General election has to be questioned. The central narrative is based upon and assessment of the main social policy issues during the Independence Referendum campaign, between 2012 and 2014. It stresses the significance in which social justice issues were almost inseparable from the wider questions of the direction of constitutional status in Scotland. Mooney argues that such interconnections have continued to shape the political climate in the period after the 2014 Referendum and they also influenced the outcome of the 2015 General Election. This is deemed to be the case not only in Scotland but also in ways that have a wider UK resonance and importance. The United Kingdom is a multilateral and pluri-national collection of territories whose coming together and separation in history has often been a matter of accident rather than design. Mooney uses this quote to explain the current position and challenge:

> Nobody asked to design a political system for Britain would ever propose the one it has. The one-and-a-bit large islands (and many smaller ones) that The Economist calls home are a hotchpotch of parliamentary systems, unevenly distributed powers and constitutional uncertainties. The set-up is as uneven as Britain's history is eventful, which is no coincidence: the causes of the mess date back centuries. The latest upheaval – Scotland's referendum on independence, which ended with a "no" vote on September 18 – has made things untidier still. (*The Economist*, September 27, 2014)

He further explains how social justice has been central to the devolution narrative since the start of the devolution process in 1999. However, this path has led to increasing pressure on the UK Welfare State and divergences in social policy between and within the component territories of the United Kingdom. The complication for Scotland is that many of the supporters of independence were less concerned with nationalist sentiment, rather expressing support for changes to promote and reinforce social justice. This appears to resonate with demands for local control in other parts of the United Kingdom, in an environment in which austerity appears to have become institutionalized in the whole of the EU. Despite claims to the contrary, Mooney argues that Scotland exceptionalism in regard to progressive and pro-welfare values does not stand up to scrutiny and evidence. Similarly, politics and its economic consequences in Scotland are not driven by concerns over 'national identity' as the mainstream Westminster political parties assume. Rather it is the question of how austerity, inequality and poverty remain issues to be combated for a devolved nation, whose identity is not in question.

We now turn to part 2 of the book entitled, *Lagging or Leading in the Rest of the UK*. The question posed here is set up a tension between the initial narrative of this collection. That is, that the Scottish question has kidnapped the devolution agenda but the other nations and regions are advancing their own and sometimes unique causes. Identity is clearly necessary to the critical discourses they are seeking to establish. Administrative and organizational change, accompanied by limited decentralized instruments, will be ultimately insufficient to contain these discourses.

The question of identity and its historical formation is particularly pertinent in Northern Ireland. As a post-conflict territory there remains a strong economic legacy of relative under-performance, poverty and the challenge of managing a welfare system that has been under strain. It is against this backdrop that Leslie Budd explores *The Economic Challenges and Opportunities for Devolved Taxation in Northern Ireland* in chapter 5. In 2018, the Northern Ireland Executive will be able to set its own rate of Corporation Tax (CT). The logic is to attract increased Foreign Direct Investment (FDI) following the apparent success of a low business tax regime in the Republic of Ireland (ROI). This logic rests upon a discourse that the success of the 'Celtic Tiger' is almost entirely due to this regime. Yet theory, evidence and data suggest that low CT rates are not high on the list of the locational factors that attract Multi-National Corporations (MNCs) to particular economic territories. Budd draws on international evidence to substantiate this conclusion.

In regard to Northern Ireland, setting its rate of CT as its southern neighbour has done at 12.5% harmonizes the effective exchange rate; currency differences notwithstanding. In this context, greater cross-border economic cooperation, a particular innovation since the Good Friday Agreement, creates a different relationship between CT rates and FDI. As Budd argues, the devolution of powers to set the CT rate should be viewed as just one instrument of a new regional industrial policy. In particular, one in which investment allowances and credits are targeted at key sectors, which attract the most FDI. In Northern Ireland these are known as the so-called MATRIX advanced sectors in which the province has an internationally competitive advantage. Moreover, connecting these sectors into Global Value Chains (GVCs) provides a substantial basis for FDI to increase output and employment. His overall point is to think more holistically in terms of industrial policy at the regional level.

The pressures to harmonize business taxation and end abuses in the EU, notwithstanding, the pursuit of the doctrine of lower corporation tax equals increased FDI is a race to the bottom, Budd argues. In the case of Northern Ireland the reduction in central government grant is estimated at between £300m and £700m, as a result of this tax change. In the absence of transitional funding arrangements, the net effect will be negative. Without this form of conditionality mentioned above and integrating this change into a regional industrial policy in order to stimulate targeted sectors, Northern Ireland's undeniable economic potential may be undermined.

In chapter 6, entitled *Commanding Economic Heights?* Rebecca Rumbul considers the economic future of Wales through a constitutional lens. She argues that the asymmetrical nature of UK decentralization, the imbalance in the political interests of the Westminster parties between Wales, Scotland and Northern Ireland, and the constitutional uncertainty surrounding a European Union (EU) referendum, form some of the most considerable influences upon Wales' economic future. She argues that without genuine and quality reform of the fiscal and legislative structures in Wales, and without financial stability, Welsh politicians and policy makers will continue in their attempts to build Welsh policy using outdated tools. This will likely be to the detriment of the future growth and prosperity of the Welsh economy. In particular, she argues that the quality of the Welsh devolution dispensation has been poor, and the incremental tweaks to the Government of Wales Acts 1998 and 2006 did very little to provide a more stable settlement. The bilateral focus of the UK devolution debate, driven by a more engaged, united and vocal Scottish public, had the effect of sidelining Welsh interests and delaying meaningful change. She argues that while the Wales Bill 2014 and the legislation to implement the St David's Day Agreement may well address some of the structural issues that have thus far limited Wales' economic potential. Without fiscal responsibility, and against a backdrop of constitutional change across the United Kingdom involving devolution elsewhere and uncertainty in Europe, it seems likely that Welsh devolution will limp along in the same neglected fashion it has for the last fifteen years.

In chapter 7, entitled *Securing Economic and Social Success: The Local Double Dividend*, Neil McInroy and Matthew Jackson shift attention to how the problems of inequality and poverty might be solved through further devolution in England. The push for devolution of powers and resources to local government and cities represents an opportunity to combine economic and social growth strategies, they argue. For this to happen, there needs to be a change in thinking in both Whitehall and the town hall to deliver more joined up, place-based policy making (in line with Bailey et al. in this volume). To realize a social return from growth, they argue, demands a more deliberative and conscious set of inclusive policies which support business growth at the same time as building enduring social and civic institutions and maximizing opportunities from collaboration and social networks.

The authors promote the notion of a 'double dividend' built on both economic and social success. Rather than viewing local communities as mere downstream recipients of economic success (as beneficiaries of actions designed to deliver 'trickle down' growth), they should be seen as active upstream parts of a system that creates success in the first place. Social success, in the form of more jobs, decent wages, rising living standards and civic pride, is thus less a mere consequence of economic development action, and more something which feeds into and sustains a virtuous local economy for all. The chapter documents the failings of past policies and makes the case for an alternative approach to achieving social and economic benefit based on what works locally. It highlights some of the opportunities and risks offered by devolution, and makes the case for social capital and networks as economic engines, promoting business citizenship, maximizing the power of procurement, developing local labour markets, community wealth building, and developing the role of anchor institutions.

Taking a similarly 'place based' approach, in chapter 8 (entitled *Beyond 'Localism'? Place-Based Industrial and Regional Policy and the 'Missing Space' in England*), David Bailey, Paul Hildreth and Lisa De Propris address the question: what might a genuinely 'place-based' strategy mean for industrial and regional policy in England? The chapter first discusses the policy model in the UK context before drawing on the international literature to outline the basic foundations of 'place-based' policy approaches, drawing out two key features, particularly as they relate to 'institutions' and to 'knowledge'. After examining key concepts in 'place-based' policy debates, such as 'communities of interest' and 'capital city and local elites', it tries to interpret them in an English policy context. The chapter then moves on to discuss a 'place-based' approach towards an understanding of the role of knowledge, linked to debates around 'smart specialisation' and contemporary industrial policy. In doing so, it shows why there is an important 'missing space' or gap in the 2010–2015 government's localism and local growth agenda between the 'national' and the 'local' and how that space might be filled through appropriate institutions and policy responses. Overall, the chapter outlines what a genuinely 'place-based' approach under the new administration might mean, in particular for Whitehall, in changing its approach towards subnational places and for local places, in seeking to realize their own potential. Furthermore, it outlines what the 'missing space' is (as a 'governance gap') and how it might be filled.

In chapter 9, Zach Wilcox explores *Prospects for Devolution to England's Small and Medium Cities*. He argues that government faces larger incentives to devolve to larger city regions because of their economic and political clout and the magnitude of change it could have on the national economy. Larger city regions also have more institutional capacity, skills and resources within their councils to drive policy and programme change. Nevertheless, he argues that small- and medium-sized cities (SMCs) offer something different; they allow government to experiment with devolution without exposing the economy to too much risk. They are more nimble and could implement change more quickly. For all cities, though, Wilcox argues that devolution will only come about when the 'Four I's align. These comprise: incentives; initiative; imposition; and institutions. Given the 'Four I's necessary for devolved power, devolution will be uneven across the country both in scope and scale depending on places' ability to meet the criteria.

Wilcox argues that government has set out the incentives and has imposed the rules of the game: metro mayors and combined authorities. That leaves local initiatives and the right institutions for local councils and government to be set out. Those small and medium cities that bring forward the right institutions will be the most successful, but designating combined authorities in the two-tier county system can be difficult to define and messy to assign, Wilcox argues. SMCs' ambition will play an important part in how much they 'get' from Government, reflecting the range of devolution in the Wave 2 City Deals. Wilcox argues that it is highly unlikely that any city, large or small, will receive another Greater Manchester-style deal, but the opportunities are nevertheless there for significant devolution in England's small and medium cities to 'revolutionise local government and drive economic growth'. Nevertheless, he argues, these 'Four I's work for and against cities based on their scale and individual characteristics.

In chapter 10, *City Dealing in Wales and Scotland: Examining the Institutional Contexts and Asymmetric Arrangements for Policy Making*, David Waite examines the logics and rationales underpinning a new round of city dealing in Wales and Scotland. Lagging behind steps made in England, such city dealing is nevertheless now firing the imagination of local leaders around the potential for metropolitan development. Originally reflecting a bilateral bidding programme involving central government and local bodies in England – with funding made available for long-term infrastructure, sector interventions and labour market programmes inter alia – Waite considers how incentives for city dealing in Scotland and Wales are being inflected by a mix of austerity, local entrepreneurialism, and the shifting logics of localism.

Yet, relative to England, these trends may exhibit somewhat different characteristics in Scotland and Wales. This is because dealing in the Celtic nations takes place within more complex governance architectures, involving an additional layer of government as well as different heritages of spatial policy. Waite argues that how such issues play out in the context of a changing and somewhat unstable UK state system – and how non-metropolitan areas feature in devolved arrangements and regional policy approaches – will shape the nature and scope of the city dealing to emerge.

Waite's final point is a pertinent one in respect of devolution and the UK economy. The final chapters of this collection are akin to J. B. Priestley's fine book *The English Journey*. In it he writes of his travels around England in 1933 and makes observations on the social problems he comes across. He concludes that democratic socialist change is needed to address these problems that are often geographically determined. The spatial and economic inequality within a London-dominated United Kingdom is a starting point for the current English journey of devolution. Indeed, it has been suggested that the Westminster Parliament should be moved to Wigan. This is redolent of Orwell's *The Road to Wigan Pier*, inspired by Priestley's book, in which he observes poverty and inequality in the North of England. There are clearly lessons from the Celtic Nations for a more comprehensive and coherent system of centre-periphery of governmental relations. This would seem to be an important building block in which devolution creates a more economically and spatially balanced United Kingdom. We trust that the critical analysis in this collection has made a contribution in advancing this narrative.

REFERENCES

Blöchliger, H., and King, D. (2006). Fiscal Autonomy of Sub-National Government, *OECD Network on Fiscal Relations Across Levels of Government Working Paper*, No. 2. Paris: Organisation for Economic Cooperation and Development.

Chapain, C., and Renney, C. (2011). Impacts of the Recession on Local Authorities, in Bailey, D., and Chapain, C. (Eds.), *The Recession and Beyond: The Role of Local Authorities in Dealing with the Downturn*. London: Routledge.

Cingano, F. (2014). Trends in Income Inequality and Its Impact on Economic Growth, *OECD Social, Employment and Migration Working Paper*, No. 163. Paris: OECD Publishing.

Diamond, P., and Carr-West, J. (2015). *Devolution. A Roadmap*. London: Local Government Information Unit.

Dorling, D., and Ballas, D. (2008), Spatial Divisions of Poverty and Wealth, in Ridge, T., and Wright, S. (Eds.), *Understanding Poverty, Wealth and Inequality: Policies and Prospects*, 103–34. Bristol: Policy Press.

The Economist. (2014a). Metropolitan Revolutions: Power Surge, 28th June.

The Economist. (2014b). Now for the English Question, 27th September 2014.

The Guardian. (2014). What Will the Scottish Referendum Mean for Leeds, Manchester or Bristol? 29th May, 2014.

Hambleton, R. (2014). Osborne's Devo Deals Disguise Centralisation, *Local Government Chronicle*, 18/12/2014, page 23.

OECD. (2015). *In It Together. Why Less Inequality Benefits All*. Paris: OECD.

Part I

LESSONS FROM A POST-REFERENDUM SCOTLAND

Chapter 1

Where Next for Scotland and the United Kingdom?

Jim Gallagher

Within the last year, the Scottish people have said two apparently contradictory things. They want to stay in the United Kingdom, and they want to be represented by the SNP. By a majority of over 10%, Scotland chose to remain British, but then, with 50% of the general election vote, chose Scottish nationalists to represent it. The partisan politics of the general election were extraordinary. The Labour vote collapsed, and the SNP showed remarkable skill in building a coalition of voters. As a result, as well as exercising dominant control over both Parliament and government in Holyrood, they are the overwhelming Scottish voice in Westminster. People committed to what Scotland has rejected, it seems, represent Scotland.

CONSTITUTIONAL CHALLENGES

This combination of results presents acute challenges for Scotland's relationship with the United Kingdom. Scotland's representatives will be seeking things that the United Kingdom will, and should, reject. Some of these may be no more than the theatre of politics – demand the unattainable, and trumpet the rejection. But amidst the rhetoric sits a real question: Is there a constitutional relationship between Scotland and the United Kingdom that satisfies Scottish aspirations and is acceptable to the United Kingdom as a whole?

Exactly what those aspirations are is not easy to see, but even if well-defined, they are not a matter for Scotland alone. In recent decades, Scottish demands for additional autonomy have been seen as largely a Scottish question pursued by Scots. The rest of the United Kingdom, or more precisely England, has by and large been tolerantly indifferent, and devolution has been shoehorned into the existing UK constitutional framework. This has

changed. Some of the reasons for the change are purely political. The referendum campaign raised the real possibility of secession, and gained English
attention. More recently, the idea that Scottish Nationalist MPs might impose
a government on England in a narrow general election was made into a major
election issue.

The proposals for more powers now on the table or demanded by nationalists press at or over the boundary of what can be described as devolution, and
raise in acute form the two long-standing rough edges of the devolution settlement: the Barnett formula, and the West Lothian question. As a result, the
discussion on Scotland's constitutional position can no longer be construed
merely as what concessions Scottish politicians can wrest from reluctant UK
ministers: this will be a negotiation with a mobilized English opinion, which
requires a serious look at the UK territorial constitution as a whole.

A CHOICE MADE: POLITICAL, ECONOMIC
AND SOCIAL UNION

The place to begin is following through the logic of the first choice made by
Scots: the referendum decision to remain in the United Kingdom.

The referendum was at least as much a test of the union as it was of the
idea of independence. Independence was a concept presented with relentless
positivity, but it was a blank canvas onto which virtually any hope or aspira-
tion could be projected. An independent Scotland could be richer, or fairer,
or greener: Who was to say that was impossible? Union with the rest of the
United Kingdom, by contrast, was a concrete reality. Perhaps its virtues could
be taken for granted, but its faults were easy to see and to criticize. In the end,
the voters seem to have concluded that the risks of change were too great. The
risks were very real, and the campaign focused on them, but it is more fruitful
to focus on the positive arguments that underlay those calculations of risk,
and so get a sense the nature of the union that was defended, and accepted,
by the electorate.

The campaign itself was like a two-year-long general election. Campaigning is ephemeral, more soundbite than seminar, with arguments relentlessly
simplified and exaggerated by the media. This was, however, a campaign
with a government on each side. The case for a separate Scotland is recorded
mainly in the Scottish government's White Paper, *Scotland's Future* (Scottish
Government, 2104), a bulky document, light on analysis but strong on reas-
surance; Scots were told they could keep the things they like about the United
Kingdom, and ditch those they did not – and even gain a place in the Eurovi-
sion song contest. The case for the Union is surprisingly well documented,
and much of the argument, heavy with underlying analysis and data, can be

found in the government's *Scotland Analysis* programme (https://www.gov.uk/search?q=Scotland+Analysis accessed 01/06/15).

The positive argument of the Better Together campaign was set out at length in June 2013 by Alistair Darling in a poorly reported lecture at Glasgow University, subsequently published as a pamphlet (Better Together, 2013). It is a case for a political union, linked to an economic union and social union. The linkages mattered much in the debate, because those arguing for independence claimed it was possible to keep the economic and social sides of the union while dissolving the political union.

The United Kingdom is a 'union state' (Mackintosh, 1968; Rokkan and Unwin, 1982). That union is a political institution, based in Scotland's case on the union of the parliaments negotiated in 1707.[1] Internally, the union is differentiated in ways that are analogous to the distribution of powers in a federal state, but it presents a single external face to the world, under single foreign and defence policy stance. Interestingly, this is something supported by more Scots than voted 'No' in the referendum (Curtice, 2013).

Formally speaking, the choice in front of the voters was whether to end the political union of the United Kingdom. However, the real debate was not about defence and foreign policy, despite some mention of Trident. Instead, it was about the other two connected aspects of the union: the United Kingdom as an economic union – a single home market, a single currency and an integrated economy – and the United Kingdom as a social union – a state that shares resources across its territory to guarantee certain levels of public services, pensions and benefits. These three aspects of the union are closely intertwined. You cannot pick and choose amongst them, and political union was the key to the other two.

To take an example, one of the biggest and most emotive arguments of the referendum campaign was whether an independent Scotland could continue to share a currency with the rest of the United Kingdom. Of course, if one truly believed in economic independence, one would argue for a separate Scottish currency, and some honest nationalists did. But the politics were obvious: voters trusted the currency they knew, so the 'Yes' campaign somewhat uneasily argued for an economic policy driven from London. The most interesting contribution to this debate was technocratic (Armstrong and Ebell, 2012). The Governor of the Bank of England (Carney, 2014) made clear his view that a stable currency union required a fiscal union, with a state authority controlling resources of at least 25% of the GDP, in UK terms about half of public spending.

You cannot have a fiscal union without a political union. Carney was making a point about the EU as well; it is a currency union (for most members) that cannot bring itself to be a fiscal union, because it lacks the necessary political cohesion. To put it in practical terms, no one in Germany pays the public spending bills in Greece: there is no democratic mandate across the Eurozone for this. But because Greece is a currency union, it cannot devalue its way out of its present economic difficulties. No sensible Scottish government would put Scotland in that position. All the neutral economic analysis[2] shared this conclusion, and it was heavily emphasized in the United Kingdom's Scotland analysis programme: a currency union requires the fiscal union. And, of course, if that is true in the case of independence, it is even more obviously so when Scotland remains inside the United Kingdom.

A fiscal union means sharing resources across the whole territory. This promotes economic stability, but public spending is driven by normative principles, rather than just economic technicalities. In a word, its distribution is justified by reference to need, even though need is very imperfectly recognized in the mechanics of resource allocation. The most obvious example is the whole social security system, driven by the needs and circumstances of individuals, who, irrespective of their geographic location, receive benefits on the basis of entitlement. As a result, the social security system acts as not only (as is well known) an automatic stabilizer over time – increasing expenditure when the economy turns down – but also a stabilizer across geographies, transferring resources to areas where employment and tax income are lower. If it did not do that, there would be a risk of a multiplier effect, with the local downturn resulting in reductions in public expenditure, exacerbating the economic bad news.

This territorial redistribution has important economic consequences. But it is, in essence, a moral proposition. Geographical differences in taxable capacity shouldn't result in differences in welfare provision. This is true in federal countries worldwide: all governments redistribute across their territories, some more comprehensively than others. Trade unionists in the United Kingdom fought at the beginning of the twentieth century to replace a failing local poor law, which could not meet needs as they arose locally as a result of economic change, with national resources mobilized for individual areas. It means that there are social rights that apply across the whole territory of the state.

So just as a fiscal union supports a currency union, it supports a common social citizenship. This, in turn, is linked to a common political citizenship. The truth is that people are willing to share with those with whom they feel they belong, with whom they have a common identity. Resource sharing within the United Kingdom is automatic and relatively painless. London taxpayers pay Liverpool pensions without really thinking about it. This is one of the characteristic signs of a nation-state: when Bismarck eventually succeeded in his project of German unification, among his first priorities was to create pan-German systems of social welfare. Social unions do not extend beyond nation-states; sharing fiscal resources across the European Union, for example, is much more difficult. German taxpayers simply don't pay Greek pensions.

So much for the internal logic of union. This matters because it is what the voters bought into, and conditions what they should get.

CHOICES MADE: POLITICAL UNION, SMITH AND 'THE VOW'

More devolution is on the agenda. Voters were also promised that a vote to stay in the United Kingdom was a vote for change, and more powers for the Scottish Parliament. Each of the major parties supporting the union had set up a commission to look at the options for further devolution. All working independently, they came to very similar conclusions about the scope for increasing tax devolution and the capacity for some devolution of welfare. The parties didn't, however, develop a single common package before the referendum vote. They agreed, instead, to come together in very short order after the referendum (together with the SNP and the Greens) to produce a settlement involving greater powers. This was all set out in a 'vow' in, of all places, the *Daily Record*. Some readings of the campaign suggest that this was a turning point, though who knows. It is important, however, to understand *all* the contents of this vow: notably, in addition to greater tax powers, it also promised retaining the Barnett formula. This process became the Smith Commission, which produced a report (The Smith Commission, 2014) in November after the vote, at extremely high speed, and whose recommendations were turned into draft clauses before the general election and are now before Parliament in the Scotland Bill.

A striking thing about the referendum campaign was the way in which it acknowledged a radical view of the union between Scotland and the rest of the United Kingdom. In accepting that the Scottish people could unilaterally choose to leave the United Kingdom, the UK government and Parliament accepted that Scotland was a nation that could make this choice. As an inevitable consequence, it follows that the United Kingdom is (and actually has always been) a multinational state. It is a state that provides the constitutional framework and the external identity for more than one nation. That has always been the case since 1707, but the expression of this separate national identity became democratic only in 1999. Before that, it was expressed in the separate Scottish church, for many, or a legal system, and in the different institutions of Scottish government. The Smith Commission adopted the Labour party idea of making this explicit by entrenching the Scottish Parliament and giving the Sewel convention legal force.

In the event, the Smith Commission produced plans that are rather more radical than had been canvassed by the parties before the referendum. The immediate post-referendum political environment, no doubt, drove this. The result is a set of devolution plans under which the Scottish Parliament will have markedly wider tax powers – essentially over income tax – and will be assigned half of the revenue of VAT in Scotland. In consequence, something approaching 60% of the Parliament's budget will be funded from its 'own resources', and nearly 40% of the tax revenue in Scotland will belong to the Scottish Parliament. Additionally, the Scottish Parliament is being given the control over about £2.5 billion of welfare spending (excluding universal credit and pensions), the ability to set the housing element of universal credit, and the power to supplement from its own resources UK benefits paid in Scotland. This latter point is of great significance (and needs better definition in the Smith legislation). For public services, the Scottish Parliament has complete spending freedom, and tax powers will enable it to spend more or less. For pensions and benefits, for example the unemployed benefit, the United Kingdom guarantees certain levels, and it would be wrong if those were dependent on how well the Scottish economy was doing. A principle of the social union is that such risks are pooled. But there is no reason why Scotland should not supplement them from its own resources if it were willing to bear the fiscal consequences.

This produces a remarkably decentralized system. The commonly used measures of decentralization inside a state are the proportion of spending decentralized below central government, and the proportion of taxation.[3] On these measures, Scotland under the Smith Commission proposals will be comparable to a Canton in Switzerland or a province in Canada:[4] an extraordinary leap from the wholly centralized United Kingdom of 1998.

The legislation now produced will require the consent of the Edinburgh Parliament as well as enactment at Westminster. Much detail requires to be sorted out, though the UK government has proposed the principles of a financial settlement. The most important question is how much less Barnett formula grants the Scottish Parliament will receive when it takes on these new tax powers. This has already been worked through in the context of the (Calman) tax powers in the Scotland Act 2012. In essence, the Scottish Parliament will take on the risk of differential economic growth in Scotland affecting its own revenues (which under Smith will be nearly 60% of the total), but will be supported by a share of UK revenues, still mostly calculated via Barnett, for the remaining 40%. This means that the Scottish Parliament will have the major say over how much is spent on Scottish public services in total, as well as the share-out between different priorities. The price, of course, is that the total spent will be more at risk from how Scotland's economy does relative to the United Kingdom.

Broadly speaking, these plans are consistent with the union as defended during the referendum campaign. They do not disrupt economic integration, nor set up borders or significant barriers to trade, investment or employment. In terms of economic union, the UK government will be responsible for less than £20 billion of direct expenditure in Scotland (Social Security), but also for Barnett transfers of another £20 billion or so. This is enough to meet Governor Carney's test of keeping the currency union stable. Scotland is taking on some economic risk, as the budget of the Scottish Parliament will be heavily influenced by the Scottish economy. Shared resources means that devolved services are not completely dependent on Scottish tax resources, but the Scottish Parliament will have a great deal of flexibility to make quite different choices on the balance between taxation and spending on public services. The fact that the most important UK welfare benefits are guaranteed means that the risks of demography and asymmetric economic shocks are shared within what can properly be described as a continuing social union. The virtually complete devolution of income tax under Smith (all rates and bands will be a devolved decision) does create some difficulties for voting on income tax in Parliament at Westminster. How this is to be resolved has not been fully settled, and it is a harbinger of potential difficulty with more ambitious devolutionary schemes.

SO WHAT ABOUT THE GENERAL ELECTION RESULT?

Getting 45% in the referendum was a big success for Scottish nationalism. Independence was previously the preferred option of about a third of the population. Some of those whose constitutional preference was for more devolution, clearly opted for independence instead. Perhaps more significant, many people who were (and are) dissatisfied with the way the United Kingdom is going – over economic policy and inequality, especially – were prepared to opt for independence as well. There is a sense in which this can be regarded as a protest vote, as it may be primarily a vote against how the United Kingdom is, rather than having started out as a principled commitment to Scottish independence, but it would be unwise to assume that it would remain so.

In Scottish elections in recent years, there has been a distinct tendency to regard elections for the Scottish Parliament and for Parliament at Westminster as of different orders. Scots seemed happy to vote one way for Westminster and another for Holyrood. In the 2010 general election, for example, the Labour Party secured more than 40% of the vote, only to lose badly to the SNP in the 2011 Scottish elections. Two years of referendum campaigning may have changed that: those who voted 'Yes' in the referendum, and perhaps others also, supported the SNP in 2015. A first past the post-electoral system gave them 56 out of Scotland's 59 MPs.

This was not a vote for independence. Independence was not on the ballot paper, and neither was it promised by the SNP. Nor is it seen as a mandate to hold a further referendum. The Scottish government's White Paper said the independence referendum was a 'once in a generation' event; a generation is arguably anything between 15 and 30 years. In terms of the SNP's campaign rhetoric, this was a vote against 'austerity', maybe against Trident, but mostly a vote for a single Scottish voice at Westminster. The SNP did, however, include constitutional changes in their manifesto, and argued that they have a mandate to pursue them. They argued for a policy of full fiscal autonomy, that is, Holyrood should be responsible for all taxes and spending in Scotland other than defence and foreign affairs, and identified a list of taxes to be devolved as priorities. It is to these ideas, under the banner of 'Devo-Max', therefore, that we now turn.

MAXING OUT ON DEVOLUTION

Before the referendum, it was clearly the ambition of the SNP that a substantial phalanx of SNP MPs should hold the balance of power at Westminster. Scottish nationalists could be relevant to the Westminster arithmetic for the first time since they helped bring down the Callaghan government in 1979, and might even have the leverage enjoyed by Irish nationalists at the end of the nineteenth century and the beginning of the twentieth century (Gallagher and McLean, 2015). But the election failed to deliver this. SNP MPs may represent Scotland, but they can only make progress on their constitutional aims with the agreement of the rest of the United Kingdom.

Just what those aims are is not clear. There has been some to-ing and fro-ing amongst SNP representatives about whether they support the manifesto policy of 'Devo-Max'. This idea surfaced at various points in the independence debate, and at one early point seemed even to be the Scottish government's favoured alternative to independence. In the event, Scottish ministers pursued 'independence-light' rather than 'devolution-max'. Since the election SNP members have been hesitant about pursuing the idea (one has been quoted as describing it as 'disastrous' if introduced soon). But at the time of writing, it seems that they now support the plan and will seek to amend the Scotland Bill to allow for it.

Devolution-max was for a time a phrase in search of a policy to give it substance. The SNP's manifesto refers to 'full fiscal responsibility', replacing the previous mantra of 'full fiscal autonomy'. Certainly, the idea that Westminster should deal with defence and foreign affairs only and Holyrood with everything else is a notion, which has a common-sense appeal for Scottish voters (Curtice, 2013). Defence and foreign affairs are obviously characteristics of an independent state. But so (as we have seen, and as the SNP themselves argued even in the event of independence) is currency and macroeconomic policy. So the model of devolution max or full fiscal responsibility looks like this:

• Defence, foreign affairs and macroeconomic management are the United Kingdom's responsibility.
• All other (domestic) policies, including pensions and benefits, are dealt with at the Scottish level.
• All taxes in Scotland are collected by the Scottish Parliament (other than VAT whose yield is completely assigned to them).
• The Scottish Parliament pays a sum to Westminster for common services, most obviously on a per capita basis, for example defence.
• Scotland would be able to borrow to finance capital expenditure and any deficit it ran.

There would be no fiscal transfers from the rest of the United Kingdom to Scotland, but a relatively small fiscal transfer from the Scottish budget to the UK government, some of which would return to create economic activity in Scotland, for example at the defence bases on the Clyde. The likely payment is under £10 billion a year, which is the amount of the so-called non-identifiable expenditure undertaken by the United Kingdom on Scotland's behalf (GERS, Scottish Government, 2014), declining as Scotland's share of inherited debt declines, within the total public expenditure in Scotland of around £65 billion a year.

SHOULD ANYONE BUY DEVO-MAX?

The Nationalist leadership might argue to their supporters that this approach can be seen as a stepping stone to full independence. The analogy with Dominion status for Ireland in 1923, leading to full independence in the 1930s, is an obvious one; hopefully, the concomitant Civil War would be avoided. It also has a commonsense attraction, as the polls show, in that the population is inclined to assume that such a system makes practical sense. After all, surely the Scottish Parliament can deal with everything domestic, leaving Westminster to deal with the outside world?

The analogy is made, sometimes, with the Channel Islands and the Isle of Man, which run their own domestic affairs, but rely on the United Kingdom for external relations. They have complete fiscal autonomy, besides other autonomy. This is an instructive comparison. These islands are something of a constitutional anomaly. They are not part of the United Kingdom, nor are they part of the European Union. They send no MPs to Westminster, they pay no UK taxes (the Isle of Man does share in the UK VAT system) and make no contribution to UK defence, and receive no financial support from the United Kingdom. They do not use the pound sterling, but instead maintain sterling reserves to match, one for one, the issue of their local pounds. They make a living, especially the Channel Islands, by being a tax haven in which wealthy individuals and companies shelter from the UK taxes. They run a balanced budget. Above all, they are very small. Taken together, their population is about that of Aberdeen, that is to say less than one-twentieth of the population of Scotland.

But would this approach work for Scotland, and what would the consequences be?

THE FISCAL AND ECONOMIC IMPLICATIONS OF 'FULL FINANCIAL RESPONSIBILITY'

The first and most significant effects for Scotland, however, would be fiscal, not constitutional. This system would imply cuts in pensions, benefits and public spending of at least 10%, and probably more. To understand why it is necessary to have a brief account of Scotland's fiscal position, this issue was extensively explored during the referendum campaign, in independent academic analysis, and by the UK government (Johnson and Phillips, 2012, Crawford and Tetlow, 2014). Those promoting independence simply denied the fiscal risks that it would produce. The Scottish government's White Paper contained fiscal numbers for one year (only 2016–2017), and made the books look no worse than the UK balance by assuming oil revenues would be 2 or 3 times higher than independent estimates suggested. Oil revenues have collapsed since the referendum oil revenues for that year are now forecast to be less than one-tenth of that Scottish government assumption.

The Table 1.1 below gives the March 2015 estimate of Scotland's fiscal position over six years.[5] The data was drawn from the Scottish government's own publications, and the UK Office of Budget Responsibility forecasts, by the Institute for Fiscal Studies, and updated by Fiscal Affairs, Scotland (Fiscal Affairs Scotland, 2015).

Broadly speaking, the total public expenditure for the benefit of Scotland is about £65–75[6] billion a year, and the total Scottish tax income is about £55–56 billion, a deficit of about £10 billion. The gap between Scotland's spending and its revenue has increased markedly because of the collapse in oil revenues, though other tax revenues are forecast to rise to some degree alongside spending as the economy grows. In very broad terms, around half of the gap today is filled by Scotland's share of the United Kingdom's borrowing, and another half by fiscal transfers from England. What the data show is that Scotland has a structural deficit greater than that of the United Kingdom, of around £8 billion a year. The additional structural deficit is substantially down to additional spending, rather than a shortfall in taxation. Most of this additional spending is concentrated on devolved expenditure, funded by the Barnett formula (Gallagher and Hinze, 2005), rather than UK expenditure such as spending on pensions and benefits.[7] In the past, this additional spending would have been covered by North Sea oil revenues, or sometimes much more than covered, if they had been available to Scotland.

This fiscal arithmetic would have been extremely painful for an independent Scotland, and it is no accident that the campaigners in favour of remaining in the United Kingdom committed to retaining the Barnett formula if Scotland voted 'No'. That is the obvious route to avoid big cuts in public spending. If it were abolished, and Scottish public expenditure were dependent only on Scottish tax revenue, spending reductions roughly equivalent to this structural deficit would be needed. This is more than 10% of the total Scottish public spending, or about 25% of the Scottish Parliament's own budget today. Scottish tax revenue would have to increase by about 15% more than that of the United Kingdom for Scotland to be better off than under the present system. The level of economic growth needed is equivalent to that of a developing country, or the increases in tax rates obviously become unsustainable. £8 billion a year would almost double Scottish income tax.

Under Devo-Max rather than independence, the arithmetic remains unchanged, and the powers of the Scottish government are smaller. In their opposition to austerity, the SNP, of course, propose additional borrowing.

Table 1.1   Scotland's Structural Deficit Compared to the United Kingdom

	2014–15	2015–16	2016–17	2017–18	2018–19	2019–20
Scotland						
Spending £bn	68.4	68.9	68.7	69.0	70.4	74.0
Onshore income £bn	52.3	54.1	56.8	59.3	62.0	65.2
Offshore income £bn	2.3	0.6	0.5	0.6	0.7	0.6
Deficit £bn	−13.8	−14.1	−11.3	−9.1	−7.8	−8.1
Deficit per head £	−2583	−2643	−2103	−1687	−1429	−1599
UK						
UK deficit per head £	−1398	−1158	−603	−193	+80	+105
Difference						
Difference per head	−1186	− 1485	−1501	−1494	−1509	−1599
Difference £bn	−6.3	−8.0	−8.1	−8.1	−8.2	−8.7

Source: Fiscal Affairs Scotland 2015, simplified.

And under full fiscal responsibility, the Scottish government would have to have borrowing powers, and indeed the UK government would have to ensure that it did not stand behind loans to the Scottish government. (It would be taking a risk over which it had no control.) But it is very hard to imagine that the markets would be prepared to lend to Scotland at the levels of deficit needed to sustain current levels of spending. That would be around 20% of tax revenue borrowed in any one year. Whatever was loaned would cost more, as Scotland would be a small economy, borrowing a high proportion of its GDP (4%+) (Armstrong and Ebell, 2014). The deficit could grow again as time goes on, because of Scotland's demographic pressures,[8] and as oil revenues dwindle even closer to zero. There would be a direct effect on public services, of course, where most of the spending bonus compared to England is to be found. There would be an indirect, multiplier effect on the Scottish economy. Even the least Keynesian economist would expect that taking as much as £8 billion out of demand would create very serious problems in the Scottish economy.

It cannot be an exaggeration, therefore, to say that full fiscal autonomy would be fiscally catastrophic for Scotland. It would certainly require public expenditure reductions substantially greater than imposed on Scotland by the previous and present governments. The policy of the SNP, to the extent that this arithmetic is acknowledged, is that full fiscal responsibility should be phased in over time, so that the tax powers that are devolved first can be used to draw the economy. Given that the level of economic growth over and above what is currently expected is around 15%, this is a quixotic ambition. If changing corporation tax and national insurance contribution rates could create additional economic growth at this level, every government would have done it by now.

The implications of such a plan are economic for the rest of the United Kingdom. The fiscal union, which underlies a common currency, would be broken, and the stability of the currency called into question. Most of that risk would be borne by Scotland, as it is by far the smaller part of the currency union – it might, for example, find that its economy was diverging from that of the United Kingdom in a way that made the sterling exchange rate inappropriate. The United Kingdom would carry the risk of a substantial onshore tax haven, potentially more damaging than the tiny Channel Islands. On the fiscal side, the United Kingdom would gain as the loss of North Sea oil revenues would be much more than offset by no longer supporting Scottish public spending.

So UK Ministers must be sorely tempted to offer full fiscal autonomy. After all, 56 out of the 59 Scottish MPs stood on that platform and 50% of Scots voted for them. The Scottish government wants it, and the fiscal arithmetic looks alluring from the point of view of the Treasury. Fiscal transfers from the rest of the United Kingdom to Scotland would cease. The UK Treasury would be something like £8 billion a year better off. Treasury ministers might even be benevolent and defer any contribution to the UK national debt, and they could still be quids in, enough to cut English income tax by nearly a penny in the pound. The sterling currency zone would be less stable, but most of that risk would be borne by Scotland. If such a deal also cut Scottish representation in the UK Parliament, removing troublesome nationalist members, a UK government might take the view there was nothing but upside for them. No more Barnett formula, no more complaint from England, no asymmetry at Westminster. The reasons why they should, and probably will, resist are, however, principled, about the nature of the United Kingdom as a union.

THE IMPLICATIONS OF FULL FISCAL AUTONOMY FOR THE SOCIAL AND WELFARE UNIONS

The nature of the social union is discussed at some length above: sharing resources guarantees equivalent levels of benefits, pensions and comparable levels of public services across the territory of the United Kingdom. It is self-evident that full fiscal autonomy would end this. Scottish public expenditure would not be supported by UK public spending, nor would Scottish taxpayers support welfare services elsewhere in the United Kingdom. Not only would the Barnett formula end, with the effects on public services already discussed, but the sharing of demographic risk in old-age pensions, or the sharing of economic risk implied in national payments of unemployment benefit and universal credit would also end. The UK government's analysis demonstrated that the demography in Scotland will differ over the coming decades from that of the United Kingdom, so that demand for pensions would be greater.[9] This is an important instrumental argument. Certainly, the evidence was that pensioners in Scotland were more likely to vote 'No', perhaps feeling the benefits of that security. But the argument is one less of self-interest than principle. Sharing across a nation-state is both a sign of common identity, and something that supports it (Eichorn, 2013).[10]

The most significant implications are political. Scotland could hardly expect to send MPs to Westminster, as they would set only English taxes (other than VAT) and legislate almost exclusively on English matters. This is exactly the position of the Channel Islands, and as we noted above, these islands are not part of the United Kingdom. So Scotland would have no, or virtually no, say in defence or foreign affairs. This is certainly not consistent with maintaining the United Kingdom as a union.

LIMITS TO DEVOLUTION: WHAT IS SCOTLAND'S
FUTURE WITHIN THE UNITED KINGDOM?

Devo-Max, or full fiscal autonomy, therefore is in the interests neither of
Scotland nor of the United Kingdom, though it is a lot worse for Scotland. It
is very clearly not in Scotland's economic interest and no rational Scottish
government should argue for it. It is certainly not consistent with the union
supported by a majority of voters in the referendum, nor with the specific
promise to sustain the Barnett formula. The Scottish people were promised
devolution, not a Channel Islands solution. Devo-Max would be tantamount
to the end of the United Kingdom, principally because it would end the fiscal
sharing across the territory, which is necessary to make a state a real union,
and it would abolish effective Scottish representation at the UK level. No
principled UK government should accept it. Have we, therefore, come to
the end of the road in developing the devolution settlement to meet Scottish
aspirations for separate identity and representation?

Nationalist ministers and MPs will press for more devolved powers,
whether or not they are consistent with maintaining the union – ideally not,
from their point of view. It seems likely they will press for full fiscal autonomy, secure in the knowledge that it will be rejected. Despite the temptation
to make nationalists face up to the reality of their rhetoric, UK ministers will
be right to reject it. It is the people of Scotland who would suffer, not those
who have misled them. There is no scope for a grand bargain with the present UK government, trading representation at Westminster for tax devolution;
in this respect, the Conservative party remains unionist. The SNP will then
press for power over specific taxes, notably corporation tax and employers'
national insurance contributions.

For some time, the SNP's policy was to cut corporation tax so as to attract
mobile international investment: the unacknowledged purpose was to attract
taxes that would be paid otherwise elsewhere in the United Kingdom.[11]
Understandably, HM Treasury has been deeply resistant to this. If, however,
plans proceed to devolve this in Northern Ireland, subject to safeguards to
prevent the loss of taxes elsewhere in the United Kingdom, pressure from
both Wales and Scotland for similar powers may be harder to resist. This
would be a distortion of competition, but perhaps a substitute for the absence
of an effective regional economic development policy. The needs of Wales
and Northern Ireland, however, are much greater than Scotland's. National
insurance is a different case. Certainly, employers' national insurance contributions are a payroll tax, and it might be that cutting them would stimulate
employment. But national insurance is also a gateway to contributory welfare
state benefits, notably the old-age pension. Devolving it would be a breach in
the social solidarity that was accepted during the referendum.

For now at least, SNP MPs do not have the leverage at Westminster to force the UK government to deliver any of these changes. They are already threatening another referendum if the government does not give them sufficient concessions. Since no concessions will ever be sufficient, this threat should be ignored. Instead, the United Kingdom should set its own agenda, delivering at pace the additional devolution already in the pipeline, and developing and communicating a better understanding of its own territorial nature. Putting change into effect has lagged behind the public appetite for greater powers to the Scottish Parliament. The Calman Commission was appointed in 2007, legislated for in 2012, and its main recommendations will become effective only in 2016 (Calman, 2008, 2009). As a result, the electorate (whose understanding of the boundaries of the devolution settlement may not be strong anyway) have yet to experience the reality of devolved fiscal power. The Smith Commission Bill cannot be allowed to take so long before giving the Scottish Parliament not just powers, but also responsibilities. More important, perhaps, will be developing and communicating effectively a common understanding of the United Kingdom as a territorial state, and moving down the road of codifying to a greater degree the UK territorial constitution. Scotland has voted for both union and for distinctiveness. Those who are willing to accept the result of both votes need to set out, explain and defend the principles of the system of devolution.

THE TERRITORIAL CONSTITUTION

One way of thinking about devolution is that it delivers federalism in a non-federal state. This sounds contradictory but, in fact, has been remarkably successful. The Scottish Parliament, like the Welsh and Northern Ireland Assemblies, has wider spending powers than many state governments in federal systems. Holyrood's lack of tax powers is being remedied: minor taxes in 2015, a share of income tax in 2016, and thereafter, the Smith Commission plans. The reaction to these plans outside Scotland demonstrates in very stark relief how the asymmetry of a devolved constitutional settlement shows where the limits to devolution might lie. The root of this is the fact that the United Kingdom Parliament is also England's Parliament, and the United Kingdom government, England's government. The first rubbing point is the most obvious. If income tax is virtually wholly devolved, then Scottish MPs in the UK Parliament will be voting on the rates of English income tax, which their constituents will not pay. This is the West Lothian question, this time with teeth.[12]

The second rubbing point is more subtle, and takes us into the territory of spending as well as taxation. Devolved Scottish taxes will only be used to fund devolved Scottish spending. But there is no devolved English budget and so the same taxes levied by the UK government will, on the face of it, fund any UK expenditure. So it might be that English income tax payers are funding expenditure in Scotland – whether on welfare, or even on devolved services via the Barnett formula. It is relatively easy to devise funding formulae that demonstrate that *changes* in English income tax are not used to fund *changes* in Scottish spending. But in the absence of a devolved English budget, and perhaps a devolved English government to manage it, it is not so easy to see that English-only taxes fund English-only spending. And when Scottish spending is markedly higher than English, and Scottish tax receipts are not, significant fiscal transfers from England to Scotland are obviously happening. The more the taxes that are wholly devolved, the greater this challenge will become.

The first problem might, in principle, be dealt with by reducing the powers or number of Scottish MPs at Westminster. This is precisely the set of issues that Gladstone wrestled with in England and Ireland at the end of the nineteenth century. In the end, giving up in despair at the complexity, he cut the Gordian knot by cutting the number of Irish MPs. This was carried through into the so-called devolution discount that applied in Northern Ireland from 1923 until 1972. Detailed proposals have been made for reducing the powers of Scottish MPs to influence England-only legislation without resort to a cut in numbers, but no detailed plans have been developed in relation to English-only taxation (Gallagher, 2012).

What Scottish pressure cannot reasonably expect to do is require that England should create its own spending programmes and taxation (and perhaps as a result, at some point, its own separate government) simply to accommodate Scottish aspirations for greater tax powers. Some in England may wish this, but most don't. An inevitable result would be the end of the Barnett formula, which was designed for a devolved, rather than federal, system. It would probably have to be replaced by some sort of needs-based system sharing out some of the proceeds of UK taxes. Many in other parts of the United Kingdom would welcome this, as it could only be to their advantage.

The key issue here is to remember, therefore, that the United Kingdom is a union of more than one nation. There are other nations than Scotland, and they have their own views, interests and proper entitlements. A striking consequence of devolution has been the rise in English identity, and the demands for English political expression. Scots who argue for special institutions to reflect their identity and allow them to make different choices from England's, sometimes struggle to answer the challenge why England should not have the same. The principle, however, is that each of the nations of the union should have both separate and shared institutions, but crucially, the separate institutions of each should be consistent with the maintenance of the union. Much of the argument in this chapter is about the extent to which separate Scottish institutions can be sustained within the union as described. Similar arguments can be made about Wales and Northern Ireland. But England is different: it is 85% of the total.

In discussing these issues, there is much loose talk of federalism. To the extent that this means full and formal federalism, with a codified constitution and four federal units, it is to misunderstand the nature of the United Kingdom as a union. The United Kingdom has never been a federal state, as it has never distinguished between English and UK government, reflecting the reality of England's size. English nationalism with the same aspirations as Scottish nationalism would end the union. But that does not mean that institutions that discharge the functions of federalism in the context of the United Kingdom cannot be devised or strengthened. To be clear, however, a separate English Parliament would not be consistent with the union, and in any event, Westminster is England's Parliament and will remain so. So, special constitutional recognition of England is different in kind and nature from that of the smaller nations in the union. This is common in federal countries: small states get special protection, often through overrepresentation, or other constitutional guarantees. Larger entities acknowledge that they will always be the majority. To put it at its simplest, the (specious) Nationalist complaint is that in the UK elections, Scotland doesn't always get the government it voted for. By contrast, England almost always does. This is simply a consequence of relative size. A similar consequence of scale is that the framework of UK guarantees will inevitably be set at an English level, even though as devolution extends within England, there will be increasing scope for variation there too. At the same time, there is clearly scope for English-only votes in the House of Commons, though the way in which this is done is important: it cannot require that there be a separate English government, even though it might in some circumstances make a UK government's job of running England harder (Gallagher, 2012).

CONCLUSION

Various proposals have been made for how such a territorial constitution might be drawn up to cover all these issues. The Labour Party before the election were committed to a constitutional convention, which might have been very wide ranging indeed – everything from the second chamber to the electoral system was suggested. Gordon Brown has recently suggested that if the government does not take up this challenge, the other political parties should run a people's constitutional convention instead. A narrower approach was suggested by the Bingham Centre for the rule of law, focusing on the legal machinery of a territorial constitution, in the form of a suggested charter for the union, building on the Smith Commission recommendation of the declaration of permanence of the Scottish Parliament (which is likely to be extended by the government to the Welsh Assembly). But constitutional arrangements are more than legal rules, just as the union is more than a purely political entity. The territorial constitution of the United Kingdom will have to set out what it seeks to achieve, and have institutions that are fit for the purpose of delivering that. Its content must include the following:

- formal constitutional recognition of the multinational nature of the union, and the entrenched status of both the devolved institutions and the national Parliament;
- a stronger institutional framework for consultation and cooperation between the different levels of government;
- a set of powers over public services, taxation and (in a different way) over welfare that enable the devolved nations to diverge from England if they wish provided they are willing to bear the consequences;
- scope for English voices to be heard effectively on English issues in the national Parliament;
- legal and institutional guarantees of economic integration, in terms of trade, investment and employment;
- effective institutions of fiscal federalism to ensure resources are distributed according to principles that guarantee the economic and social cohesion of the union;
- well-defined social and economic, as well as civil and political, rights, which guide the allocation of resources and which are guaranteed at a minimum level across the whole territory of the union; and
- the same clear principles of national guarantees and the scope for local choice within national frameworks apply equally within England.

Most of all, however, the UK territorial constitution is a story that needs to be communicated. There is a positive tale to tell, unconstrained by negativity forced on pro-union campaigners obliged to argue for a 'No' vote and to call out the risks of independence. It is an explanation of how a union safeguards economic and social rights, as well as how it allows the smaller nations to take a different path from the English approach if they are willing to do so. This is a tale that explains to the Scots, Welsh and Northern Irish on the one hand and the English on the other how the devolved nations have the scope to make different choices, over taxation, spending and welfare, and why and how the same freedoms can be exercised within England. The arguments exist, and were accepted by Scotland. The case is there to be made to the whole United Kingdom.

NOTES

1. See Kidd, 2008, for an explanation of how union was not the same as incorporation, but rather a Scottish plan for dealing with a powerful neighbour.

2. See for example Armstrong and Ebell, 2014.

3. See OECD Fiscal Decentralisation database.

4. Indeed, in one critical respect it is more so: federal governments typically put conditions on financial transfers made to state governments, but this is not the case in the United Kingdom.

5. Since then, the oil forecasts have fallen further.

6. It should be noted that this assessment of expenditure, carried out by the Scottish government (in GERS) includes a per capita contribution to the UK national debt. In the event of independence, the Scottish government argued that there might be a case for smaller contribution, on the basis that Scotland had contributed more historically through North Sea oil revenues. But as Ashcroft, 2013, has calculated, this fails to take into account that Scotland has also enjoyed over that period a substantially higher public expenditure. Indeed, he concludes that most of the additional revenue has been spent, or there is a different profile from the tax income, in Scotland. The United Kingdom has been Scotland's Oil Fund.

7. See HM Treasury, Public Expenditure Statistical Analysis for comparative data.

8. See Scotland analysis: Work and pensions.

9. See Scotland analysis: Work and pensions.

10. Interestingly, over the 10 years since the start of devolution, Scots have, in fact, become more conscious of their British identity rather than less.

11. Corporation tax is a tax that is easy to avoid if there are differential rates across the territories in which a company operates. Ireland has made a living for some decades by attracting international companies to register their profits in that jurisdiction, even if the underlying economic activity is elsewhere.

12. It does not arise in 2016 with the partial devolution of income tax under Calman as a UK-wide rate of tax remains.

REFERENCES

Armstrong, A., and Ebell, M. (2012). Scotland's Currency and Fiscal Choices, *National Institute Economic Review*, 219: 4–9.

Armstrong, A., and Ebell, M. (2014). *Commentary: Monetary Unions and Fiscal Constraints*, 227: 4–7, at www.niesr.ac.uk/publications/commentary-monetary-unions-and-fiscal-constraints (accessed 01/06/15).

Ashcroft, B., (2013). Has Scotland Already Spent Its Oil Fund?, *Scottish Economy Watch*, July 2013, at www.scottisheconomywatch.com/ (accessed 01/06/15).

Better Together. (2013, 2014). *We Belong Together: The Case for a United Kingdom*, July 2013, at http://b.3cdn.net/better/8e048b7c5f09e96602_jem6bc28d.pdf (accessed 01/06/15).

Calman Commission. (2008). *The Future of Scottish Devolution within the Union: A First Report*, Edinburgh: Commission on Scottish Devolution.

Calman Commission. (2009). *Serving Scotland Better: Scotland and the United King-dom in the 21st Century*, Edinburgh: Commission on Scottish Devolution.

Carney, M. (2014). *The Economics of Currency Unions*, Lecture to the Scottish Council for Development and Industry, January 2014, at www.bankofengland. co.uk/publications/Documents/speeches/2014/speech706.pdf (accessed 01/06/15).

Crawford, R., and Tetlow, G. (2014). Fiscal Challenges and Opportunities for an Independent Scotland, *National Institute Economic Review*, 227: 40–53.

Curtice, J., (2013). *So Where Does Scotland Stand on More Devolution?* ScotCen Social Research 2013, at www.natcen.ac.uk/media/282285/ssa13-devo-max-brief-ing-report.pdf (accessed 01/06/15).

Department of Work and Pensions. (2014). *Scotland Analysis: Work and pensions*, 24 April 2014, London: Stationary Office.

Eichorn, J. (2013). *There Was No Rise in Scottish Nationalism: Understanding the SNP Victory*, at blogs.lse.ac.uk (accessed 01/06/15).

Fiscal Affairs Scotland. (2015). *Supplement on GERS 2015*, Glasgow March 2015, at www.fiscalaffairsscotland.co.uk/wp-content/uploads/2015/03/Supplement-on-GERS-2015-rev-180315.pdf (accessed 01/06/15).

Gallagher, J. (2012). England and the Union: *How and Why to Answer the West Lothian Question*, IPPR, London, at www.ippr.org/publications/ (accessed 01/06/15).

Gallagher, J., and Hinze, D. (2005). *Financing Options for Devolved Government in the UK*, University of Glasgow, at www.gla.ac.uk/media/media_22218_en.pdf (accessed 01/06/15).

Gallagher, J., and Maclean, I. (2015). *Nationalists at Westminster Scotland and Ireland a Century Apart,* Nuffield College Working Paper, at www.nuffield.ox.ac.uk/News/Documents/Nationalists-at-Westminster-GG01-2015.pdf (accessed 01/06/15).

HM Treasury. (2014). *Public Expenditure Statistical Analysis*, at www.gov.uk/govern-ment/statistics/public-expenditure-statistical-analyses-2014 (accessed 01/06/15).

Johnson, P., and Phillips, D. (2012). "Scottish Independence: The Fiscal Context", *Institute for Fiscal Studies, Briefing Note BN135*, London: Institute for Fiscal Stud-ies, at www.ifs.org.uk/bns/bn135.pdf (accessed 01/06/15).

Kidd, C. (2008). *Union and Unionisms: Political Thought in Scotland, 1500–2000*. Cambridge: Cambridge University Press.

Mackintosh, J. P. (1968). *The Devolution of Power*, Harmondsworth: Penguin Books.

Maclean, I., Gallagher, J., and Lodge, G. (2014). *Scotland's Choices*. Edinburgh: Edinburgh University Press, 2nd edition.

Rokkan, S., and Unwin, D. (Eds.) (1982). *The Politics of Territorial Identity: Studies in European Regionalism*, London: Sage Publications.

Scottish Government. (2014). *Scotland's Future*, at www.gov.scot/resource/0043/00439021.pdf (accessed 01/06/15).

Scottish Government. (2014a). *Government Expenditure and Revenues in Scotland,* at www.gov.scot/Topics/Statistics/Browse/Economy/GERS (accessed 01/06/15).

Organisation for Economic Cooperation and Development (OECD). (2015). Fiscal Decentralisation Database, at www.oecd.org/tax/federalism/oecdfiscaldecentrali-sationdatabase.htm (accessed 01/06/15).

The Smith Commission. (2014). *Report of the Smith Commission for Further Devo-lution of Powers to the Scottish Parliament*, Edinburgh: The Smith Commission.

Chapter 2

The Aftermath of the Scottish Referendum

A New Fiscal Settlement for the United Kingdom?

David Bell

INTRODUCTION

In the referendum of September 2014, the proposal that Scotland should become an independent country failed. Yet, in the last few days of the campaign, when a 'yes' vote seemed possible, the leaders of the three main Westminster political parties made a 'vow' that Scotland would be granted additional fiscal powers should the outcome of the referendum be a rejection of independence. As soon as the negative result was confirmed, the Prime Minister, David Cameron, set up a commission under Lord Smith of Kelvin to propose sweeping additional fiscal powers for the Scottish Parliament. Draft legislation was produced in January 2015. Some variant of this is likely to become law before the end of the year ¥2015.

In Wales, following the report of the Commission on Devolution in Wales (2012), proposals for further devolution were published in February 2015 following the St David's Day Agreement between the main political parties in Wales. These also had significant fiscal implications, including setting a floor on the relative funding that Wales receives through the Barnett formula and the granting of power to allow the Welsh Parliament to hold a referendum on income tax powers.

Meanwhile, the UK government has agreed to examine the possibility of allowing the Northern Irish executive to set the rate of corporation tax in Northern Ireland. This proposal stems from the 'Rebalancing the Northern Ireland economy' consultation paper produced in 2011.

The United Kingdom has had one of the most centralized fiscal structures among the major industrialized economies. Fiscal powers are more widely distributed between national and sub-national governments (SNGs) in the

United States, Germany, Japan and Canada than in the United Kingdom. During all of the postwar period, the only sub-national tax power in the United Kingdom has been granted to local authorities and applies to domestic and commercial property.

However, given the political chain of events in Scotland, Wales and Northern Ireland, the U.K.'s fiscal structure seems likely to experience radical change. Is this simply a knee-jerk political response to this affection with the centralized nature of the British state or is it a rational course of action that will enhance the welfare of citizens throughout the United Kingdom? This chapter seeks to explain the changes that are in train and to argue that they are not built on a clear set of principles or motivations.

The structure of the chapter is as follows: In Section 2 we discuss the rationale for fiscal federalism – the allocation of tax powers to different levels of government, looking briefly at how it operates in practice in three developed countries. In the following section, we discuss the evolution of additional fiscal powers in Scotland. Section 4 discusses full fiscal autonomy for Scotland, arguing that it is unlikely to come about in the near future. The final section concludes.

FISCAL FEDERALISM

The early literature on fiscal decentralization was based on the premise that preferences for public goods vary spatially. This assumption is quite limiting, since the range of true public goods is relatively small. It is sometimes confused with the belief that preferences for public provision of services such as health and education, which are merit goods rather than public goods, vary from area to area within a country. Nevertheless, ignoring this important distinction, the early fiscal federalism literature asserted that the central state, though always willing to act in the interests of all its citizens, is unable to assemble the information on how preferences vary across its territory and so cannot design policies that maximize the welfare of all its citizens. One solution is to devolve some functions to a lower level of government that is better informed about citizens' preferences and can therefore take more appropriate local policy actions.

The contributions of Tiebout (1956) and Oates (1972) were central to the development of these arguments. Oates developed the 'decentralisation theorem', which suggested that allowing (better-informed) SNGs to make decisions around the supply of local public goods would be welfare enhancing. Other arguments in favour of fiscal decentralization included the argument that the powers of a monopolistic central state should be limited by the countervailing force of strong SNGs, where 'strength' would necessarily imply fiscal powers (Weingast, 1995).

The arguments relating to fiscal federalism have evolved over time. In particular, theories that fall under the umbrella of 'second generation' fiscal federalism (see Oates, 2005) have focused on issues of political economy, information asymmetry and strategic interaction. For example, if preferences do vary spatially, centralized decision making in a national legislature would result in conflict between representatives from different SNGs. Their objective might be to form winning coalitions that best reflect their preferences, even if this means compromising of what they regard as an ideal outcome.

Whether decentralization trumps a centralized legislative framework then depends on the dynamics of political coalitions and how they interact. Other arguments around the economic benefits of decentralization include its ability to foster 'yardstick competition' over the efficiency of public goods provision (Schleifer, 1985): the recognition that 'policy experimentation' may be more easily fostered within a decentralized political structure (Strumpf, 2002) and the benefits of increased accountability that more localized decision making can bring.

Whatever the theoretical arguments, it is clear that fiscal decentralization is relatively common in both developed and developing countries. See, for example, Boadway and Shah (2009), and Cotarelli and Guergill (2014). Many countries embed fiscal decentralization within their constitutions. Thus, any encroachment of central government on SNG tax powers may be an issue of constitutional law and cannot be readily altered. Further, although the courts provide an important mechanism for adjudicating disputes between central and sub-national governments, some countries also have institutions whose role is to adjudicate on disputes between SNGs and their national governments and between SNG governments who may take a differing view on the outcomes of fiscal rules and allocations.

Constitutional provisions and institutional arrangements enable SNGs to vary the public services that they provide. However, they frequently also have a distributive role – to ensure that different SNGs have the capacity to provide a standard or minimum level of public service. This is known as 'horizontal fiscal equity' and frequently involves explicit transfers from relatively rich regions to those that are relatively poor. Clearly, all parties to such arrangements have to be willing participants. One difficulty in establishing such a framework within the United Kingdom is that the SNP is unlikely to be a willing partner in the establishment of such agreements and it currently has a very strong political voice.

Such issues do not exist in Australia. And thus, for example, the role of the Commonwealth Grants Commission is to assess the relative fiscal capacities of the States and Territories and to recommend how tax revenues should be allocated among them (Commonwealth Grants Commission, 2015). It views the establishment of horizontal fiscal equity across the states and territories as among its key objectives. This often means fiscal transfers from states like New South Wales and Victoria to the less affluent parts of Australia. One of its key principles is that each state should have the capacity to provide the same level of public services after equalization payments have been made. However, the states are not mandated to provide this level of service: tax rates and levels of service provision are determined at the state level.

Equalization payments are guaranteed by the Canadian constitution. The Canada Act 1982, which amended the constitution, included the rights of the poorer provinces to equalization payments. Subsection 36(2) of the Constitution Act, 1982, states that 'Parliament and the government of Canada are committed to the principle of making equalization payments to ensure that provincial governments have sufficient revenues to provide reasonably comparable levels of public services at reasonably comparable levels of taxation'. Thus, equalization payments are made to provinces where the application of average tax rates taxes would fall short of the national average tax yield. In contrast to the United Kingdom, provinces are allowed to keep a proportion of royalties from natural resource exploitation, but compensating payments are made to poorer provinces where there are no natural resource rents. The United Kingdom has been consistently unwilling to allow Scotland any share of oil and gas revenues. In contrast, in Canada, Alberta keeps a significant proportion of the oil and gas revenues generated within its borders.

In Germany, complicated tax sharing arrangements are in place, which are designed to ensure horizontal and vertical fiscal equity (Werner, 2003). The equalization system among the federal states (Länderfinanzausgleich) is based on Article 107 of the German constitution, which was designed to protect the weaker länder. Equalization takes place both horizontally and vertically. Germany uses a share of Value-Added Tax (VAT) to establish vertical fiscal balance and then horizontal redistribution to achieve horizontal equity. Table 2.1 shows how the main taxes in Germany were allocated between the federal government, the Länder and communities in 2001.

Table 2.1   Fiscal Allocation by Level of Government in Germany

	Federal Government	Länder	Communities	Revenues 2001
Consumption Tax	100%			€61 bn
Inheritance Tax		100%		€3 bn
Property Tax			100%	€9 bn
Personal Income Tax	42.5%	42.5%	15%	€141 bn
Value added tax	51.4%	46.4%	2.2%	€139 bn
Corporation tax	50%	50%		−€0.4 bn
Interest rebate	44%	44%	12%	€30 bn
Trade tax	14.8%	7.7%	77.5%	€25 bn

Source: Werner and Shah (2005).

The key point from this discussion is that many developed countries have systems in place to allocate fiscal responsibilities between different levels of government. These reallocations are based on a shared view of horizontal and fiscal equalization. They inevitably involve disputes and consequently are often contested by the interested parties (Prud'homme, 1995). Because of their importance to the supply of public services and to levels of taxation, these disputes often lead to change in their design. However, most countries have systems and institutions that prevent such change leading to constitutional crises. This does not appear to be the case in the United Kingdom.

The current proposals for fiscal devolution in the United Kingdom are not the product of any systematic approach to issues of fiscal equity; instead, they appear to be based on political response to constitutional threats. This is not a good starting point: there has been no systematic evaluation of the costs and benefits of fiscal decentralization and little discussion of the constitutional or institutional issues involved. Further complicating the issue is the highly asymmetric nature of the proposals, with Scotland potentially being granted very significant fiscal powers, Wales somewhat less and Northern Ireland a very small extension to its fiscal capacity. The debate on devolution within England has been limited to the extension of additional spending powers to some cities in the North and to discussion of tax-raising powers in both London and the Northern cities.

In the next section, we focus on the changes to fiscal powers in Scotland. They contrast sharply with the models and processes associated with fiscal federalism that have been described in this section.

DEVELOPMENTS IN SCOTLAND

Scotland has been at the centre of the UK debate on increased fiscal powers. The political success of the Scottish National Party was an important driver of this debate on enhanced powers. Unionist parties have tended to accept the (untested) argument that enhanced tax powers would stem the political advance of the SNP. Thus, in 1998, when the Scottish Parliament was established, it was given the power to vary the basic rate of income tax by 3p in the pound. This power was never used.

Following the 2007 Scottish Parliamentary election, after which the SNP formed a minority government, the main Unionist parties in the parliament established a commission to consider further possibilities for the extension of devolution. The Commission on Scottish Devolution (2009) made a number of proposals, many of which were included in the Scotland Act 2012. Its main fiscal provisions were for the Scottish Parliament to assume control over Stamp Duty Land Tax (SDLT) (a tax on property transactions), Landfill

Tax and, most importantly, partial control over income tax. The value of these taxes in 2015–2016 is around £0.4 billion for SDLT, £0.1 billion for Landfill Tax and £4.7 billion for the Scottish Rate of Income Tax (SRIT). SRIT is clearly the most important of the three fiscal measures. Its operation is described in Figure 2.1.

In Figure 2.1, the horizontal axis measures personal income, while the vertical axis shows income tax rates. Thus, no income taxes are payable up to the current personal allowance of approximately £10,000; thereafter, the basic rate of income tax is levied at 20p in the pound up to approximately £42,000, when the higher rate becomes applicable. Figure 2.1 does not show the additional rate of 45p in the pound, which is levied on incomes over £150,000. The SRIT operates by taking 10p from each income tax band: thus the Scottish Government will receive half of all basic rate income tax payments and one-quarter of all higher rate income tax payments in Scotland. The hatched area in Figure 2.1 shows this. The total value of payments to HMRC from SRIT will be around £4.7 billion. HM Treasury will retain the remaining income tax raised in Scotland.

The SRIT mechanism, first, forces the Scottish Government into making a decision about income tax since its block grant from the Westminster Government will be reduced based on the assumption that the tax will be levied at 10p in the pound. Second, the mechanism is restrictive in that it prevents the Scottish Government from changing the size of basic, higher and additional bands and the rate of progression between bands. This means that the Scottish government cannot have a more 'progressive' income tax structure than that in the rest of the United Kingdom. Marginal income tax rates will still be controlled by the UK government.

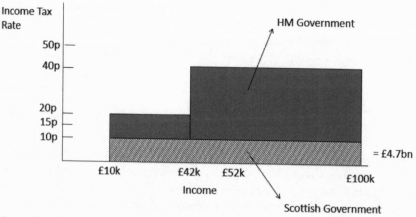

Figure 2.1   The Scottish Rate of Income Tax

The three tax powers included in the Scotland Act 2012 will be further supplemented if the Scotland Bill 2015 is enacted. As a result of the 'vow' and the subsequent Smith Commission, the proposal is that Scotland takes full control over income tax other than the definition of taxable income, the setting of the personal allowance and the taxation of savings and investment income. This will enable it to set tax rates and bands above the personal allowance as it sees fit. Hence, future Scottish governments will be in a position to fundamentally change the structure of income tax relative to the rest of the United Kingdom. It could make the structure more or less progressive depending on its political complexion relative to that of the governing party in the UK Parliament.

In addition, the Scottish Government will be assigned 10%/T% of the VAT revenues raised in Scotland where T% is the UK VAT rate (currently 20%). Therefore, at current rates, the Scottish Government will be assigned half of the VAT revenues raised in Scotland. This will have no particular implications for policy, since this is simply an 'assigned' tax. The Scottish Government will not have the power to change the structure of VAT in any way.

Finally, under the Scotland Bill 2015, Scotland will also be given the power to set Air Passenger Duty. The Scottish Government has long argued that this duty is an obstacle to the development of the Scottish tourist industry. This new power will allow it to redesign this measure, changing the incentives for air travellers to and from Scotland. Of course, if rates are cut and the revenue from that tax falls, other tax and spending plans will have to adjust.

Figure 2.2 shows how far these additional tax powers will increase the share of revenues raised in Scotland that are retained by the Scottish Parliament. Each panel shows the taxes that are levied on activity in Scotland or within Scottish territorial waters. Each rectangle within the panel is proportionate to the size of revenues derived from that source. Hence, the rectangles associated with income tax, national insurance and VAT tend to dominate within each panel. Each panel also shows how revenues are allocated between the UK Parliament (Westminster) and the Scottish Parliament (Holyrood). The panels show the development of fiscal powers and the consequent increasing attribution of revenues to the Scottish Parliament over the last few years; the first panel shows the situation prior to the introduction of the Scotland Act 2012. At that time, the only major fiscal instruments available in Scotland were council tax and non-domestic rates. Although these are in theory controlled by local authorities, the Scottish Government has frequently intervened to influence their structure. One of the most notable interventions has been the freezing of Council Tax, a measure introduced by the minority SNP government in 2007 and which is still in force. Though it is argued that this measure particularly benefits more affluent homeowners, the opposition to the measure has been muted.

David Bell

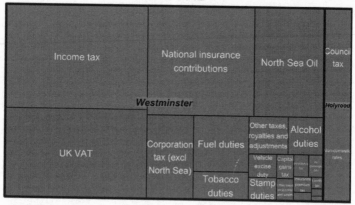

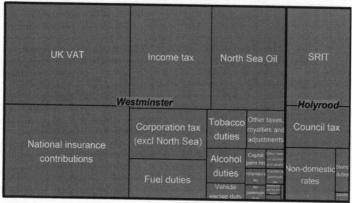

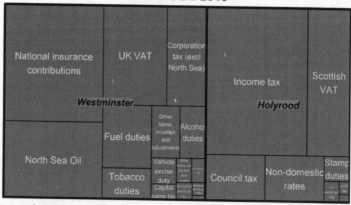

Figure 2.2   **Changing Structure of Scotland's Fiscal Powers**

Together, council tax and non-domestic rates accounted for around 8.1% of total Scottish revenues (including a geographic share of North Sea oil revenues) in 2012–2013. Compared with most developed countries, this implies that the Scottish Government retained (or at least was responsible for) only a very small proportion of the revenues raised within its boundaries. This is described as a large 'vertical fiscal imbalance'. The Scotland Act 2012 will raise that proportion to around 19% when it is fully implemented in fiscal year 2016–2017. (Although the Scottish Government is now responsible for levying Landfill Tax and Stamp Duty Land Tax, it has taken four years to establish the administrative structures within HMRC necessary to support SRIT and, therefore, the Scottish Finance Secretary will announce the rate of SRIT in his next draft budget, expected in November or December 2015.)

The second panel in Figure 2.2 shows a significant shift in the balance between those taxes for which Holyrood is responsible and those that are remitted to Westminster. The key additional elements are SRIT, Stamp Duty Land Tax and Landfill Tax. The final panel in Figure 2.2 shows the likely division of fiscal responsibilities between Westminster and Holyrood should the Scotland Bill 2015 be enacted. With the addition of all of the income tax, half of VAT revenues, and Air Passenger Duty, the Scottish Parliament will retain around 41% of revenues raised in Scotland.

An international perspective on these changes in revenue-raising powers can be seen in Figure 2.3. This is drawn from OECD data and shows the

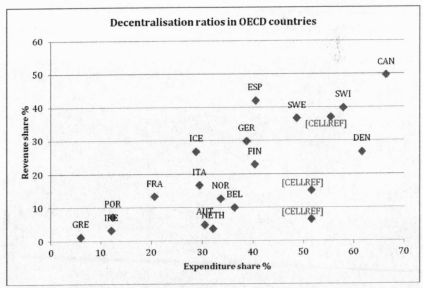

Figure 2.3   Decentralisation of Expenditure and Revenue Raising in OECD Countries.
Source: OECD Fiscal Federalism Database.

proportion of revenues retained by sub-national governments (horizontal axis) against the proportion of expenditure for which sub-national governments are responsible (vertical axis). Most sub-national governments spend significantly more than they raise in taxes.

Scotland has extensive responsibilities for spending within its borders on services that benefit its citizens, covering areas such as health, education, culture, transport and economic development. Hence, as Figure 2.3 shows, its expenditure share is well above the OECD average. The changes in revenue-raising responsibilities just described will propel it towards the top of the OECD league in terms of revenue share. Only countries such as Switzerland and Canada have more extensive subnational control over revenue raising and spending responsibilities.

Figure 2.3 shows some increase in spending responsibilities between the Scotland Act 2012 and the Scotland Bill 2015. This relates to the powers over welfare spending that are included in the Scotland Bill. The welfare powers to be transferred to the Scottish Parliament are shown in Figure 2.4. Again, the size of the rectangles is proportional to the amount spent on the various benefits and, again, the division between Westminster and Holyrood responsibilities is highlighted. Following the changes, around £2.5 billion will be transferred to the Scottish Government to distribute on benefits such as Disability Living Allowance, Attendance Allowance, Carers' Allowance etc. The total benefits expenditure in Scotland in 2013–2014 was £14.4 billion.

The transfer of welfare powers is perhaps more surprising than the transfer of revenue-raising capabilities. It marks a significant reversal of the post-war consensus around the universality of social insurance within the United

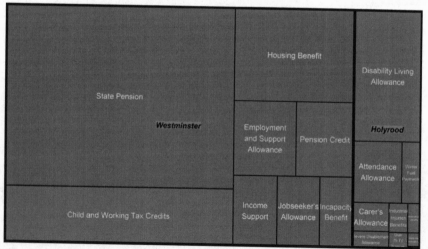

Figure 2.4   Welfare Powers to Be Transferred to the Scottish Parliament

Kingdom,[1] a system that was built around the idea of pooling risk across the whole of the United Kingdom against adverse events such as unemployment, homelessness, illness, poverty in old age and bereavement.

One of the many complications associated with the transfer of welfare powers is their inter-relatedness both with each other and with the tax system. Thus, for example, some benefits are paid net of income tax and therefore decisions made by the Scottish Government could affect the level of benefits paid by the UK Government. Some benefits trigger other payments and, again, this can lead to intergovernmental transfers. For example, mobility-related disability benefits can 'passport' individuals into lower vehicle excise duty and lower VAT on vehicle leases. Conceivably, under this new division of responsibilities, changes to benefit regulations made by the Scottish Parliament could have revenue implications for the UK Treasury.

A further complication with the transfer of welfare powers is that benefit expenditure in the United Kingdom is drawn from 'Annually Managed Expenditure' (AME). The Scottish Budget is effectively drawn from a different pot of UK Government cash known as Departmental Expenditure Limits (DEL). The reason for this division is that DEL can reasonably be managed over a longer time horizon than AME, which is essentially demand driven. The issue that arises, therefore, is how the welfare expenditure for which the Scottish Government becomes responsible will be treated within the Scottish Government's accounts. If it is transferred into DEL, then its funding will be subject to competition from other government priorities such as health and education. If this is not the case, then how will the Scottish Government divide its budget between its welfare responsibilities and other expenditure? This is complicated further by the interactions that undoubtedly take place between expenditures that are classified as DEL and those as AME. For example, Attendance Allowance is funded from AME and described as a benefit 'to help with personal care because you're physically or mentally disabled and you're aged 65 or over' (Department for Work and Pensions, 2015). Yet, Scotland has a policy to provide those aged 65+ with 'free personal care', which is drawn from its DEL budget. Suppose that Scotland is able to make savings in meeting the overall costs of disability by more closely integrating Attendance Allowance with other forms of support for those who need personal care. How will this be accounted for and how will it affect transfers from the UK Government to the Scottish Government to support its new welfare responsibilities? There are clearly a great many uncertainties associated with the transfer of welfare powers.

The issue of transfers between the Scottish and UK Governments is critical to understanding the incentives – risks and rewards – that follow from the substantial increase in revenue raising and spending powers for the Scottish Government that is currently in train. This argument further generalizes to the Welsh and Northern Irish cases. Transfers of responsibility for a tax to a sub-national government increase its incentive to maximize revenue from that tax. Transfers of welfare spending to a sub-national government increase its incentive to control welfare spending. But the UK Government has committed to maintaining the Barnett formula and, although the Scottish Government argues with increasingly weakening conviction for 'full fiscal autonomy', which would mean the end of Barnett, in reality all of the devolved parliaments are also committed to its continuation.

However, Barnett has to be amended when tax and spending powers are transferred. The block grant that is determined by the Barnett formula has to be adjusted to take account of these new powers. And the way that it is adjusted will influence the risks and rewards that the Scottish, Welsh and Northern Irish Parliaments confront. This leads to a discussion of the somewhat arcane topic of the 'Block Grant Adjustment' (BGA). Nevertheless, the setting of the BGA is central to understanding the likely economic and fiscal effects of the transfer of tax and welfare powers to these governments.

The BGA works as follows: in the first year of its operation, the Barnett formula block grant is reduced by the same amount as the devolved parliament raises in tax. This means that HM Treasury is neither better nor worse off as a result of the introduction of the tax power. For the sake of argument, let us focus on income tax being raised by the Scottish Government. The key question is this: How should the block grant be adjusted after the first year?

If the BGA was simply equated to the tax revenues raised by the Scottish Parliament each year, there would be no change in the Scottish budget compared with what would have happened under the Barnett formula. The Scottish Government would raise a certain amount of tax and each year the same amount would be withdrawn from its block grant from HM Treasury. Unless the devolved parliament was willing to use its tax powers actively to change tax rates or tax bands and so raise or lower tax revenues, the whole exercise would be pointless. There would be no effect on the devolved parliament's budget except that it would have to meet the administrative costs of establishing and running the new tax arrangements.

This is not what will happen. After year 1, the BGA will be increased by the rate of growth of the tax base in the rest of the United Kingdom. The faster the economic growth outside Scotland is, the larger will be the deduction from Scotland's block grant. This method of adjusting the BGA is known as the indexed deduction method and was devised by Holtham (2009). Its design establishes the incentives that will face the Scottish Government when it takes control of income tax. These are depicted in Figure 2.5, which shows how the block grant will be determined in the first and second years following the introduction of income tax powers in Scotland.

The Indexed Deduction Method

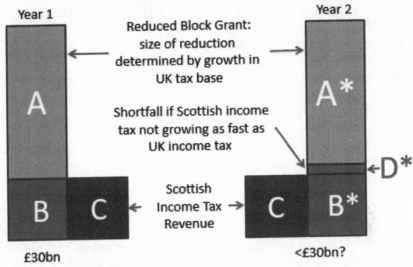

Figure 2.5   The Block Grant Adjustment

Assume that prior to the introduction of the tax power, Scotland's block grant is around £30 billion (A + B in Figure 2.5) and that income tax revenues are around £11 billion (C in Figure 2.5). In Year 1 of the new income tax power, to ensure that the UK and Scottish budgets are unaffected, £11 billion will be deducted from the Scottish block grant. In Year 2, the Scottish income tax base does not expand and income tax revenues stay fixed at £11 billion. However, as a result of more rapid economic growth outside Scotland, the rest of the UK income tax base increases by 5%. The deduction from the Scottish block grant therefore increases by 5%, taking it to £11.55 billion (B* + D* in Figure 2.5). The net effect is that Scottish income tax revenues are insufficient to compensate for the loss of block grant, leaving a shortfall of £550 million (D* in Figure 2.5) in the Scottish budget. It will be £29.45 billion rather than £30 billion, while the UK Government's budget will increase by £550 million compared with the Barnett formula outcome. (The media have failed to notice that the establishment of SRIT gives the UK Government, concerned about public spending outside Scotland, the incentive to ensure that UK economic growth should be concentrated outside Scotland.)

The design of the BGA therefore gives the Scottish Government an incentive to grow its tax base more rapidly than in the rest of the United Kingdom. The income tax power and the design of the BGA may provide this incentive, but it is not clear that the tax power itself is an effective mechanism for stimulating such growth. Variations in income tax may influence labour supply at the margin, but policies around the development of physical and human capital, innovation and market behaviour are more commonly thought to be the origins of effective growth policy.

One positive aspect of the indexed deduction method is that it protects the devolved government's budget from external economic shocks that affect the whole of the UK economy: in these circumstances, tax base growth would be reduced equally across the whole of the United Kingdom and the BGA would be unaffected. Hence the external shock would have no differential effect on the size of the devolved parliament's budget relative to that in the United Kingdom. Either government could take fiscal action in response to the external shock.

This discussion illustrates the more general point that the incentives implicit in the transfer of fiscal powers to the devolved parliaments may be somewhat opaque. Because they are dependent on detailed regulations that will not be included in the legislation, their precise detail may be fashioned by bilateral negotiation between the relevant devolved government and the corresponding UK department, often HM Treasury. This has certainly been the experience of Scotland in relation to the determination of the BGA.

As far as the welfare powers are concerned, a decision will have to be made on the increase in the Scottish budget that will be necessary to compensate it for the additional expenditure responsibilities that it is adopting. Again, the structure of this budgetary adjustment will determine the incentives that the Scottish Government will face. The welfare powers being transferred to Scotland mostly concerned disability: one mechanism for adjusting the annual transfer to the Scottish Government might be to index it to relative disability trends in Scotland and the rest of the United Kingdom. This kind of arrangement would, of course, be open to challenge, and one might wish to consider what mechanism could be in place to ensure that a fair and acceptable solution is established.

Such mechanisms would be unnecessary if, instead, Scotland took complete responsibility for taxation and spending within its boundaries. This is described as full fiscal autonomy, and is discussed in the next section.

FULL FISCAL AUTONOMY

Full fiscal autonomy is the most extreme form of fiscal decentralization. Sub-national governments become entirely responsible for their own spending and taxes. Each sub-national government makes a payment to the central government to pay for central government services, such as defence, foreign affairs, international aid etc. The Scottish Government has argued that this is the most desirable form of fiscal arrangement short of independence (Scottish Government, 2009).

Nevertheless, instances where this kind of arrangement has been put in place are relatively rare. The case most frequently cited is that of the Basque Country and Navarra in Spain, where the GDP per head is significantly higher than the Spanish average. However, it would be unwise to infer causality from this observation. Higher GDP per head may have led to fiscal decentralization rather than vice versa. Indeed, there is no consensus on the evidence that decentralization stimulates economic growth: indeed, if anything, the evidence points in the opposite direction (see, for example, Baskaran and Feld, 2013).

The Basque Country has full fiscal autonomy in all taxes except VAT (where EU regulations prevent sub-national autonomy). These powers and how they compare with the other, less fiscally independent 'autonomous communities' in Spain are shown in Table 2.2.

The Basque Country pays a 'quota' or 'cupo' to the Spanish Government to maintain central state expenditures for defence, foreign policy, debt interest

Table 2.2 Allocation of Tax Powers within Spanish Autonomous Communities Including the Basque Country and Navarra

Main Taxes in Spain	Legislative Powers of the Basque Country and Navarra	Legislative Powers of Common System Autonomous Communities
Personal Income Tax	Total Regulation of the Tax	Tax rates (must have the same number of tax brackets as the state tax), tax credits under certain conditions
Corporation tax	Total regulation of the tax	None
Tax on income of non-residents	Regulation of the tax only in the case of permanent establishments in the charter territory	None
Wealth tax	Total regulation of the tax	Tax Rates, Minimum Threshold, Tax Credits
Death and gift taxes	Total regulation of the tax	Deductions (Mainly for Family Circumstances) Tax Rates, Deduction and Tax Credits, Tax Administration Regulations
Taxes on transfers and official documents	Total regulation of the tax	Tax rates, tax credits, tax administration
Value added tax	None	None
Excise duties	None	None

Source: Zubiri (2007), Ruiz-Almendral (2012).

etc. The Spanish Government has retained responsibility for welfare benefits including pensions and unemployment benefits. In respect of borrowing, the powers available to the Basque Country are no different from the autonomous communities but it tends to have better credit ratings.

Importantly, the Basque Country has agreed with the Spanish Government that it will respect some general principles in respect of its tax policies. These relate to solidarity, correspondence with the structure of state taxation, coordination, tax harmonization, mutual collaboration and compliance with treaties and international agreements signed by the Spanish state. (Colino, 2013)

Thus, the Basque Country is subject to decisions made by the Spanish Government around issues such as macroeconomic stability, fiscal consolidation and debt. It also benefits from at least 60 to 80% more per capita funding than other autonomous communities. This has, for example, allowed it to spend twice as much as the Spanish average on health, education and social services.

Tax rates in the Basque Country are not greatly different from the rest of Spain. Personal income tax rates are slightly higher and more progressive and there are more tax credits conditional on family circumstances. The rate of corporation tax is slightly lower. (Colino, 2013). The Basque Country is an interesting example that is possibly the closest practical example of full fiscal autonomy. However, although it clearly enjoys a great deal of freedom in designing its tax system, there are subtle constraints on its action, which lead to outcomes that are not substantially different from those in other parts of Spain.

Could full fiscal autonomy operate successfully in Scotland? This issue has been the subject of considerable speculation since the referendum and particularly since the outcome of the general election that resulted in 56 of Scotland's 59 MPs coming from the Scottish National Party. However, the view of independent analysts has been that, at least in the short to medium term, full fiscal autonomy would not be viable. There are two important constraints on its implementation. First, the United Kindom is in the midst of a major fiscal consolidation following the financial crisis of 2009. Second, the price of oil, which is the most important determinant of UK oil and gas revenues, has collapsed over the last year, leading to a massive downgrade in the projections of future revenues. Prior to the independence referendum, it was broadly believed that higher public spending per head in Scotland was broadly compensated by the revenues from oil and gas, which are largely located in Scottish territorial waters. This no longer seems to be the case. Historic and projected oil revenues along with the movement in the oil price are shown in Figure 2.6.

There has been a remarkable fall in oil revenues from almost £12 billion in 2008–2009 to £4 billion in 2013–2014. And because of the precipitous fall

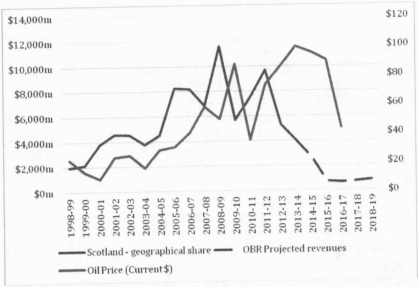

Figure 2.6   Oil Revenues from Scottish Territorial Waters, OBR Projections of Future oil Revenues, and the Oil Price ($US) (Right-Hand Axis). *Source*: Scottish Government: Government Expenditure and Revenue in Scotland, US Energy Information Administration.

in the oil price, future projections alongside issues such as more difficult and costly exploration and decommissioning costs suggest that there will be no short- to medium-term recovery in oil revenues and, indeed, oil revenues will continue to fall.

The decline in oil revenues means that the fiscal situation for Scotland is now considerably more difficult. The argument that the decline in oil revenues weakens the case for full fiscal autonomy has been put by Phillips (2015). He argues that following the decline in the oil price, the Scottish budget deficit in 2015–2016 will be larger than the UK deficit. The Scottish deficit will be around 8.6% of the GDP compared with a 4% deficit for the United Kingdom as a whole. Closing the gap between the Scottish deficit and the UK deficit would mean reductions in spending in Scotland or increases in taxation of around £7.6 billion. Projections of future deficits do not suggest that a delay in closing the gap would make it any easier.

The key difference between Scotland and the Basque Country is that the latter enjoys significantly higher living standards than the rest of Spain and can generate sufficient tax revenues to make its fiscal position manageable, whereas Scotland, following the fall in the oil price, is in a more difficult position. As a result, it is unlikely that there will be significant short-run polit-ical pressure from within Scotland for a move towards full fiscal autonomy.

CONCLUSION

This chapter has briefly reviewed some of the arguments around fiscal federalism in theory and in practice. Compared with other developed countries, the United Kingdom has no consistent approach to, or commitment to, creating fiscal equity across its various nations and regions. It lacks the legal and institutional framework to put such mechanisms in place.

As a result, it does not have the kind of legal or institutional framework that is available in other countries to resolve conflicts over which level of government should levy which tax. Neither is there much empirical evidence from the United Kingdom on the tax structures most likely to promote economic efficiency.

We have reviewed the fiscal measures that have already been put in place for Scotland and those that are proposed under the Scotland Bill 2015. Whether these will be followed by additional powers in Wales and Northern Ireland is not entirely clear, but if this occurs, the structure of taxation in the United States will be extremely complex, asymmetric, lacking in any clear underlying principles or logic and without the institutional or legal structure that might help to resolve conflicts.

The risks and rewards associated with current and prospective fiscal changes cannot be considered independently of the Barnett formula. In particular, the design of the block grant adjustment (BGA) is critical to understanding the incentives that will face the Scottish Government if it hopes to increase its budget for public spending. Critical to this will be its ability to increase the size of its tax base more rapidly than that in the rest of the United Kingdom.

The new fiscal powers associated with the Scotland Bill 2015 will further extend the share of revenues raised in Scotland that are retained by the Scottish Government. It will have among the highest shares of retained revenue in the OECD. Whether these can be used to stimulate economic growth is much more questionable: the international evidence does not suggest that there is a clear causal link between tax decentralization and increased economic growth. Indeed, the evidence suggests that the effects range from neutral to negative.

The outcome of the general election might suggest that the Scottish people wish to see additional tax and welfare powers, beyond those already included in the Scotland Bill, to be devolved to Scotland. This suggests that the support for the postwar consensus around social insurance and risk pooling across the whole of the United Kingdom is disappearing rapidly, at least as far as Scotland is concerned.

However, the fall in the oil price since 2014 makes the economics of Scotland's virtually complete fiscal separation from the rest of the United

Kingdom (FFA) very dubious in the short to medium term. Scotland appears to be benefiting economically from risk sharing while simultaneously rejecting it politically.

NOTE

1. Although Northern Ireland has had its own social security system for some time, it has always followed the rates and categories of benefit set in the rest of the United Kingdom. Indeed, when the Northern Ireland Executive recently failed to pass the necessary legislation to introduce Universal Credit, it found itself paying fines to HM Treasury for the savings in benefit expenditure that it had 'failed' to make.

REFERENCES

Baskaran, T., and Feld, L. P. (2013). Fiscal Decentralization and Economic Growth in OECD Countries: Is There a Relationship?, *Public Finance Review*, 41, 4: 421–45.

Boadway, R., and Shah, A. (2009). *Fiscal Federalism: Principles and Practice of Multiorder Governance*. Cambridge: Cambridge University Press.

Colino, C. (2013). Devolution-Max à la Basque: A Model for a Scotland within the UK?, *David Hume Institute, Research Paper*.

Commission on Devolution in Wales. (2012). (accessed at: http://bit.ly/1HFAW8a, 4/7/2015) (accessed 10/06/2015).

Commission on Scottish Devolution. (2009). (accessed at: http://bit.ly/1faODSf, 4/7/2015) (accessed 10/06/2015).

Commonwealth Grants Commission. (2015). (accessed at: https://www.cgc.gov.au/ on 4/7/2015) (accessed 10/06/2015).

Cottarelli, C., and Guergil, M. (Eds.) (2014). *Designing a European Fiscal Union: Lessons from the Experience of Fiscal Federations,* (Vol. 34,) London: Routledge.

Department of Work and Pensions. (2015). *Attendance Allowance,* London: DWP, https://www.gov.uk/government/uploads/system/uploads/attachment_data/file/447485/aa1a-interactive-jul-2015.pdf (accessed 01/2015).

Oates, W. E. (1972). *Fiscal Federalism*, New York: Harcourt Brace Jovanovich.

Oates, W. E. (2005). Toward a Second-Generation Theory of Fiscal Federalism. *International Tax and Public Finance*, 12, 4: 349–73.

Prud'Homme, R. (1995). The Dangers of Decentralization. *The World Bank Research Observer*, 10, 2: 201–20.

Phillips, D. (2015). Full Fiscal Autonomy Delayed? The SNP's Plans for Further Devolution to Scotland, *Institute for Fiscal Studies*, Accessed at: http://www.ifs.org.uk/publications/7722 3/7/2015 (accessed 10/06/2015).

Ruiz Almendral, V. (2012). Sharing Taxes and Sharing the Deficit in Spanish Fiscal Federalism, *eJournal of Tax Research*, 10, 1: 88–125.

Shleifer, A. (1985). A Theory of Yardstick Competition, *The RAND Journal of Economics*, 319–27.

David Bell

Scottish Government. (2009). Fiscal Autonomy in Scotland: The Case for Change and Options for Reform, http://www.gov.scot/Resource/Doc/261814/0078318.pdf (accessed 03/07/2015).

Strumpf, K. (2002). Does Government Decentralization Increase Policy Innovation? *Journal of Public Economic Theory*, 4: 207–41.

Tiebout, C. M. (1956). A Pure Theory of Local Expenditures. *The Journal of Political Economy*, 64, 5: 416–24.

Weingast, B. R. (1995). The Economic Role of Political Institutions: Market-Preserving Federalism and Economic Development, *Journal of Law and Economic Organization*, 11: 1–3.

Werner, J. (2003). El Federalismo Fiscal Aleman: En Estado de Fluctuacion in Zergak, *Gaceta Tributaria Del Pais Vasco*, 25: 81–113.

Werner, J., and Shah, A. (2005). Fiscal Equalisation in Germany. Washington: World Bank Paper. Accessed January, 21: 2011. http://info.worldbank.org/etools/docs/library/241116/FiscalEqualisationInGermany.pdf

Zubiri, I. (2007). Los sistemas forales: características, resultados y su posible generalización. En Lago, S. (Ed.) *La financiación del Estado de las autonomías: perspectivas de futuro,* Madrid: Instituto de Estudios Fiscales, 355–88.

Chapter 3

Local Tax Reform in Scotland

Fiscal Decentralization or Political Solution?

Kenneth Gibb and Linda Christie

INTRODUCTION

The current system of local taxation in Scotland, the council tax, is being fundamentally reviewed. Sir Peter Burt, the chair of the 2006 Local Government Finance Review Committee (the Scottish Executive rejected its property tax proposals outright), recently identified a key problem with designing taxes: *'Louis XIV's finance minister said the art of tax was like plucking the goose – to obtain the largest possible amount of feathers with the smallest possible amount of hissing'* (*The Herald*, June 17, 2015, p. 10).

Alongside debates concerning the fiscal and economic consequences of the additional devolution proposals made by the Smith Commission for Scotland, whether there should be more powers granted to Wales and the more ad hoc city-region questions arising from City Deals, the taxing and funding position of local government remains unresolved, complex and contentious. In Scotland, however, there is the chance of movement, as the result of the Commission on Local Taxation Reform (CLTR), which has the remit to look at the reform or abolition of council tax and to address (if it chooses to) the council tax freeze, now in its eighth continuous year. However, the Commission's brief does not extend to non-domestic taxation; nor does it include the balance between grant in aid and local revenues, or the system of grant allocation and the broader debate between local government autonomy and central government influence and control.

The CLTR was announced in late 2014, and set up in the spring of 2015 with a view to collect evidence, do its analysis and report in the autumn of 2015 in time for the development of party manifestos for the Spring 2016 Scottish election. It is a broad-based commission featuring all the major political parties (absenting only the Scottish Conservatives, who are pursuing their own 'low tax' commission), independents and relevant professional bodies, and is co-chaired by the local government minister and the convener of the Convention of Scottish Local Authorities (and is serviced by a Secretariat drawn from government and COSLA officials).

The Commission remit is to identify and examine alternatives to the Council Tax that would deliver a *fairer system of local taxation*. In doing so, the Commission will consider the following:

• the impacts on individuals, households and inequalities in income and wealth.
• the wider impacts, including housing market and land use.
• administration and collection, including transition and subsequent operation.
• potential timetables for transition, given the 2017 Local Government elections.
• the impacts on supporting local democracy, that is financial accountability and autonomy.
• The revenue raising capacity of the alternatives.

In the light of the CLTR's work[1] this chapter will do the following: First, it will set out how the council tax works and describe the problems it is commonly associated with. It will also set the council tax in its contemporary taxation, finance and policy context, including recent history in Scotland. Second, it will examine the arguments for and against the deployment of five strategies of reform – reformed council tax, a new property tax, a land value tax, a new local income tax or some combination of property and income taxes. The third and main section draws on a recent international evidence review of local taxation by the authors for the CLTR and in particular looks at what we know about efforts elsewhere to reform property taxes (Gibb and Christie, 2015). The final section asks, given the limited remit of the Commission, what the possible or desirable, and the likely outcomes we might expect to see are, and how these might form the basis for something more durable.

THE COUNCIL TAX: HOW WE GOT HERE AND WHY IT IS A PROBLEM

The council tax was an inherently political solution to the considerable difficulties of the Community Charge (commonly known as the 'poll tax'). It was to be a new hybrid tax that would be collectable (unlike the poll tax) and avoid a return to the (apparently) discredited domestic rates system (Gibb, 1988; 1992). The objective with the new council tax was to neutralize what had become the toxic politics of local taxation, but to do so in such a way that retained the less salient but nonetheless attractive features of the poll tax system of local government finance, such as personal discounts for single adults and single-person households (and the overarching grant system and nationalization of non-domestic rates).

The council tax was a compromise, a fix that would allow normal political life to resume. Nearly twenty-five years later, it is easy to say that without active management this was unlikely to work well over such a time horizon. However, the setting up of the council tax had a much shorter time horizon, it was done quickly and did not carefully consider the long-term (unintended) consequences.

What are the key features of the council tax as it now applies in Scotland? First, it is based on property values set at 1991 prices (or if built subsequently or resold – properties are valued at an imputed 1991 value). Only in Wales have council tax valuations been updated since 1991 (in 2007). Actively not carrying out a general periodic revaluation stems from the political desire to avoid the previous problems with rates revaluations. This instinct not to revalue is cumulative and harder to unwind the longer time goes on. Almy (2013) argues that these tendencies to soften property taxation lead to 'legislative neglect'.

Second, the council tax is a hybrid tax with elements of a property tax but also retaining features of the poll tax; chiefly, personal discounts were offered to single-adult households. Along with exempted properties, this means that a little over a half (55%) of Scottish dwellings are liable for the full council tax.

Third, properties were banded into 7 (later 8) bands such that each property within a band in a given local authority faces the same gross liability. A council in principle sets the Band D tax liability and all other bands are a fixed percentage of Band D. The actual payments for each band were deliberately compressed in terms of their differentials. As Table 3.1 displays, this meant that in Scotland, those with the lowest values (under £27,000 in 1991 values) paid 2/3 of the reference Band D and those in the highest Band (H), with properties exceeding £212,000 in 1991 values, paid twice the level of Band D. We can also see from Figure 3.1 that the bandings do not relate well to the proportions of properties in each band, with more than 3/5 of all properties in the lowest three bands and only one per cent in the top band.

The Burt Review in 2006 noted that they could not find any other country that taxed property, but which also used a banding system of some kind. However, in 2013, the Irish government decided to introduce a new property tax, which incorporated 19 bands (Gibb and Christie, 2015). For the UK council tax, comparing Band A with Band H, we see that properties are at least nine times more expensive but pay only three times more in council tax (and more expensive Band H properties, for instance in excess of a million,

Table 3.1   **Scottish Council Tax System**

Band	% of All Dwellings (2013)	Value Range (1991)	Percentage of D
A	21	Up to £27,000	67
B	24	£27,001–35,000	78
C	16	£35,001–45,000	89
D	13	£45,001–58,000	100
E	13	£58,001–80,000	122
F	7	£80,001–106,000	144
G	5	£106,001–212,000	167
H	1	£212,001 or more	200

continue to pay only three times more than the lowest valued properties). The system, in other words, has been designed to reduce the council tax liability on homeowners and particularly those with higher value properties.

Fourth, council tax also has a means-tested rebate system to help those on low incomes, providing up to 100% support for those on social security such as income support. This changed after the 2010 UK General Election when in England, Council Tax Benefit was cut by 10% and decentralized. In Scotland, the Scottish Government chose to pay the 10% from the Block and broadly retain the old system under the new name of Council Tax Reduction.

DIFFICULTIES WITH COUNCIL TAX

First, there is the failure to carry out regular general revaluations. While we understand the political calculation behind simply not revaluing, the long-term effect is corrosive. Not only is increasing resource required to value new properties back to 1991 values; but more importantly, we have no sense of the adequacy of the banding today. Have properties and their neighbourhoods remained static in relative terms and not risen or fallen with economic and social change? Of course not. Burt (2006) noted that between broadly 1993 and 2005, Scottish house prices rose by around 90% while in the same period Band D council tax increased by 10% – this also masks wider local variation.

Second, council tax is regressive in two important ways. First, as a proportion of property value, lower-valued properties pay a larger proportion of their value in council tax than do higher-valued properties. To the extent that the distribution of property values proxies for wealth, this is not fair in a progressive sense. This is a direct consequence of the banding weighting system. Second, the Burt Review in 2006 also suggested that lower decile income groups tend to pay an increasing share of their income in council tax, but that it falls once we are over the median level of income. Households in the top two deciles pay the lowest proportion of their income in council tax.

It is also the case that the poorest 10% appear to pay more than anyone else despite income-related assistance.

Council tax liability is also non-neutral with respect to location in different parts of the country. In their work for the Joseph Rowntree Foundation, Chris Leishman and colleagues (2014) report that council tax as a proportion of property value was higher in low-value northern English regions compared to London and South East England.

Local tax needs to be collectable and council tax scores well on that criteria, but it does less well in terms of buoyancy and yield. The tax base is fundamentally inelastic – it does not increase until more homes are built or there is a general revaluation – thus, yield increase is much more dependent on tax rate increases, that is, the Band D rate. Moreover, and in part because of this structural feature of the tax rate for the council tax, in Scotland there has now been eight years of council tax freeze, reducing the real contribution of the council tax and its share of local government revenue. The freeze also reduces the autonomy and accountability of elected local governments since there is, in effect, no taxable variation to meet local spending platforms (Commission on Strengthening Local Democracy, 2014).

THE LOCAL GOVERNMENT FINANCE CONTEXT

Council tax is the residual element in the system and in principle is the element local government has discretion over along with, to a limited extent, the scope to draw on fees and charges, and, more recently, by dipping into reserves. Central Government grant in part tries to compensate for differences in local spending need, but also provides support for specific services and on a per capita basis redistributes non-domestic rate income back to local governments.

In an early presentation to the CLTR, the head of CIPFA Scotland, Don Peebles,[2] laid out key points about local government finance and the council tax context in Scotland:

- The net spending by councils in 2013–2014 was £12.55 billion. The revenue to pay for that spending came from Scottish Government Grant (£7.225 b), and non-domestic rate income (£2.436 b), while other income and reserves accounted for £0.877 billion, leaving £1.977 billion raised by the council tax.
- The annual cost of the council tax freeze begun in 2008–2009 was £70 million from the Scottish Block. In the second year, to retain the level of support, the annual cost was £140 million, the following year, £210 million, such that by the current year (2015–2016), the cost per annum of the

council tax freeze is £560 million. In cash terms, the cumulative overall loss to the Scottish Block is £2.52 billion.

There are four main political contextual factors pertaining to the council tax in Scotland. First, in 2006, the then Labour–Lib Dem coalition rejected the substantial inquiry into local tax chaired by Peter Burt, before it was published (and to be fair, all the parties rejected it). This inquiry proposed a flat rate percentage property tax, regularly revalued, on capital values (the approach adopted from 2007 in Northern Ireland). Second, the SNP minority government (2007–2011) hatched a plan to use the 3p in the pound income tax discretionary power (the so-called *Tartan Tax*) to shift domestic local tax to a flat rate common level across Scotland (i.e., ending *local* taxation altogether). This, however, would not generate sufficient revenues and was subsequently dropped.

Third, and as mentioned earlier, for eight successive years, there has been a council tax freeze paid for out of the Block programme wherein councils are 'fined' by grant reduction if they choose not to continue with the freeze. This has been promoted as a way of reducing household bills, but, of course, it is of greatest benefit to those with higher council tax bands. Finally, the decision to launch a broad-based and multi-party commission approach at the end of 2014 is now under way with a view to providing analysis and options for reform for the political parties to include in their electoral platform for the spring of 2016. The broad base of the current commission contrasts strongly with the expert team led by Sir Peter Burt appointed by the Scottish Executive.

FIVE APPROACHES TO LOCAL TAX REFORM

Council tax was designed to be the most inoffensive tax possible with which to salve unruly homeowners, but its design arguably undermined its long-term coherence as a valid form of taxation. The implication for the CLTR is what this means for the fundamental choice between reform and abolition. Are adjustments in the form of re-banding, re-weighting bands and/or offering a commitment to regular general revaluations sufficient to establish a durable, fair and efficient form of taxation, or is it necessary to abolish council tax and look at more radical alternatives?

A long list of writers and reports on good local taxes have proposed criteria with which to assess alternative taxation arrangements (e.g., Layfield, 1976; DoE, 1986; Gibb, 1988; Hollis et al., 1992; Burt, 2006). The standard criteria can be grouped into four categories:

• several dimensions of the *feasibility* of the tax: often, these are necessary conditions. How much would it cost to set up and run them? What is the likely take-up of tax and will there be problems of collectability? A key issue is the stability of the tax base; that is, is it subject to volatility because of changes to local economic circumstances or might the tax itself induce mobility, which in turn has implications for the local tax base?;

- how *fair* is the tax? At one level, this is simple – what proportion of income for different income groups is devoted to paying the local tax? However, the incidence of a tax is rarely as straightforward, especially with respect to property taxes, which can be interpreted as a housing services tax or as a wealth tax. Others argue that local taxes are a payment for services more akin to a user price;
- *accountability* is an important factor. How visible or salient is the tax and can voting taxpayers clearly link tax liabilities to the spending decisions of their local government?;
- finally, local taxes have *wider impacts* on the overall tax burden, on local economies and property markets and may contribute to other fiscal goals, for example, widening the tax base and reducing revenue risk, shifting tax burdens to specific parts of the economy and capitalizing tax differentials into property prices.

What are the options for the CLTR? Assuming that the status quo is not on the table, we can also rule out new sales taxes for EU tax harmonization reasons and we would not expect to see any return to a poll tax; therefore, the options that are open to the CLTR broadly are as follows:

- reform of the existing council tax;
- a new property tax resembling the Burt proposal or the 2007 Northern Ireland Rates reform;
- land Valuation taxation;
- local taxes based on income taxation systems;
- A combination of property and income taxes.

REFORMING THE COUNCIL TAX?

The standard minimalist reform of council tax involves adding extra bands, particularly to capture very high property values and to propose a general revaluation. In a piece in the *Financial Times* (A Fiscal Fix for a Peculiarly Flawed Property Tax, April 2015), John Muellbauer goes much further and sets out a case in favour of reforming rather than replacing council tax, including, of course, a general revaluation.

Muellbauer argues that council tax should be more progressive. He would make the first £40,000 of property value free of tax, taking 'hundreds of thousands out of the poverty trap' of means-tested support. At the same time, he would add a higher band for properties over £5 million. He recognizes that a key problem with property taxes is the asset-rich but cash-poor household. He argues for offering all council tax payers a tax deferral in return for a government equity share in the property (1% per year) with a small discount for continuing to pay in cash.

From an economic point of view, Muellbauer argues that this would increase the efficient use of the housing stock. More revenue from council tax could be used to reduce reliance on stamp duty (following the Mirrlees Review agenda of seeking to cut stamp duty), and capitalization effects would raise house prices in areas of low value and reduce them at the upper end of the market. Overall, this would reduce expected capital appreciation, which is argued to be better for younger households, economic performance and the wider housing system. It might also deter speculative foreign invest-ment in high-value property.

The proposal involves a further element of nationalizing council tax with the government rather than councils operating the deferral system (although councils would receive a cash sum equivalent to the deferred payment each year). This does not really do anything to increase local democratic account-ability or to help councils raise more revenue locally. Along with pressure to continue with council tax freezes, it does not reverse the process of centraliza-tion of local government finance that goes back to the 1980s. A second con-cern is that despite the proposed general revaluation, an increasing proportion of households would no longer be liable to pay the tax because of the £40,000 allowance (adding to the current long list of exemptions). The trade-off is between liability, progressivity and local accountability. Third, the proposal, undoubtedly clever and pragmatic, does little other than add a very high value band to address the compression of liabilities across council tax bands as a result of the way it is weighted relative to Band D.

A NEW TAX ON PROPERTY

The simplest way forward with a property tax would be to implement the Burt Review proposal from 2006 or, indeed, the system in place in Northern Ire-land introduced in 2007. This would be a tax on the assessed capital value of domestic property. The tax base would be a regularly revalued capital value based on individual sales values, where necessary extrapolated to non-traded or rented properties. The tax rate would be set by each local government, presumably grafted on to the existing grant and other income sources of the present system of local government finance. This would inevitably include a degree of central control or limitation over the discretion of local councils to set tax rates autonomously.

Burt proposed a single tax on the capital value of property, with tax bills capped on high-value properties. There would be statutory regular revaluations premised on a revenue neutral yield. How would low income households be supported with property tax payments? One might imagine a combination of means-tested rebates and tax deferrals (now underway in Northern Ireland but with very low take-up).

A fundamental question is whether or not property taxes are regressive, let alone how we perceive them to be. There is no simple answer, unfortunately, because the question turns on the debate about property tax *incidence*. In the literature, there are essentially four views about the true incidence of property taxation: (1) As a tax on housing services, it is regressive as housing generally constitutes a relatively larger share of consumption by poor people. (2) As a tax on capital, it is essentially progressive since capital as a rule is relatively more held by the rich – this is often stressed by those who wish to shift tax more to wealth and on to unproductive assets such as second-hand housing. (3) Others argue that the uplift in land values is untaxed and earns landowners economic rents. They take the view that this distortion needs to be taxed in order to also reduce inequities arising from the private benefit from planning permission and infrastructure investment public goods. (4) Those who view property taxes as essentially benefits taxes tend to think it makes little sense to consider whether the price of public services, or indeed anything else, is regressive – it is voluntary exchange and does not raise any question of incidence.

Often, the empirical work makes assumptions about the nature of the tax's incidence before it assesses distributional outcomes – so the results that are subsequently found are not surprising. This does not help the debate and sharpens the divisions between analysts and economists on the one hand and voters, politicians and pressure groups on the other.

A general rule in this subject area is that well-designed land and property taxes are attractive to academics and commentators but generally unpopular with taxpayers, who often view them as *presumptive* taxes, that is, something imposed on them, highly visible (e.g., actively paid for rather than deducted at source) and based on challengeable valuations. This, then, often leads to politicians trying to soften the impact of property taxes and, in particular, responding to the high saliency of property taxes by using a battery of policies to lessen this unpopularity and perceived regressivity (such as the cash-poor, asset-rich problem). In the United States, these are known as 'circuit-breakers'. Often, these measures turn out to be more like middle-class subsidies. Many of these schemes have distributional and other (arguably) unintended or cumulative consequences. Across the OECD (Slack and Bird, 2014), these include the following:

- banding, as in the case of the UK council tax, though, in principle, the weights chosen between each band relative to the benchmark could be

organized in different ways compared to what presently happens in the
United Kingdom;

- caps on tax bills. This is a common way of reducing the cost-of-living
effects of annual increases that are perceived to be politically challenging
– this may involve real or nominal freezes, other limits to increases, with
more or less discretion for local governments within such systems. There
are also instances of constitutionally binding limits on tax bill increases
such as Proposition 13 in California;
- property tax reliefs and exemptions are, in general, terms that are universal
but everywhere different in their specifics. Many types of property or land
uses have exemptions or other concessions, as do household circumstances
in some countries. At the same time, property tax in both the domestic and
non-domestic settings may be allowance for tax deductibility for property
taxes;
- deferrals, rebates and abatements are widely used, again varying in their
national specifics. Deferring payments till the point of sale or as a lien on
estates is generally not popular with taxpayers. Rebate schemes focus on
low current incomes and face the high cost of delivering means-tested benefits, even if well targeted;
- income-related 'circuit-breakers' that might protect households from paying an excessive share of income on property taxes or do so on some kind
of sliding scale. These are common in North America;
- progressive tax rates imply higher property tax liabilities for higher income
groups (though this is usually accompanied by a ceiling or cap on liabilities). For instance, there is a well-known progressive rate approach in New
York City though it cautions more generally against the risks of fiscal
mobility with such schemes (Northern Ireland Assembly, 2007);
- delays in revaluation – this can be a form of regressive subsidy to the extent
that the property tax is a wealth tax and housing wealth is held more by
higher income groups who would benefit from the failure to uplift property
values through regular revaluation.

The point is that these strategies often undermine the property tax and reduce
the very benefits that their proponents advocated for in the first place. They
are all not obviously progressive either (e.g., capping or freezing liabilities or
postponing revaluation).

A LAND VALUE TAX

Land Value Taxation (LVT) has a long pedigree going back to Ricardo,
Henry George, Churchill and Lloyd George. This idea of taxing land alone,

normally at its highest and best land use (i.e., in the United Kingdom its existing use or the use it has specific planning permission for), is seen as a tax on the ownership of the land asset rather than a tax on its economic use or development (McCluskey et al., 2007; Dye and England, 2010; Wightman, 2010). In that sense, the tax is one on economic rent and is economically efficient and much lauded by economists as well as land reformers (Mirrlees et al., 2011). The key principle is that if we consider granting planning permission as a specific benefit accruing to the landowner who benefits from uplift in land value and associated infrastructure investments by the state, the tax acts as a fee for this benefit. It could, therefore, play the role of the proposed offsetting tax on development that was supposed to accompany the UK national land planning permission system after World War II (but has never, despite different iterations, worked).

As an exercise for the Green party, Wightman (2010) calculated a broadly revenue-neutral LVT replacement of council tax premised on land constituting just over 24% of property value and setting the tax rate at 3.16% of land value. This would lead to 75% of properties in Bands A–D facing lower tax liabilities, but all properties in Bands F–H paying more: a significant first-round distributional impact – though one would anticipate that the market would respond to the tax over time, which might, through general equilibrium capitalization processes, induce second-round effects. Note also that non-domestic rates would also be included in the LVT system.

Should LVT be a national or a local tax? Muellbauer and Mclean argue from different perspectives regarding whether it would be better to adopt a national LVT as part of the policy menu to improve the efficiency of the housing market (Muellbauer, 2005) or as a local tax reflecting spatial land and planning issues locally (McLean 2005). Wightman also argues that the LVT might employ a national element, for example, 1% on value and the rest set locally, so as to capture the non-local elements of land value variation (where that part of the revenues is redistributed back to councils on a per capita basis).

Although LVT or site value taxation, as it is also known, has been deployed in many places and remains in use today (Wightman, 2010; Dye and England, 2010),[3] the tax is clearly radical and would imply significant redistribution. Issues would therefore arise as to how to lessen the impact on asset-rich cash-poor households or, indeed, lower income households more generally. Here, proponents like Wightman share the views of Muellbauer on council tax reform, that is, adopt generous allowances and tax deferral options for low income households.

While the economic theoretical arguments are widely supported, the perceived issues arising from redistribution as well as from the costs and feasibility of setting up the tax base are also non-trivial. There will need to be a comprehensive valuation of all land and this will need to be regularly updated and revalued periodically. Neither is impossible or, in fact, particularly difficult – but it is a necessary condition and as with all property taxes, it is essential that regular revaluation is carried out.

SHIFTING TO LOCAL INCOMES

Replacing council tax or, indeed, property taxes in general with a local income tax is a long-established option and has considerable political support. Many countries deploy local income taxes, often supplementing other local taxes.[4] Some systems also distinguish between truly local taxes, or assigned national income taxes redistributed locally, or, systems that split the two in some way (and would also need to decide the extent to which tax rates are set locally and whether they are limited in some fashion). Any system based on income tax would need to address this structural question. The tax base would normally be earned income and would need to affix income earned to place of residence and not place of employment. Of course, there is no fundamental reason why other forms of income accruing to households could not also be included other than simplicity and transparency (and, indeed, that would be more consistent with the national income tax system – Burt, 2006).

A local income tax would normally be added to the national income tax structure and set of allowances. In other words, it would be as progressive as is the national system. The common sense view is that this is the basis of a 'fair' system measured in terms of current incomes, and is widely supported in public or social attitudes surveys (Burt, 2006), though the decision not to tax property may be viewed as less progressive in terms of the taxation of wealth. Again, the debate is about the correct interpretation of tax incidence and whether or not the focus should be on the progressivity of a given tax or the tax burden as a whole. The extensive use of local income tax is also associated in countries like Denmark with a different balance of services by local government in the form of greater decentralization of core welfare functions such as health care.

In 2006, Burt reported estimates of the levels of tax liability associated with a shift to complete reliance on a revenue-neutral domestic local income tax (p. 98). This indicated that if it was only levied on the basic rate of income tax, an additional rate of 7.9% would be required; if it was levied on the basic and higher rate, this would require a local income tax rate of 6.8%; and if levied on all income (including unearned), it would require a tax of 5.7%. These are non-trivial levels and would interact with means-tested benefit withdrawal and commencing paying tax for low income households.

Local income taxes face specific challenges on a number of fronts. First of all, unlike property, taxes on income are volatile and elastic. The tax base is mobile, increasingly so, and there is a danger that differential tax rates may induce mobility, that tax can be avoided and not collected as planned. In many of the countries more reliant on income taxes, corporate income taxes often make up an important share of tax revenues and these are also subject to fiscal mobility and tax avoidance questions. These tax flight issues operate across boundaries of local authority. The tax yield for a local income tax depends on three factors: the number of taxable units, the tax rates and local economic conditions (Burt, 2006) – deficits and surpluses may be more common, requiring financing and more short-run central government intervention.

Second, local income tax is a tax on productive economic activity and may be detrimental to economic growth in a way that well-designed taxes on land and property (inherently less productive) are not. Linked to this is the idea that additional taxes on income may lead to a net reduction in labour supply depending on the balance of income and substitution effects – this is why a sense of the size of the local tax rates implied is so important. Burt (2006) tried to model this and also found that there is some evidence that high combined national and local income taxes discourage entrepreneurship.

Burt (2006, p. 2) summarized, for the committee, the criticisms of a local income tax:

- the tax base should be as broad as possible. Around one-third of UK tax receipts already come from UK income tax. A property tax on the other hand would widen the tax base;
- wealth, as well as income, should be taxed. Again, depending on your view of the incidence question, property may be viewed as a store of wealth;
- additional income tax is a disincentive to work;
- yield would be more volatile than under a property tax, and runs revenue risks because of more mobile taxable units (i.e., people engaging in 'fiscal flight');
- local income tax is a 'fair tax' 'only if it is levied on all income but this would be extremely complex and expensive to do so'. Only applying the tax to earned income 'would arguably not be "fair"'.

A final issue is, of course, the phased introduction of greater devolved income tax powers in Scotland and the establishing of Revenue Scotland. Does that make it a good or a bad time to contemplate a further income tax operating locally?

COMBINING PROPERTY AND INCOME TAXES

A striking feature of the Burt analysis was that 23 out of the 28 countries studied adopted multiple local taxes – usually a combination of property and income taxes. However, Burt (2006) argues that public opinion does not support the introduction of supplementary taxes because it is perceived to be a way of creating more tax revenues rather than redistributing existing levels of revenue (i.e., a neutral overall yield). Any effort to introduce such taxes to supplement either a reformed council tax or a new property tax undoubtedly needs to address this saliency issue.

On the other hand, there may be value in developing multiple local taxes, of which income tax is one component, and in which the net overall tax take is revenue neutral (i.e., the same tax take as presently with the council tax alone). We discuss this more fully below but note in passing that Slack's (2013) contribution compares and contrasts the local fiscal powers open to a number of leading global cities (London, Paris, New York, Tokyo, Madrid, Berlin). She finds that all of them bar London had access to at least five local sources of revenue. London relies wholly on the council tax.

What are the arguments for a combined tax revenue-neutral approach? First, logically, the two taxes would individually have less marginal impact on households, introducing a degree of progressivity and limiting the burden of the property tax. This would also alter the distributional outcome of the local tax burden. Second, this would be a simpler alternative to applying circuit breakers to the property tax and may actually allow the authorities to develop a more pure property tax, albeit with a more modest yield (pragmatically, this may help overcome the residual resistance to property taxes).

Third, Hollis et al. (1992) develop a coherent argument in favour of linking local tax type to service provision – services more related to redistributive/ need functions could be funded by a combination of national grants and local income tax while more local amenity- or facility-related services would be funded by property taxes. A similar division might logically be applied to non-domestic or business property taxes.

Burt (2006), however, strongly argued against multiple taxes in general and income tax as a supplementary tax to the property tax on the grounds that it would be perceived as a revenue increase by taxpayers, that it would be more complex, less transparent and more costly to operate. All these challenges would need to be overcome if a multiple tax solution was to be advanced.

INTERNATIONAL EVIDENCE FOR REFORMING LOCAL TAXES

A number of local tax options, in abstract terms, may therefore be on the table. However, there is a further critical hurdle – the actual process and strategy of undertaking and implementing local tax reform is fraught with potential difficulty. There has been considerable recent interest and assessment, in particular, of property tax reform internationally (Norregaard, 2013; Gibb and Christie, 2015). Several countries have recently introduced reforms and many more are evidently contemplating change.[5] Many countries and systems of local government wrestle with the potential of property taxes versus the limited political room for manoeuvre they feel they can operate within.

Slack and Bird (2014) distinguish four general issues for property tax reform: establishing the preferred tax base, how to assess the tax base, how to set the tax rate and thus the tax bill, and how to run the system itself. Almy (2013) concludes that *'unless the tax structure is simple enough to be efficiently administered, and fair enough to gain the confidence of the population, administrative reform by itself will not succeed.'*

Slack and Bird (2014) also analyse the challenges and possible ways forward with reform. From their detailed comparative study of national property tax systems, they identify six principal challenges and differentiate ways forward as a result of those challenges into promising ones and those that are less promising.

1. salience: The high visibility of the tax requires change to be transitioned and improvements in local services to go alongside tax reform;
2. liquidity Constraints (e.g., the cash-poor asset-rich problem): These suggest deferral and other payment options and against value phasing-in change;
3. perceived regressivity on current income measures: This suggests a range of ways of reducing this impact, including low income exemptions;
4. volatility in terms of large movements in individual taxpayer bills: The authors argue for annual evaluations and for phasing-in reform;
5. presumptive tax: The antagonism to the form of tax requires education and consultation, phasing-in and good systems of appeal;
6. inelasticity: The tax base is less buoyant than incomes and this is a problem for revenue risk rather than the tax payer and is another argument for more regular, that is annual, revaluations.

Most of the 'challenges' demonstrate common problematic approaches to reform, for instance, property tax capping and limiting tax assessment/revaluation as well as a range of attempts to make property taxes more progressive. Slack and Bird (2014) argue that thinking about incidence in terms of tax reform involving property taxation is inherently problematic since the regressivity or otherwise is difficult to measure, because we are dealing with the effects in the income distribution of a largely capitalized tax on a particular form of gross wealth (as we noted earlier, estimates typically reflect the ex ante assumptions made about the nature of property tax incidence). Overall, reform is multi-dimensional, political and complex:

Property tax reforms could clearly be designed and implemented much more sensibly than appears to have been the case. To do so, however, countries need to recognise clearly both the nature of the task facing would-be reformers and also the complexity of the task they face . . . inextricably related to very long-lived assets and often deep-rooted social beliefs and norms. (Slack and Bird, 2014, p. 26)

What does this mean for Scotland and the CLTR? First, any reform of the status quo requires the recognition that key constraints have to be removed for effective reform such as the council tax freeze or the failure to regularly revalue. Second, reformers would need to take head-on the issues of salience and the presumptive nature of the tax. Tax ideas will have to be clearly and credibly communicated, political and professional support will be required to lend credibility and help educate, and strategies will have to be deployed to address these 'deep-rooted social beliefs and norms'. This persuasion-based focus may seem a little nebulous but political and public support will be essential, as will the public ventilation of arguments about reducing revenue risk, widening the tax base and shifting taxes away from productive assets to things such as property. It will also be vital to be seen to deliver on promises regarding help for lower income groups and demonstration of revenue neutrality.

Third, the Scottish discussion needs to be grounded in the long-term economic and social cost of not reforming. Furthermore, if change is only cosmetic and merely tinkers with the underlying status quo, future politicians will inevitably be saddled with confronting this problem in the future.

The international evidence, finally, does also indicate that positive reform can be delivered and that property tax can be successfully reformed or introduced. It needs to be done carefully and transparently, and probably needs to involve careful transition over a decent period of time in order to protect losers from the change.

CONCLUSIONS: WHAT MIGHT ACTUALLY HAPPEN?

Local Government Finance as a System

It is perhaps useful to distinguish between first best and second best outcomes in terms of reform proposals emerging from the Commission. In doing so, we also need to recognize the narrow terms of the CLTR in that it does not deal with non-domestic taxation, the balance of funding between grant and tax, and it does not speak to these wider questions of what local government does relative to what central government does and how that is financed. Nonetheless, it is possible to suggest moves and policy changes that would both shift

Scotland to a better local tax system (as assessed against our simple criteria discussed in Section 3 above) and leave the door open for complementary and evolutionary changes to the wider system of local government finance (Lyons, 2007; Gallagher et al., 2007).

To be clear, improving the tax system is necessary but not sufficient: there needs to be further reform work setting out how the wider local government finance system needs to be reformed, and in turn the functions and geography of local government should operate in order to produce a sustainable, efficient and fair system. The Commission on Strengthening Local Democracy (2014) reminds us that the constitutional position of local government needs to be part of the reform process with a shift in the balance in favour of the autonomy of local government relative to the capacity of central government to impose freezes on taxation.

Remaining at the level of the system, international evidence suggests that many countries have non-consistent systems locally, that is different bundles of taxes and ways of setting tax rates locally (Gibb and Christie, 2015). We are living through a period of uncertain constitutional change and innovations; for instance, City Deals offer relatively ad hoc privileged financing situations for specific councils, cities and their hinterlands. One might argue, therefore, that this might be positively viewed as a flexibility that affords different financing opportunities for a range of contexts. That might be an argument one could sustain with a generally fair and consistent system in place which could then be added to – but when our financial functions and geographies are themselves presently relatively incoherent and that undermine principles of territorial equity and equalization, then it is harder to make the case for such a variable geometry in Scotland or the United Kingdom. There is a lot that has to be done first before one might consider a multiple local system of taxes and grants

Reforming Local Taxes

Focusing on the CLTR brief, merely providing the minimal changes to the council tax (a general revaluation and extra bands) does not resolve the fundamental problems that characterize the council tax. Such reforms would be a sticking plaster approach. The purist Burt-style property tax solution is a rational, well-thought-through balance of radicalism, principles and evidence. However, it is not clear to us that the political sands have shifted in its favour; certainly not as a sole tax funding local government. Interestingly, it is also not clear at all that local income taxes have overcome their technical problems (e.g., fiscal flight and revenue risk) or that they are as straightforwardly popular with the political parties as once was the case. The revenue-neutral tax rates estimated for Burt do look quite high and would be difficult to sell for a potential First Minister in the election.

Land value taxation has much in principle to recommend it, though while it can be seen to work effectively elsewhere, it faces major obstacles, not least establishing a comprehensive new form of taxation and also dealing with the political fallout for the big distributional swings it will generate. This has to be set against the positive land use and property market benefits that would accumulate over time for such a form of tax. We suspect that makes LVT less likely to be the candidate for reform after the election, but it is still a first best option.

On balance, we are not convinced by Burt's arguments about multiple taxes. A second best solution therefore would be to follow the principle set out by Hollis et al. (1992) who proposed property taxes on local amenity and facility services and a supplementary income tax on redistributive or need-based services alongside grant in aid. This can and should be set up on a revenue-neutral basis with current council tax revenue, and, crucially, with the freeze abandoned, local voters can subsequently determine whether future spending and tax increases are acceptable or not. We have seen that most systems have multiple taxes and also that many large and innovative city economies have more than one tax to work from. It should be the same in Scotland. The property tax element will by definition be more modest in yield terms than the council tax and could take the simpler route of the Burt capital value flat rate percentage tax or could be more adventurous and work with an LVT model (though we probably on balance tend towards the argument for deploying LVT as a national tax).

This property tax and supplementary income tax approach would lessen the fairness problems property taxes face but there would be benefits from the technical superiority of the property tax element. It would be revenue-neutral as proposed and would keep the door open for further changes such as re-localizing non-domestic rates and re-energizing local accountability. The combination would need to be carefully modelled under different scenarios, but it should be able to reduce the reliance on caps or other circuit breakers on property tax liabilities. It should also overcome worries about fiscal flight because either tax element will be that much smaller in yield or tax liability terms than if there was only one tax. Depending on their mix, there need be less reliance on means-tested benefits but there remains a need for a statutory periodic revaluation and persuasive communication and political buy-in. A final issue will be how one transitions from the existing system to the new approach – that will need to be carefully thought through, but a goal of implementation should be to minimize the maximum losses any below-average-income household might face in a given year.

While the above is a second best approach given the limits to more radical reform, we would still make the case for first best property taxes combined with land value tax at a national level. But we recognize the practical limitations as well as the politics of the situation. As a first stage, we would like to see two things happen as a result of the CLTR and then to allow reform to move at a good, though not hasty, pace. First, there needs to be a recognition that neither the council tax freeze nor limited reform to the council tax are acceptable. Second, also framed negatively, there should be decisive rejection of local income tax as anything other than a supplement to a smaller-yield property tax. With those decisions made (if they can be), the reform process moves on to look at the type of property tax and low-income protection, and the transitioning required to implement it.

At this point (in early summer 2015), other than a willingness to listen to all sides of the arguments, we have no sense of where the Commission will go and whether it can achieve consensus. How willing are the politicians to contemplate real change and reform, and ending the freeze? Who knows? Many are not confident, however, about the appetite for purposeful change. It may be that the 2015 Commission will be a considered progressive step along the road rather than the definitive solution. But the worst outcome would be not settling things and at some point in the future having to go through all this again when next our leading politicians feel something has to be done or are forced to do something.

NOTES

1. The authors have presented evidence to the CLTR on an independent basis, specifically a historical overview of local government finance and commissioned work to review international evidence.

2. http://localtaxcommission.scot

3. Dye and England point to Australia, New Zealand and South Africa, as well as Estonia and Fiji. Examples also exist within the United States: Connecticut, Hawaii, Pennsylvania and Virginia. Other commentators (e.g., Wightman's 2015 presentation to the Commission) have cited examples from across Africa (e.g., Namibia), the Americas (e.g., Argentina), Asia (e.g., Japan) and other parts of Europe (e.g., Denmark, Latvia).

4. Generally, within the EU, income taxes dominate. In Belgium, Denmark, Finland, Germany, Iceland, Luxembourg, Norway, Sweden and Switzerland, more than 80 per cent of tax revenues are derived from personal and/or corporate income tax.

5. The main examples are Denmark, Estonia, Hungary, Iceland, Latvia, Lithuania, Macedonia, Netherlands, Russia, Sweden, Greece, Ireland and the United Kingdom (council tax in 1993 and, separately, Northern Ireland rates in 2007).

REFERENCES

Almy, R. (2013). *Property Tax Regimes in Europe,* UN Habitat, Brussels: United Nations.

Bird, R., and Slack, E. (2014). *International Handbook of Land and Property Taxation,* Cheltenham: Edward Elgar.

Bird, R., Slack, E., and Tassonyi, A. (2012). *A Tale of Two Taxes: Property Tax Reform in Ontario,* Cambridge, Mass.: Lincoln Institute of Land Policy.

Burt. (2006). *A Fairer Way: Report by the Local Government Finance Committee,* Edinburgh: Local Government Finance Committee.

Commission on Strengthening Local Democracy. (2014). *Effective Democracy: Reconnecting with Communities.* www.localdemocracy.info.

Department of Environment. (1986). *Paying for Local Government.* HMSO: London.

Dye, R., and England, R. (2010). *Assessing the Theory and Practice of Land Value Taxation.* Washington, DC: Lincoln Institute of Land Policy.

Gallagher, J., Gibb, K., and Mills, C. (2007). Rethinking Central Local Government Relations in Scotland: Back to the Future? *David Hume Institute/University of Glasgow, Hume Occasional Paper* 70. Glasgow: University of Glasgow.

Gibb, K. (1988). The Community Charge and Local Government Finance, *Centre for Housing Research Discussion Paper 20.* University of Glasgow.

Gibb, K. (1992). The Council Tax: The Distributional Implications of Returning to a Tax on Property, *Scottish Journal of Political Economy,* 39: 302–17.

Gibb, K., and Christie, L. (2015). Interim Summary: Literature Review for the Commission on Local Taxation, *Mimeo,* Policy Scotland, University of Glasgow.

Hollis, G., et al. (1992). *Alternatives to the Community Charge,* London: Deloitte Coopers/Joseph.

Layfield Committee. (1976). Report of the Committee of Inquiry into Local Government Finance. HMSO: London.

Leishman, C., Bramley, G., Stephens, M., Watkins, D., and Young, G. (2014). *After the Council Tax.* Joseph Rowntree Foundation: York.

Local Government Finance Review Committee. (2006). *A Fairer Way ('The Burt Review').* Chair: Sir Peter Burt. Crown Copyright HM Stationary Office: Edinburgh.

Lyons, M. (2007). Lyons Inquiry into Local Government – Final Report, London.

McLean, I. (2005). The Politics of Land Tax - Then and Now, in D. Maxwell, and A. Vigor (Eds.), *Time for Land Value Tax?* IPPR/Department of Politics and International Relations. Oxford: Oxford University.

McCluskey, W., Lay-Cheng, L., and Davis, P. (2007). Land Value Taxation: An International Overview. *American Journal of Economics and Sociology,* 56. 2: 207–14.

Mirrlees, J., Stuart A., et al. (2011). *Tax by Design: The Mirrlees Review,* Oxford, UK. Oxford University Press.

Muellbauer, J. (2005). Property Taxation and the Economy, in D. Maxwell, and A. Vigor (Eds.), *Time for Land Value Tax?* IPPR/Department of Politics and International Relations. Oxford: Oxford University.

Norregaard, J. (2013). Taxing Immovable Property: Revenue Potential and Implementation Challenges. Washington: International Monetary Fund. *IMF Working Paper.*

Northern Ireland Assembly. (2007). An International Comparison of Local Government Taxation, *Research and Library Services Research Paper*, 10/07, Belfast: Northern Ireland Assembly.

Peebles, D. (2015). Council Tax in the Context of Local Government Finance – Presentation to the Commission on Local Taxation. Available online at: http://localtaxcommission.scot/wp-content/uploads/Don-Peebles-Intro-to-Local-Government-Finance.pdf (accessed 01/06/15).

Slack, E. (2013). *International Comparison of Global City Financing*, Report to the London Finance Corporation. London: London Finance Corporation.

Slack, E., and Bird, R. (2014). The Political Economy of Property Tax Reform. *OECD Working Papers on Fiscal Federalism*, No. 18, Paris: Organisation for Economic Co-Operation and Development Publishing.

Wightman, A. (2010). *A Land Value Tax for Scotland: Fair, Efficient, Sustainable.* Edinburgh: Scottish Green Party.

Chapter 4

Questions of Social Justice and Social Welfare in Post-Independence Referendum Scotland

Gerry Mooney

INTRODUCTION

The political spotlight has in recent years been on Scotland in ways rarely – if ever – seen before. The reasons for this are clearly evident – the September 2014 Scottish Independence Referendum and the May 2015 General Election, as it played out in Scotland. It has long been recognized that Scotland has a distinctive political – and policy – landscape. Since at least the 1970s, voters in Scotland were increasingly voting in ways that were different from other countries in the United Kingdom, and not least when compared with England. Taken together, the 2014 and 2015 votes not only reflect the continuation of such divergences and the wider process of political polarization, but have also contributed to these processes in ways that, at least before 2012, were largely unpredictable.

Both events experienced, albeit in ways that were simultaneously similar and distinctive, the interrelationship between constitutional questions, nationalism and a range of issues that fall under the general label of 'social justice'. With respect to the latter, in particular, questions around the future direction of the welfare state, and of social welfare and social policy more generally, were central to the ongoing debates about the future direction of Scotland and around the type of society that people in Scotland wished for. Social welfare has also come to occupy a key role in the Scottish National Party's (and the Scottish Government's) visions of what a future Independent Scotland could look like.

This chapter therefore questions the many claims that have been advanced that the Scottish Independence debate and, in particular, the arguments made by the pro-Independence YES campaign, were fuelled by nationalist issues and an increasing sense of Scottishness and of a Scottish national identity. In

Chapter 1, reflecting on the 2014 Referendum and the 2015 General Election outcomes, Jim Gallagher highlights that voters in Scotland *'have said two apparently contradictory things'*. As is now well known, there was a 55% NO to the Scottish Independence vote in the former while eight months or so later, in the May 2015 General Election, 50% of the Scottish electorate voted for the Party of Scottish Independence, the SNP. However, by focusing on the ways in which social justice issues featured in both events, we can develop a more nuanced understanding that arguably looks beneath this apparent contradiction.

The discussion that unfolds in this chapter then explores some of the main social policy issues that were mobilized during the Independence Referendum campaign, between 2012 and 2014. It focuses primarily on the ways through which social justice issues were almost inseparable from the wider questions of the constitutional status direction of Scotland. It is argued that such interconnections have continued to shape the political climate in the period after the 2014 Referendum and they also influenced the outcome of the 2015 General Election, particularly in Scotland, but also in ways that have a wider UK resonance and importance. These are no longer, if they ever properly were, issues for Scotland alone.

THE POLITICAL LANDSCAPE OF SCOTLAND: SETTING THE POLITICAL AND POLICY CONTEXT

Both the 2014 Independence Referendum and the 2015 General Election will be recognized as historic moments in Scottish politics – and perhaps also for UK politics more generally. It has become a new political common sense to state that politics in the United Kingdom will never be the same following these two events. Both events, while path breaking in different ways, also highlight once again the increasing fragility of the United Kingdom.

The United Kingdom is not the unified entity that many claim it to be. Here history, living history, plays an important role in shaping the changes that have been taking place in recent years. The United Kingdom itself has always been a union state – a multinational union of different nations. It is a pluri-national state consisting of several countries, brought together in what is represented, if now even more problematically than in the past, as one nation, (British!). The history of the coming-togetherness (and in the context of the Irish Republic, the separation) of different countries of these islands to form the United Kingdom, matters immensely to where we find ourselves now. The enduring history of the United Kingdom's turbulent and volatile past works to shape the present and the future:

Nobody asked to design a political system for Britain would ever propose the one it has. The one-and-a-bit large islands (and many smaller ones) that The Economist calls home are a hotchpotch of parliamentary systems, unevenly distributed powers and constitutional uncertainties. The set-up is as uneven as Britain's history is eventful, which is no coincidence: the causes of the mess date back centuries. The latest upheaval – Scotland's referendum on independence, which ended with a 'no' vote on September 18 – has made things untidier still. (*The Economist*, September 27, 2014)

In this historical overview, the Scottish Independence Referendum can be best understood as only the latest stage in the evolving story of the political and constitutional structures of the United Kingdom. In turn, both the 2014 Referendum and the 2015 General Election have been generally understood as laying down the basis for further evolution – evolution that might now lead to the breakup of the United Kingdom, or at least the fragmentation of what we today understand as the United Kingdom.

For many observers reflecting on the past three to four decades, a period that has seen the rise and fall, and the rise again of the SNP, such evolution and the potential fragmentation is being driven by a rise in Celtic nationalism, not least in Scotland (leaving aside the thorny issue of Irish nationalism in the context of Northern Ireland).

However, and while this may also apply to some within Scotland, the external view of the Scottish Independence Referendum, and the issues that drove the demand for a ballot, have largely been mistaken. The dominant viewpoint is that this was first and foremost an issue of national identity – a case of rising nationalism. Likewise, the SNP's unheralded success in the May 2015 General Election is also regarded by some as reflecting rising nationalist sentiment in Scotland.

It would be wrong to completely discount the role of nationalism. The SNP are first and foremost a nationalist party, even if it is a nationalism of a peculiarly Scottish kind and one that they claim rejects ethnic and racialized forms of nationalism in favour of a more all-encompassing 'civic' nationalism. Aside from the SNP, there are other nationalists and people who also see the struggle for Scottish Independence in nationalist terms – as being a necessity for 'Scotland' and the 'Scottish Nation.'

However, both the 2014 and 2015 votes were not primarily nationalist – of any kind. Scottish nationalist viewpoints and aspirations, while evident in the pro-Independence YES movement, were entirely entangled with other issues that cannot be adequately understood and seen as 'nationalist'.

The main argument advanced in this chapter is that social welfare and social justice issues were central to the entire Independence debate, during the Referendum itself, and this has continued to shape post-Independence

Referendum politics also. While the notion of social justice is highly contentious, with all political parties claiming that their policies are driven by
social justice ambitions, there is, nonetheless, considerable evidence that this
notion has been deployed by Scotland's two main political parties since the
early days of devolution, and it is also evident throughout the entire period of
devolution (Mooney and Scott, 2005; Mooney, 2014a).

Scottish Devolution, Policy Divergences and Social Justice

From the commencement of Scottish devolution in 1999, the issue of social
justice has occupied a prominent place in Scottish political rhetoric and in
claims about particular policies (Mooney and Scott, 2012). The then First
Minister, Labour's Donald Dewar, reflected on the re-establishment of the
first devolved Scottish Parliament that:

> We are committed to promoting social justice and equality of opportunity for
> everyone in Scotland . . . we can build on the commitment to social justice
> which lies at the heart of political and civic life in Scotland. We need to harness
> the efforts of many to the greater good of all, and establish social justice as the
> hallmark of Scottish society. (Dewar, 1999)

Fourteen years later, leading politicians from the two main sides of the Independence argument claimed that social justice was a defining feature of Scotland's future. Ex-Labour Leader and Fife-based MP Gordon Brown (2014a)
also claimed that social justice lies at the heart of Scottish political values but
commended the current union as 'a union of social justice'. The SNP Scottish
Government's vision for Independence, *Scotland's Future: Your Guide to an
Independent Scotland*, published in November 2013, also made claims to the
centrality of social justice, not only as the founding principle of an Independent Scotland, but also as a key driver of policy and as playing to uniquely
Scottish values and aspirations:

> The Scottish Government's vision is of a Scotland, fit for the 21st century
> and beyond, which is founded on the fundamental principles of equality and
> human rights and characterised by our economic success and social justice and
> the ability of our people to have control over the decisions which affect them:
> the opportunity for all Scotland's people to play a part in our future. (Nicola
> Sturgeon, Deputy First Minister, Scottish Government, 2013)

Social justice and a commitment to a 'fairer' welfare state have long been
presented as reflecting Scottishness in some shape or form. For the SNP, of
course, such goals could only be delivered by full Independence for Scotland. However, during the 2012–2014 Independence campaign and since
the Referendum itself in September 2014, there is clear evidence that much

more political capital was being invested in claims around social justice and social welfare. For example, the approaches of both the Scottish and UK governments to the economic and financial crisis of 2007–2008 were sharply different in important respects (Bell, 2010). Of course, the main fiscal policy areas that relate to the economy are currently reserved to the Westminster parliament.

The SNP Scottish Parliament has disputed and criticized UK Government welfare policies continuously from the launch of 'austerity' policies immediately after the Conservative and Liberal Democrat Coalition Government took office in May 2010. Such critiques reached a new level during the two-year period before the September 2014 Referendum. For the arguments in this chapter, this was important for a number of reasons. First of all, issues of social welfare became even more pivotal in the political debates taking place in Scotland. Returning to the claim made at the outset, questions of competing constitutional futures, territorial politics, of national identity and social policy, became even more strongly interconnected. Post-Independence Referendum, this was also the case in the debates around what future powers could be devolved to Scotland following the report of the Smith Commission in November 2014.

SCOTLAND'S CONSTITUTIONAL DEBATE AND THE END OF THE UK WELFARE STATE?

The question of the future of the UK welfare state is in some respects not new. Since the 1970s, the welfare state, here taken to include various forms of welfare benefits, education, housing, health, personal social services and so on, has undergone significant changes. Much of this has been driven by the policies of successive UK Governments that have sought to 'reform' welfare. This includes not only far-reaching changes in the nature of the welfare benefits system itself, characterized by a general shift to a work-first model, increasing conditionality and reductions in entitlements, but also privatization of key areas of welfare service delivery and a greater reliance on private companies as well as on charities and other not-for-profit organizations.

However, another driver that has arguably contributed to the growing fragmentation of the UK welfare state has been devolution. This has worked to enhance pre-devolution differences in welfare policies and practices, and in the organization of the NHS, and personal social services, among others. The result has been the development of a welfare state in which the 'UK-ness' is now reduced largely to the provision of key welfare benefits, employability and, of course, much of taxation.

Arguably, it is in Scotland where the divergences driven by devolution appear most significant. Since 1999, successive Scottish Governments have introduced free prescriptions for all, abolition of fees for higher education students resident in Scotland, free travel for the over 1960s, and free personal care for the elderly. Taken together, these policies point to and reflect much more visible differences between Scotland and other parts of the United Kingdom, not least England (see Keating, 2010; Greer, 2009; McLean, Gallagher and Lodge, 2013; Mooney and Scott, 2012; Mooney and Wright, 2009).

The growing divergences in social policy making across the different component parts of the United Kingdom has also contributed in no small way to the arguments advanced by politicians from different political traditions in Scotland that devolution has made a difference and continues to make a difference, that further devolution could lead to even more differences, positive differences that will enable Scottish governments to meet specific Scottish needs and address Scottish social problems.

In both the 2014 Independence Referendum and the May 2015 UK General Election campaigns, a key plank in the SNP platform that the policies pursued by successive UK governments have not only led to the dilution of the 'UK-ness' of the welfare system, a central issue that Labour politicians struggled to reject in the 2014 Independence Referendum campaign in their arguments that UK-wide solidarity was to Scotland's advantage, but that it is only through full Independence that Scotland would hold on to something approaching the 'classic' 'golden age' of the UK welfare state. This would be enabled by an Independent Scottish administration reversing UK government reforms, cuts and reductions in entitlements etc., as well as introducing new policies that have their basis in social democratic and social justice approaches to welfare and public service delivery more generally.

In the 2014 Referendum, Labour, as the leading unionist party in Scotland, argued that the provision of more devolution, as expressed in the post-September 2014 era in the recommendations of the Smith Commission (see chapter by Jim Gallagher), would also provide Scotland with the capacity to introduce policies that would reduce the impact of the UK Coalition Government and now UK Conservative Government cuts and reforms in welfare. Both sides in the Independence debate, therefore, were advocating sharply different degrees of constitutional change that largely shared the same promise of a more uniquely Scottish approach to welfare, even if for Labour this was built upon continuing UK-solidarity and the pooling of resources and risks on a UK-wide level.

In the YES for Independence campaign, social welfare occupied centre stage in the arguments advanced for Independence, and this has continued throughout the period since the September 2014 Referendum, into the May 2015 UK General Election campaign and beyond.

SOCIAL WELFARE IN THE CASE FOR AND
AGAINST SCOTTISH INDEPENDENCE

The YES for Independence campaign comprised a diverse range of groups and organizations. While the SNP occupied much of the centre stage in this, it would be completely mistaken to interpret from this, as many have unfortunately done, that the YES campaign was led by issues of national identity and nationalism. As with the huge success of the SNP in the May 2015 General Election in Scotland, gaining 56 of the 59 MPs on 50% of the vote, the vast majority of those supporting Scottish Independence were not in any way 'nationalist'. The YES movement reflected a wide range of struggles over UK Government 'austerity' policies and welfare 'reforms', opposition to nuclear weapons, environmental issues, anti-privatization and other issues.

The issues that galvanized the YES campaign and which gave it much of its vitality cannot be easily dismissed as 'nationalist', but they are more adequately understood as social justice issues. That a number of different political ideologies and traditions were reflected in the YES campaign, for instance the Scottish Green Party and the Scottish Socialist Party, also played a significant part, and many new organizations emerged and coalesced around the pro-Independence argument, also means that there are different, sometimes sharply so, understandings of social justice, but the SNP aside, the majority of YES campaigners and supporters viewed Independence as a means to an end, a 'fairer' or more socially just Scotland, not constitutional change as a goal in itself.

The social and political geography of voting in the 2014 Referendum also highlights that for many in the YES camp, it was social justice and social welfare issues that won them over to the Independence cause – the promise that in an Independent Scotland, there would be a much fairer and more just welfare system, more fairness and prosperity for all. It was apparent in the early hours of Friday morning September 19, 2014, that the income-deprived areas were voting YES in large numbers. The four areas with a majority YES vote, Dundee, Glasgow City and its two neighbouring Clydeside areas, West Dunbartonshire to the West and North Lanarkshire to its immediate East, contain the most deprived areas in Scotland. In areas with a marginal NO vote (of between less than 1% and 3%), Inverclyde (centred on the towns of Greenock, Gourock and Port Glasgow to the West of Glasgow), North Ayrshire, which is based around Irvine New Town (the largest part), the Garnock Valley (Kilbirnie, Dalry, etc.), East Ayrshire (Kilmarnock and surrounding areas), and in Renfrewshire (centred on Paisley, which also returned a YES vote), there was a clear split between areas of poverty and (relative and absolute) affluence.

To turn to the NO vote, here we can also identify the importance of social welfare and social justice issues. Together with fears of job losses in the event of Independence, something that was marked in key Labour heartlands such as in Fife, economic position and age were crucial factors in the NO vote: the more elderly and affluent the voters, the more likely they were to vote NO. This is the group with the strongest allegiances to (and memories of!) the post-1945 settlement and the idea of a UK-wide welfare state that is supported and resourced on a UK-wide basis. Others were persuaded to vote NO by anxieties that Independence would erode the remaining commitment on a UK-wide basis to some kind of collective welfare provision, which in turn would lead to a rapid deterioration in services and entitlements, reflected in the idea of a 'race to the bottom' with a residual, poor quality welfare system emerging.

The future of pension provision, welfare entitlements and the welfare state more generally was used by the two sides in the debate, with YES advocating that the future of the welfare state was only secure with Independence and the NO campaign claiming that Independence would lead to an end to cross-UK transfers and, therefore, a decline in services. Voters were pulled in both directions around this issue, but among older voters there is evidence that the fear of the erosion of UK-wide pensions was a significant factor in helping to return a NO vote from that section of the population. Further, it was the fact that the YES campaign fought its cause across a range of social welfare/social justice issues that saw it win 45% in the Independence Referendum. And it was the same social movement that also drove the SNP to its stunning success in May 2015. Had the YES campaign 'only' been concerned with Independence, in isolation from all the other issues raised here (and there are more!), arguably the SNP would not have done as well in May 2015. It is evident that the national question was entirely tied up with social justice matters that have continued to give it strength in the post-2014 Independence Referendum era.

THE 2014 INDEPENDENCE REFERENDUM AND BEYOND

The 2014 Referendum highlights a complex and uneven intra-regional political geography of Scotland, which itself reflects the fractured and divided nature of modern Scottish society. While social welfare issues were a key fault line in the wider constitutional debate, it was only one of a number of fault lines that worked to divide opinions and voters.

Despite the rejection of Independence, however, it was clear from the 45% who voted for Independence and from a significant proportion of the 55% NO voters, that all parties involved in the debate recognized that more powers than those to be implemented in 2016 as a result of the Scotland Act (2012) (Scottish Parliament, 2012) are needed, even if the degree of further devolution has been hotly contested. During the final days of the Referendum campaign, there was the now (in)famous 'Vow' (published on the front page of the *Daily Record* newspaper on September 16), from Labour, Conservative and Liberal parties that further powers would be considered and established within a reasonable time period. '*Permanent and extensive new powers for Scotland will be delivered*' was the stated vow to the Scottish electorate. For many, this was interpreted largely as powers that would give Scotland greater control over welfare and the ability to raise the expenditure required to reduce the impact of some of the then UK Coalition Government attacks on welfare spending and on benefit levels.

On the morning of Friday September 19, David Cameron announced the establishment of a commission under Lord Smith of Kelvin, to report by the end of November 2014, on additional powers for Scotland. However, and in another irony, the results of a Referendum on Scottish Independence and future powers for Scotland came to be tied to how such changes would impact on other countries of the United Kingdom, and in particular on England. Since then, the idea of English Votes for English Laws (EVEL) has become common currency in political debate about the future constitutional settlements of the United Kingdom as a whole, and this has continued in the months that have followed the 2015 General Election.

However, a commitment to move towards new legislation for extended powers for the Scottish Parliament by 2015 was a relatively clear outcome of the referendum process. It was clear that both YES as well as many NO voters were not voting for the status quo, but for substantial change – indeed, for powers that approximate to something close to 'Devo-Max'. Gordon Brown, who played a key role in the NO campaign in its final stages, in a speech at Loanhead Miners Welfare Club in Midlothian on September 9, 2014, announced that with a NO vote there would be cross-party agreement on new powers for Scotland, which would be, in his own words, tantamount to '*a modern form of Scottish home rule*'. Days earlier, in another speech he announced, seemingly with the support of David Cameron and Ed Miliband, '*we are going to be within a year or two, as close to a federal state as you can be in a country where one nation is 85% of the population*' (Brown, 2014b).

According to Lord Ashcroft on the day post-result poll, 25% of NO voters voted that way because they believed that Scotland would receive significant devolved powers while remaining a part of the United Kingdom (Ashcroft, 2014). The key visible result of this was, of course, the establishment by the UK Government, in the days following the Referendum, of the Smith Commission (Smith Commission, 2014) to investigate and report on the provision of additional devolved powers for Scotland.

One difficulty that now affects the main UK parties is that the Scottish Independence Referendum outcome, and the promise of additional powers for Scotland, has raised expectations that are well beyond the proposals that have emerged in the Smith Commission. Further, none of the main UK parties are advocating anything that comes remotely close to devolution-maximum. In turn, of course, this plays directly into the hands of the SNP who have become the party, not of Independence, at least in the short term, but the party now campaigning to ensure that the promises made in the September 'vow' are fully implemented – that is, something approaching devolution-max. This was also central to the SNP's arguments in May 2015. It was its ability to argue that the promises made in the pre-Referendum 'vow' were likely not to be met that won over many voters, including a sizable number who had voted against Independence only eight months previously.

CONCLUSION

Social justice, social welfare and nationalism have come together in very particular ways in the context of contemporary Scotland. Welfare is high on the political agenda, and opposition to UK government policies have been central to the debate about the country's constitutional future. In May 2015, the SNP campaigned on a strongly anti-austerity platform, even if its overall understanding of austerity and its track record on austerity can be criticized (see Mooney, 2015). The argument that the Tories are out of touch with the needs of Scotland and with the aspirations of Scottish voters is hardly a novel claim. What is new is that this can also now be said of the Labour Party in Scotland. This has led to claims that Scotland is now very much at odds with England. To quote Simon Heffer:

> There is now as clear a division of political and social values between Scotland and England as there has been since 1707. (Heffer, 2015: 28)

The idea that Scotland has a set of values, progressive and pro-welfare values, that are distinctively Scottish has long been questioned, with successive attitudinal surveys providing little evidence to sustain such a view. Nonetheless, such a view remains politically powerful in the Scottish context – but this is also in turn used by many commentators outside (and not just a few inside either) Scotland to claim that Scotland has been gripped by an 'irrational' nationalism and that voters in Scotland were '*in the grip of religious fervour*' (Michael White in *The Guardian*, May 13, 2015). Claims that national identity was the key factor in shaping voting intentions are seriously mistaken (see Eichhorn, 2015; Thomson, 2015).

These claims play down the fact that social welfare and opposition to austerity were key to both the 2014 Referendum and the outcomes of the 2015 General Election in Scotland. However, the argument made in this chapter is not that nationalism was completely irrelevant but that it was interrelated with other issues in crucial ways. That welfare issues have become even more entangled with constitutional debates and questions of national futures today is not surprising. This was central to discussions in the post-World War II period of Britishness. UK-wide institutions such as the NHS and social security have long been held up as pivotal elements in the Union, a union that in many respects has been a 'welfare union'. There is a powerful narrative that the historical development of the welfare state in post-1945 Britain played an important role in binding the United Kingdom together, forging Britain as a nation.

In this respect, divergences in social welfare as well as in claims for transfers of more power to Scotland are not unique (Keating, 2010; McLean et al., 2013). Indeed, Beland and Lecours' (2008) study of nationalism and social policy in Scotland, Quebec and Flanders highlight the importance of social policy as an instrument of territorial differentiation in struggles over political autonomy. The political and policy landscape of contemporary Scotland has been increasingly shaped by resistance, both at a Scottish Government level and on the ground, to social welfare and 'austerity' policy objectives of the UK Coalition Government.

It was widely claimed that with a NO result, the Scottish Independence Referendum would have 'secured the Union for a generation'. However, few would now, in the aftermath of the Referendum and the 2015 General Election, put much weight on this view. The pace of political change in Scotland has been unprecedented. The SNP have attained what looks like a hegemonic position in Scotland in a relatively short space of time. It is the second largest political party in the United Kingdom with over 100,000 members; it has 56 of the 59 Scottish MPs and looks likely to sweep the board with an even larger majority than it enjoyed in 2011 in the May 2016 Scottish Parliament election. It has made huge inroads into Labour's traditional heartlands in Glasgow and the rest of West Central Scotland and is attracting in huge numbers many who had previously always voted Labour.

The 2014 Independence Referendum has been transformative in that a new era in Scottish politics has emerged. The SNP stands against a greatly diminished Labour Party as the defender of Scottish social democracy. In important respects, it outflanks Labour on the left, implements and supports the kinds of policies that were once largely the preserve of the pre-Blair Labour Party, of 'old Labour'. Opposing austerity, defending welfare, welcoming new immigrants and promising to rid Scotland of nuclear weapons have all played well for the SNP.

It is perhaps difficult to convey in writing to those outside Scotland the enormity of the result of the 2015 General Election in Scotland. Newspaper and media headlines from around the United Kingdom and from the rest of the world talk of 'the end of Britain'; that British politics have been 'blown apart'; that a 'psychological change' has gripped Scotland'; that the 'end of the United Kingdom is inevitable'. A huge amount of media output and academic and political commentary has in the period since May 7 been devoted to explaining what happened in Scotland and why the SNP have been so successful. As ever, there is no one factor at work here and the weight given to different contributing factors reflects the politics and different standpoints of those writing. But despite the differing perspectives, there was a shared view that the outcomes of the 2015 General Election in Scotland were 'seismic', of 'earthquake' proportions.

However, this seismic shift hasn't emerged from nowhere. The rise of the SNP has been signalled since at least 2007 when it formed a minority Scottish Government. Then, as now, it campaigned on a range of social issues, while holding on to its cherished goal of full independence for Scotland. It is achieving success not least because its primary opponents, the Labour Party, have proved to be very weak, unable to speak to voters in Scotland while at the same time speaking also to the so-called aspirational voters in 'middle England', and in the South East of England in particular (outside London). Many who now talk of Scotland being a different place are right to some extent, but there is also something of a misunderstanding that Scotland has always been a different place – differences inscribed in the Act of Union in 1707. 'Scotland' has risen to the top of the social, political, economic and cultural agenda – not just in Scotland – but on a UK-wide basis. The 2015 General Election campaign saw Scotland in the spotlight as rarely before. Since May 2015, the SNP are constantly in the UK news while the promise of some sort of devolution for England also reflects that developments in Scotland over the past few years have re-ignited other interconnected debates about the United Kingdom's territorial arrangements. There are different dynamics and emerging renewed tensions, contradictions and ambivalences. In all of this, social welfare issues are pivotal in that they point to and are utilized in claims about the fair or unfair distribution of resources across the pluri-national United Kingdom.

These issues are destabilizing the UK union in ways that have not been seen before. Finally, and to return to an earlier theme, Scottish politics is not driven by concerns over 'national identity'. Scottishness is not up for discussion (even if this is a long-awaited subject for deconstruction); no one is disputing that there is a country called Scotland and that there is a long-existing nation, the Scots. While there has been a growth in the number of people who see themselves first and foremost as Scottish, it is not this that is shaping politics on the ground. The Conservatives, the Labour Party and the Liberal Democrats would dearly love to be able to dismiss political developments in Scotland simply as a short-lived outburst of nationalism and irrationality. Yet, the Tories have not been slow to engage in anti-Scottish rhetoric before and since the 2015 General Election (see Brown, 2015). The failure to see that more correctly it is very much the issues around austerity, poverty and inequality that have driven people to support the SNP's somewhat weak alternative vision, means that a second referendum on Scottish Independence becomes even closer.

REFERENCES

Ashcroft. (2014). *Post Referendum Scotland Poll 18–9 September*, Accessed at http:// lordashcroftpolls.com/wp-content/uploads/2014/09/Lord-Ashcroft-Polls-Referendum-day-poll-summary-1409191.pdf

Béland, D., and Lecours, A. (2008). *Nationalism and Social Policy: The Politics of Territorial Solidarity*, Oxford: Oxford University Press.

Bell, D. (2010). Devolution in a Recession: Who'd Have Thought It Would Come to This? in G. Lodge, and K. Schmuecker. (Eds.), *Devolution in Practice 2010*, London: IPPR.

Brown, G. (2014a). *My Scotland, Our Britain: A Future Worth Sharing.* London: Simon & Schuster.

Brown, G. (2014b). A stronger Scotland in a Stronger UK, *Progress*, 5 September.

Brown, G. (2015). Britain's Already Fragile Union Is at Risk–Not from Scotland but Its Own Government, *The Guardian*, June 12.

Dewar, D. (1999). *Preface to Social Justice – A Scotland Where Everyone Matters*, Edinburgh: Scottish Executive.

Eichhorn, J. (2015). There was no Rise in Scottish Nationalism: Understanding the SNP Victory, *LSE British Politics and Policy Blog*, May 14, Available at: http:// blogs.lse.ac.uk/politicsandpolicy/there-was-no-rise-in-scottish-nationalism-understanding-the-snp-victory/ (accessed 01/06/15).

Greer, S. L. (Ed.). (2009). *Devolution and Social Citizenship in the UK*, Bristol: Policy Press.

Heffer, S. (2015). Why David Cameron May Not Have Long to Savour His Success, *New Statesman*, 22–28 May.

Keating, M. (2010). *The Government of Scotland: Public Policy Making after Devolution, (Second Edition)*, Edinburgh: Edinburgh University Press.

McLean, J., Gallagher, J., and Lodge, G. (2013). *Scotland's Choices: The Referendum and What Happens Afterwards*, Edinburgh: Edinburgh University Press.

Mooney, G. (2014a). Campaigns Fight to Define what Scottish Social Justice Means, *The Conversation*, September 15, Available at: https://theconversation.com/ campaigns-fight-to-define-what-scottish-social-justice-means-31699 (accessed 01/06/15).

Mooney, G. (2014b). Poverty, "Austerity" and Scotland's Constitutional Future, in J. McKendrick, G. Mooney, J. Dickie, G. Scott, and P. Kelly. (Eds.), *Poverty in Scotland 2014: The Independence Referendum and Beyond*, London: CPAG.

Mooney, G. (2015). Anti-Austerity Backlash Is Moving Up a Gear, *The Conversation*, June 1, Available at: https://theconversation.com/anti-austerity-backlash-is-moving-up-a-gear-even-in-progressive-scotland-42454 (accessed 01/06/15).

Mooney, G., and Wright, S. (2009). Introduction: Social Policy in the Devolved Scotland: Towards a Scottish Welfare State?, *Social Policy and Society*, 8, 3: 361–65.

Mooney, G., and Scott, G. (Eds.) (2012). *Social Justice and Social Policy in Scotland*, Bristol: Policy Press.

Scottish Government. (2013). *Scotland's Future: Your Guide to an Independent Scotland*, Edinburgh: The Scottish Government.

Smith Commission. (2014). *Report of the Smith Commission for Further Devolution of Powers to the Scottish Parliament*, Edinburgh: The Smith Commission.

Thomson, A. (2015). When Will English Politicians Understand Scotland and the SNP?, Channel 4 Blog, May 8, Available at: http://blogs.channel4.com/alex-thomsons-view/english-politicians-understand-scotland-snp/9573 (accessed 01/06/15).

Part II

LAGGING OR LEADING IN THE REST OF THE UNITED KINGDOM

Chapter 5

Economic Challenges and Opportunities of Devolved Corporate Taxation in Northern Ireland[1]

Leslie Budd

INTRODUCTION

The relationship between fiscal decentralization and economic growth is an ambiguous one, which is something that is often overlooked by proponents of decentralization. The original Oates theorem stated that:

> In multilevel governments, each level of government (including the central government) will maximise social and economic welfare within its own jurisdiction. (Oates, 1993; 4)

Yet, this has been taken as a general endorsement of the utility of devolution in itself rather than focusing on how decentralized fiscal instruments can directly affect growth, output and employment, as well as other objectives of socio-economic welfare. Much of the literature that is quoted in favour of fiscal decentralization fails to take account of differences between 'administrative' and 'substantive' decentralization – that is, between what amounts to expenditure and revenue transfers from central government and those that sub-national governments have discretion over in their territories (Thornton, 2007). Thus, higher levels of sub-national revenue and spending shares do not necessarily indicate a greater local autonomy over public resources. This observation is very pertinent to the United Kingdom in that it lacks a coherent cross-cutting system of centre-periphery governmental relations. At present, the experience of devolution of the four nations of the United Kingdom appears to be inchoate and incoherent.

As can be seen from the expert contributions on Scotland in this volume, changes in the sub-national control of revenue raising can have complex and sometimes perverse effects. In order to sustain a broad tax base (a range of categories in order to raise the optimal amount of revenue) in federal systems, some taxes are more appropriately set at national levels. Thus, the degree of decentralization of tax functions and categories may have a limited impact on devolved governmental powers. With this in mind, the one taxation category that elicits demands for greater local control is Corporation Tax (CT) or the equivalent tax on business profits elsewhere. In particular, the claim is made that lowering the rate of CT stimulates greater Foreign Direct Investment (FDI), leading to increased output and employment. For many proponents of this reform, it represents a 'silver bullet'[2] as though it was *The Lone Ranger* riding to the rescue of economically under-performing sub-national territories.

In the case of Northern Ireland, it has been granted the right to set its own rate of corporation tax (CT) from April 2018. The proposed rate is 12.5% down from the current whole UK rate of 20%. As a consequence, there will be a reduction of UK central government grant, estimated at between £300m and £700m (Independent Commission on Funding and Finance for Wales Commission, 2010). The granting of local discretion over CT is in part influenced by Northern Ireland's neighbour, the Republic of Ireland (ROI), where the rate is already 12.5%. This internationally comparative low rate is central to a discourse that states that cutting corporation tax stimulates FDI and thus economic growth. In one way, this cross-border harmonization makes sense in that it equalizes what can be called an effective exchange rate: currency differences notwithstanding. The danger is that policy makers may enviously look across the border at the economic 'silver bullet' of the lower rate of tax. There are two important differences, however. First, the ROI is a larger independent economy that is a formal member of the EU and the Eurozone with direct access to a much larger market. Second, following the example of levying an effectively zero rate for US companies who use loopholes in US tax legislation, for example Apple and Google, is a case of a 'race to the bottom' that the Northern Ireland Executive should be loathe to follow.[3]

As this chapter explores, the issue of setting a lower rate of CT for Northern Ireland, in order to stimulate increased FDI, is to locate it as part of a set of instruments within a framework that can be called regional industrial policy. That is, using the full range of tax credits and allowances to target key sectors, which attract value-additive activities. In Northern Ireland, they have been identified in its economic strategy as the MATRIX[4] growth sectors, the details of which are discussed below (Northern Ireland Executive, 2014a). These are the ones in which Northern Ireland has a and competitive advantage and which tend to attract the most amount of FDI.

This chapter attempts to construct an analysis based upon the possibilities of changes in CT being part of a comprehensive regional industrial policy that brings benefits to an economy that to date has underperformed. The next section gives an overview on the general issues about CT changes being the agency of increased FDI. The subsequent section gives an overview of the performance of the Northern Ireland economy in a comparative context. The final section sets out a more detailed analysis of the challenges and opportunities of changing the CT regime in regard to its impact on FDI.

DO CORPORATION TAX RATES STIMULATE FOREIGN DIRECT INVESTMENT (FDI)?

National evidence on the relationship between cuts in CT and stimulating FDI is variable. In a small open economy like New Zealand, its corporation tax was around the global median of 30% in 2009, reduced from 33% the previous year (Inland Revenue, 2011). Yet, evidence from the same body shows that FDI as a percentage of GDP has oscillated slightly around a median of 50% for the last decade (ibid). In other words, the internal concern that New Zealand had a high rate of company taxation is not borne out by international comparisons and the effect on its domestic tax take. The New Zealand government noted, albeit equivocally:

> One reason for the potential concern about New Zealand's relatively high company tax rate is that this may make it less attractive for foreigners to invest in New Zealand. This has been cited as a potential concern by recent tax reviews. A recent survey found that, on average across different studies, a 1 percentage point cut in the company tax rate leads to a 3.72 percent increase in foreign direct investment (FDI). However, there are many significant non-tax factors, which affect FDI, and these differ between countries . . . .
>
> Taken at face value, the studies would suggest that cutting New Zealand's company rate from 33% to 30% in 2008 would have boosted FDI by about 11 percent (a difference of about 5.5 percent of GDP from about 50 percent to roughly 55.5 percent of GDP). In fact, since 2008 there has been a small decline in FDI, although it is difficult to know what would have happened in the absence of the tax change and international turmoil in recent years with the global financial crisis. Other things considered, one would have predicted the company rate cut would have had some effect in boosting FDI but the data provide no evidence of an upswing. (ibid)

Similarly, there have been heroic claims that the success of the Celtic Tiger economy of the Republic of Ireland (ROI) was due to cutting rates of corporation tax to internationally comparative low levels. This myth has been perpetuated by many in the ROI itself and those in the United Kingdom who are seeking greater devolution of taxation powers. Like many myths, it is based on a grain of truth, but it is just that – a grain.

A catenation of complex events provides a more factual analysis. In respect of the ROI, a corporation tax rate of 12.5% has been 'the poster-child' of the assertion that it created the necessary and sufficient condition for the growth of Celtic Tiger economy. Indeed, it is often referred to as the (my emphasis) industrial policy in government circles (Shaxson, 2012). This both misunderstands the role of company taxation in industrial policy and rewrites an imagined past, as shown in Figure 5.1 below. This figure tracks ROI Gross National Product (GNP) per capita as a percentage of the EU average in relation to changes in the rates of corporation tax since the mid-1950s (ibid).

As can be seen, the inflection point in the take-off of the Celtic Tiger economy was joining the Single European Market (SEM) in 1993. In fact, it can be argued that the marginal increase in corporation tax over the period shows that there is no correlation with rapid growth. By matching the capacities and capabilities of the Irish economy with a much bigger external market, its attractiveness for FDI, as one source of growth, increased. Ireland's key selling point for its largest provider of the United States FDI (56% in 2014) is a combination of English language; close cultural historical and economic connections; an educated workforce; and its membership of the SEM and Eurozone. Although research has shown that corporation tax rates

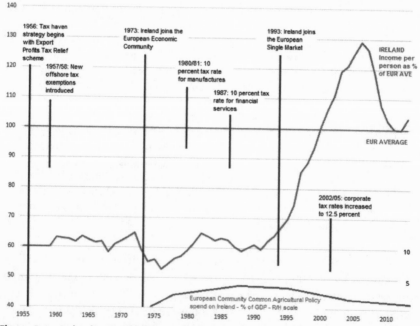

Figure 5.1 Ireland's GNP/Capita, Relative to EU GNP/Capita Against Tax Changes 1955–2013. *Source*: Shaxson (2012).

are negatively correlated with FDI in Ireland, one has to distinguish between different types of FDI (Lawless, McCoy, Morgenroth, and O'Toole, 2014). That is, directly 'value-additive' activities, especially manufacturing and tax transfer-planning activities, in particular, financial services.

The crucial point, however, is not the nominal rate of corporation tax but the effective rate. In Ireland, there is a series of tax credits and arrangements that have come into disrepute as companies located in off-shore tax havens, for example Luxembourg and Bermuda, have become the largest FDI donors after the United States. Many of these firms attract a zero rate and effectively operate as brass name-plates rather than real FDI leading to increased economic growth and employment in the recipient country. The consensus that the attractiveness of the ROI for FDI inflows is solely a function of its rate of corporation tax is shown to be wanting. Like most discourses centred on a single consensus, a degree of complexity is hidden as the report published by the United Nations Conference on Trade and Development (UNCTAD) noted:

> The role of incentives in promoting FDI has been the subject of many studies, but their relative advantages and disadvantages have never been clearly established. There have been some spectacular successes as well as notable failures in their role as facilitators of FDI. As a factor in attracting FDI, incentives are secondary to more fundamental determinants, such as market size, access to raw materials and availability of skilled labour. Investors generally tend to adopt a two-stage process when evaluating countries as investment locations. In the first stage, they screen countries based on their fundamental determinants. Only those countries that pass these criteria go on to the next stage of evaluation where tax rates, grants and other incentives may become important. Thus, it is generally recognized that investment incentives have only moderate importance in attracting FDI. UNCTAD (2000, 11)

Later evidence, as summarized in Table 5.1, reinforces this conclusion.

Table 5.1   Relative Importance of Factors Affecting Decisions on Location

	Manufacturing	Non-Manufacturing
Total labour costs	55%–73%	76%–87%
Transportation	1%–15%	0%–1%
Utility cost	2%–9%	2%–8%
Financing and depreciation	10%–22%	5%–18%
Taxes *of which:*	7%–13%	3%–7%
Property taxes	2%–3%	n/a
Other	0%–1%	n/a
Income taxes	5%–10%	3%–7%

Source: © KMPG LLC 2006. All rights reserved.

In respect of Northern Ireland itself, the Price Waterhouse Coopers (PWC) report of 2011, *Corporation Tax: Game changer or Game Over?* observed:

> Low Corporation tax is not a key driver of investment for FDI locating in the UK, ranking 17th in a list that prioritised: language, culture and values; infrastructure; skills and proximity to markets. (PWC, 2011; 11)

The evidence starts to become overwhelming so that a three-part question can be posed for proponents of the discourse of CT cut equals increased FDI: Where's the theory? Where's the evidence? Where's the data? In trying to address this question, we have to look at the context of the performance of the Northern Ireland economy over time.

THE PERFORMANCE OF THE NORTHERN IRELAND ECONOMY

In 2012, Northern Ireland accounted for about 3% of the UK population but 2% of the national income. It had the lowest Gross Value Added (GVA), a sectoral-based measure of output and productivity, of the four nations of the United Kingdom. In 2013, it had the highest economic inactivity rate at 28.2% and the second lowest weekly median wages. Table 5.2 gives the regional distribution of total GVA per head in the United Kingdom.

The comparative regional/national trajectory of GVA over time is shown in Figure 5.2 below.

Table 5.2   Total Nominal GVA by Region/Country

	Total GVA (£ Billion)		
	2011	2012	Percentage Change
London	303.4	309.3	2.0
South East	196.1	202.6	3.3
North West	127.9	130.6	2.2
East	114.3	116.1	1.6
Scotland	105.9	106.3	0.4
South West	100.4	101.6	1.2
West Midlands	97.1	98.3	1.3
Yorkshire and The Humber	92.5	93.3	1.0
East Midlands	79.7	79.7	0.0
Wales	46.5	47.3	1.9
North East	41.2	41.9	1.7
Northern Ireland	29.1	29.4	1.2
United Kingdom	1,360.9	1,383.1	1.6

Source: ONS (2014).

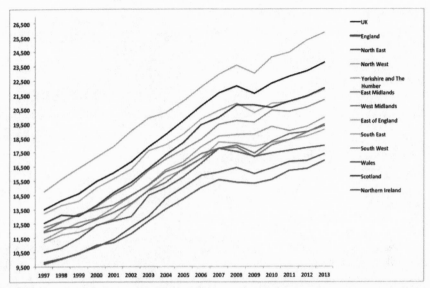

Figure 5.2   Workplace Based GVA Per Head by Region/Nation at Current Basic Prices: 2000–2012 (£). *Source*: ONS (2014).

As can be seen, just prior to the Global Financial Crisis (GFC), the trajectory of per capita GVA was closing in on that of East and West Midlands. Since then the rate of increase has been slower compared to nearly all other nations and regions in the United Kingdom. The slowing down of economic aggregates in Northern Ireland and in forecasts is set out in Table 5.3 below.

It is clear that although Northern Ireland is recovering from recession, as a result of a number of factors including budgetary pressures, the rate is slower than in the rest of the United Kingdom and the EU. In such an environment, policy makers are looking to measures to stimulate the economy over the longer term. Northern Ireland has the only contiguous border with another EU Member State in the United Kingdom, and one that is a large recipient of FDI so that there is a cross-border externality in this regard. Indeed, Northern Ireland is an increasingly attractive site for FDI within the United Kingdom as shown in Table 5.4 below.

What is apparent from this table is that although Northern Ireland performs above average in the high-value-added category for projects and jobs, it is well above average for low VA jobs. The picture is bifurcated in respect of low-value-added jobs created in that they tend to be in the business and financial services category. This type of FDI is often associated with call centre employment in either domestic firms contracting out their services to directly foreign ones or those undertaken directly by the latter. This outcome is one of the challenges for the Northern Ireland economy in that although

Table 5.3   Economic Forecasts for NI, UK and EU

% p.a.	2014	2015	2016	2017	2018
	Northern Ireland				
GVA growth rate	2.8	2.9	2.6	1.8	1.5
Unemployment (ILO) rate	7.1	6.7	7.2	7.7	8.6
Employment growth	1.7	1.2	0.8	0.9	0.4
GVA growth rate	2.8	2.9	2.6	1.8	1.5
	United Kingdom				
GDP growth rate	2.4	2.2	2.6	2.7	2.7
Unemployment (ILO) rate	7.1	7.0	6.6	6.1	5.6
Annual Employment growth	1.6	1.1	0.8	0.8	0.4
	European Union				
GDP growth rate	1.2	1.8	2.1	2.2	2.3
Unemployment (ILO) rate	11.8	11.5	11.0	11.2	9.5
Employment growth	0.8	1.2	1.3	1.1	1.1

Source: Northern Ireland Centre for Economic Policy (NICEP) (2014).

Table 5.4   Comparison of Value-Added of FDI into Northern Ireland, UK and ROI

Value Added	% of FDI Projects Attracted (2006–2010)			% of New Jobs Attracted (2006–2010)		
	NI	UK	ROI	NI	UK	ROI
Very High	44.3	39.4	46.7	37.3	20.4	41.6
High	12.1	15.8	16.1	16.5	16.8	11.2
Medium	14.1	18.0	15.8	10.5	13.4	18.9
Low	16.8	17.5	16.9	6.0	36.1	19.8
Very Low	12.8	9.2	4.5	29.7	13.4	8.5

Source: FDI Intelligence (2012).

it is well represented in advanced sectors, the distribution of the benefits of these sectors and the FDI they attract is not widespread. This is due to a number of cyclical and structural factors that are not easily managed in the short run. It is in this context that devolved powers oversetting the rate of CT looks attractive. The caveat is that the challenges and opportunities have to be weighed carefully.

BACKGROUND TO DEVOLVED CORPORATION TAX AND FDI

The Northern Ireland Research and Information Service Briefing Paper *A Review of Literature Regarding the Determinants of Foreign Direct Investment (FDI)* (Donnelly, 2014) gives a fair summary and overview of the issues concerning the drivers of inward FDI and, in particular, the role of CT. With the announcement of Northern Ireland being permitted to set a rate equivalent to that of the ROI, there has been a renewed interest in and focus on the role of cutting taxes on corporate activities in attracting FDI. This takes place against the background of particular global companies exploiting tax differences within the European Union. In particular, the ending of the 'double Irish'[5] loophole has created an overemphasis on the role of corporate taxation in attracting FDI. In assessing the economic challenges and opportunities of devolved corporate taxation, a number of issues arise:

- the new tax environment within which the Northern Ireland economy would operate will be different from that hitherto so that multiplier effects and the tax elasticity of supply may be dissimilar to those currently estimated;
- estimating the net impact on the fiscal position from tax changes and the reduction of the corresponding amount of block grant, and the transitional arrangements and their timing is uncertain;
- high-profile European Union (EU) cases being brought against global companies for tax avoidance, accompanied by public pressure and campaigns, will lead to greater pressures to harmonize corporation tax rates within the EU;
- the degree to which the Azores Judgment[6] would impinge on discretionary changes in corporation tax rates by being viewed as a form of state aid, balanced by pressures to renegotiate associated regulations;
- the possibility of a new constitutional settlement in the United Kingdom leading to more devolved fiscal powers may lead to greater tax competition between devolved nations and regions;
- by changing the effective exchange rate of business operating on both sides of the border with the ROI, an All Island approach may give Northern Ireland access to a larger market and encourage more innovation hubs: both are key drivers of FDI;
- distinguishing between investment/income and employment generating FDI as a result of cutting the rate of corporation tax. The former includes the MATRIX sectors whilst the latter includes financial services (particularly back-office functions) and other tradable services;
- the locational stability of the different sectoral composition of FDI. For example, financial and business services are more globally mobile than aerospace and advanced engineering;
- targeting the key MATRIX sectors may stimulate greater innovation and cluster development leading to increased productivity through process innovation.

There is a link to attracting FDI in key sectors and cross-border cooperation in innovation. This is set out in the structural relationships of a strategic framework to promote cross-border cooperation that is set out in Figure 5.3 below:

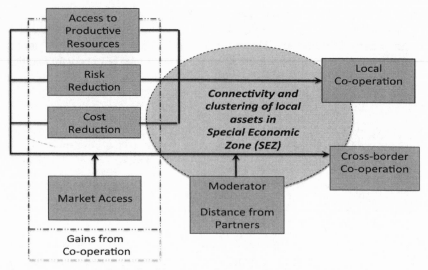

Figure 5.3   Structural Relationships Determining Local and Cross-Border Co-Operation.
Source: Roper (2006).

A series of innovation hubs with designated special economic zones
(SEZs) (not necessarily contiguous) that focus on connecting the key economic activities identified in the NI Economic Strategy would help combat this diffusion. The proposed harmonization of CT in both economies
opens up the possibility of creating incentives for embedding cross-border
economic cooperation. This harmonization changes the relative prices of
doing business across the border (in other words, the effective exchange
rate). Zero CT within the innovation hubs and differential rates within the
rest of the SEZs for a limited period, with conditionality, should strengthen
intra-firm linkages, particularly supply chains of these key activities. Much
of the innovation activity on both sides of the border is related to branch
plants of Multi-National Corporations (MNCs) focused on exports. Greater
real and virtual connectivity is an important component of sustaining this
form of FDI and the linkages between MNCs and local firms. These linkages are also important for sustaining local demand. Creating a nexus of
related activities can stimulate local domestic demand across the border.
These activities include retail; tourism; culture; sport and leisure and their
infrastructure (sports stadia; retail parks) and other community assets. Furthermore, developing agri-business that is environmentally sustainable also
stimulates agri-tourism.

The ROI has also had a successful history of attracting FDI. Overall FDI
fell from 23.9% of the Irish GDP in 2009 to 10.5% in 2011, but rebounded
to 19.4% in 2012. The sectors most represented in inward FDI are the life

Table 5.5 Selected Fiscal Measures to Promote Investment and Technological Upgrading

Tax Incentive & Mechanism	Objectives	Coverage	Advantages & Drawbacks (Partly Depend on Objectives)
1. Corporate tax instruments: *Reduced corporate tax rates (Not period – see tax holidays).*	To reduce effective tax rate (take) with waivers or reductions.	Broad coverage of profitable income-generating firms or targeted base of selected activities, sectors or firms. Does not apply to unprofitable firms.	• Tax rate has to be below global norm 35–40% for full effect; • Lower tax rates confer benefits over a longer time; • Less immediate benefits to income-generating firms; • Reductions in corporate tax rates can reward old capital more.
1a. Broad base: *Reduced corporate tax rate on all firms (e.g., Hong Kong)*	To minimize market distortions.	Broad firm base.	• Simplified system; fewer market distortions. • Perceived to be fair – affects all firms in the same way. • Confers LT benefits more slowly and rewards old capital.
1b. Selective Approach: *Reduced corporate tax rates for selected activities and sectors.*	To target beneficial industries and activities of perceived advantage.	Specific targeted industries and activities; Existing firms and/or potential investors.	• Important signalling effects about government commitment and commitments to stimulate FDI; • Generally easier to implement than general reforms; • Results depend on sector choice; may distort the market
2. Tax holidays and temporary rebates *Operate through a waiver or exempt/reduced periods for corporate tax.*	To provide support to firms in specific activities, especially new firms in their start-up phase. To encourage new investment	Popular in developing countries with a discretionary approach. Can be used to target specific industries and activities, for existing forms and/or potential investors	• Discretionary approach; risks introducing market distortions. • Flexible, according to government objectives; • Immediate benefits to firms/start-ups as soon as they earn income; • May reward founding business start-ups, rather than ongoing investments in existing companies; and LT investments; • Potential for tax planning across periods and revenue leakage • May reward ST investments in 'footloose' industries.

(Continued)

Table 5.5 Selected Fiscal Measures to Promote Investment and Technological Upgrading *(Continued)*

Tax Incentive & Mechanism	Objectives	Coverage	Advantages & Drawbacks *(Partly Depend on Objectives)*
3. Investment tax allowances: • accelerated depreciation; • expenditure allowances; • tax credits.	To support expansion in existing firms; To encourage long-term investment.	Widely used in industrialized countries; Cover firms making investments; Generally focus on specific sectors	• Promote LT capital investments and current spending, causing less revenue leakage than tax holidays; • Promote new investment; • High inflation erodes value of annual depreciation allowances.
3a. Refundable tax allowances *Refunds from government at later date.*	As above	Firms making investments	• With refundable write-off allowances, investment costs and risks can be shared by government with investors. • Where non-refundable, existing companies reap benefits • Long-term projects (e.g., infrastructure) suffer cf. rapid income-earners
4. Exemptions on customs duties or local indirect taxes (e.g., EPZs)	To encourage export/import activities for TT	Generally for targeted sectors, activities, EPZs.	• Use of customs exemptions has been restricted by trade treaties • Dependent on capacity of custom/tax administrations
5. Outright grants and upfront subsidies; Subsidized loans	To facilitate establishment of business and investment	Rarely used by DCs due to upfront costs; Used for targeted sectors.	• Flexible and can directly address objectives, but depend on capacity of tax administrations and may be open to abuse.

Source: Biggs (2007).

sciences; ICT; international financial services; content design; and engineering, as well as mobile projects from Irish food multinationals. The demonstrated effect of a successful record of inward FDI (70% of total employment in FDI-related activities is accounted for by US firms) in sectors that correspond to those promoted in the Northern Ireland Economic Strategy can act as a stimulus to cross-border activities (Northern Ireland Executive, 2014a). The MATRIX sectors are the nearest equivalent and are being promoted to generate most growth in Northern Ireland: Telecommunications and ICT; Life and Health Sciences; Agrifood; Advanced Materials; and Advanced Engineering. Table 5.5 above gives an overview of some of the effects arising from devolved CT. The shaded areas represent the current policy choices (rows 1b and 3) with the highlighted text (row 3a) being a future possibility. The degree to which other incentives and mechanisms will be introduced will depend upon the impact of changes in corporation tax. These may be positive and negative, but at present the size and scale linkages between increased FDI investment growth and employment are uncertain.

The importance of widening and deepening the attractiveness of the MATRIX sectors to FDI is clearly crucial. Outside of the targeted sectors, there are also a number of growing economic activities that also stimulate FDI. These include culture, sport, and tourism, all of which are underpinned by creative industries and are also important in cross-border economic cooperation. The status of Northern Ireland as a site for FDI within the EU, particularly for those companies from the emerging market is partially demonstrated in Table 5.6 that shows a sample of the performance of Northern Ireland's top twenty companies and their origin.

Table 5.6   Sample of Northern Ireland's Top 20 Companies (2013)

Company	Employment	Turnover (£m)	Activity	Origin
1. Moy Park	10914	1089.6	Food Processing	Brazil
3. Bombardier	4990	492.8	Aerospace	Canada
5. Four Seasons Health	4710	97.1	Nursing & Care Homes	NI
8. Dunbia	3300	701.0	Food Processing	NI
10. Caterpillar	2923	771.4	Capital equipment	US
11. Almac Group	2917	275.5	Pharmaceuticals	US
13. Resource (NI)	2538	35.3	Business support services	ROI
16. First Source Solutions	2293	55.9	Business support services	India
18. Ulster Bank	2185	n/a	Banking	UK
19. Teleperformance	2010	32.5	Business support services	France
20. Allstate (NI)			IT/Insurance	US

Source: Belfast Telegraph (2014).

Evidence of the significance of these developments is identified in the *Innovation Strategy for Northern Ireland 2014–2025* and a number of EU-funded projects (Northern Ireland Executive, 2014b). Related to these apparently subsidiary activities is the question of infrastructure and connectivity, within Northern Ireland, the rest of the United Kingdom and the EU, as well as across the border with the ROI. In this regard, air traffic, broadband and energy utilities are strategically crucial as the economy seeks to be a more globally attractive site for FDI and for sustaining associated economic development.

An important consideration in delivering the economic benefits of these targeted sectors is building upon existing and developing new Global Value Chains (GVCs). GCVS are defined as follows:

> The different processes in different parts of the world that each add value to the goods or services being produced. By joining a global value chain, small enterprises have the ability to transform their business into an international operation offering greater opportunities. (http://dictionary.cambridge.org/dictionary/business-english/global-value-chain, accessed 30/06/15)

International production, trade and investments are increasingly organized within GVCs in which the different stages of the production process are located across different countries. Globalization motivates companies to restructure their operations internationally through outsourcing and offshoring of activities through FDI. They do, however, also encourage re-shoring back to a home base as the dynamics of the global economy evolve. Firms try to optimize their production processes by locating the various stages across different sites. The last few decades have witnessed a strong trend towards the international dispersion of value chain activities such as design, production, marketing, distribution and business services (Bailey and De Propris, 2014).

In the United Kingdom, over 75% of Business Expenditure on Research and Development (BERD) is accounted for by manufacturing. Likewise, MATRIX-type sectors are the source of significant demand for business and financial services. These services are both globally tradable and form an important part of the economic framework of any economy. They also are part of key GVCs underpinning others in strategic sectors in an economy. There are also significant forward and backward linkages between and across GVCs. But perhaps just as notable are the spillovers into domestically based activities. These include adoption of process innovation to increase productivity, skills development and formation, and quality standards, as well as creating a source of demand for new activities.

These are the kinds of interactions with GVC formation associated with targeted MATRIX sectors that are likely to be the agency of linking cuts in

CT to increased FDI. The links between GVCs and associated clusters, especially business and financial services, are also likely to increase investment, growth and employment (De Propris and Hamdouch, 2013). The consequent widening of the tax base should then ensue. Northern Ireland has been noted for its success in the reform of local government taxation 2007. The essential issue in respect of devolved CT is the transition arrangements and timing of these changes. In other words, a more comprehensive calculus of the impact of changes in CT in stimulating FDI is needed, especially in a small but open economic territory such as Northern Ireland.[7]

DEVOLVED CORPORATION TAX:
CHALLENGES AND OPPORTUNITIES

Some of the challenges are implicit in the key issues set out above. The main one is the degree to which reductions in CT can compensate for any reduction in the block grant. This takes place against the size of the contribution of different taxes to government revenues, shown per person across the nations of the United Kingdom in Figure 5.4 below.

The other associated challenge is that the CT base is relatively small in Northern Ireland because of the size distribution of firms:

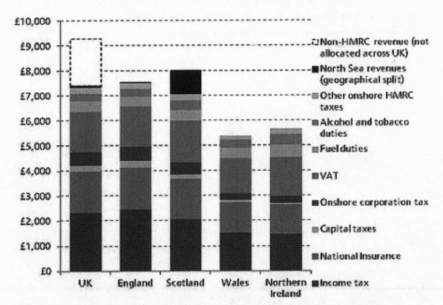

Figure 5.4 Government Revenue Per Person Across the UK, 2012–2013. *Source*: ©Institute for Fiscal Studies http://www.ifs.org.uk/publications/6881.

Leslie Budd

1. Over three-quarters of VAT and/or PAYE registered businesses with a main (or registered) address in Northern Ireland had a total employment of less than five.
2. In March 2013, businesses with a total employment of less than 50 accounted for approximately 98% of all VAT and/or PAYE registered businesses in Northern Ireland.
3. Businesses with 50–249 employees accounted for 1.5% of the total.
4. Businesses with a 250+ total employment accounted for 0.3%.
5. Businesses with a total employment of less than 10 accounted for 89.0% of the Northern Ireland total.

Similarly, the total contribution of corporation tax to the UK Exchequer has been consistently small, peaking at 2.0% in 2005–2007, then declining since, as shown in Table 5.7.

The other significant challenge is what will be the actual FDI multipliers from tax reductions. For every 1% lowering in corporation tax, the increase in FDI will vary from 1% to 5% according to the OECD (OECD, 2012). In some estimates, the upper range is 6.7%, but this was made prior to the GFC and the global economy's current under-performance.

One significant factor is what the net trade-off cost of the reduction of the tax rate to 12.5%, and the accompanying reduction in the block grant, will be. HM Treasury estimates cuts in the latter of between £300m (3.7%) and £700m (8.7%) per annum. Gerald Holtham estimates that, even if the cut were just £300 million, then compensating for that loss would require an

Table 5.7 Corporate Tax (Onshore) Receipts Across the United Kingdom (£m)

	UK	England	%	Wales	%	Scotland	%	Northern Ireland	%
1999–00	33054	29187	88.3	760	2.3	2578	7.8	529	1.6
2000–01	30092	26571	88.3	692	2.3	2347	7.8	481	1.6
2001–02	28526	25188	88.3	656	2.3	2225	7.8	456	1.6
2002–03	25606	22610	88.3	589	2.3	1997	7.8	410	1.6
2003–04	25020	22043	88.1	600	2.4	1927	7.7	425	1.7
2004–05	29810	26143	87.7	715	2.4	2355	7.9	566	1.9
2005–06	43522	39276	87.7	829	2.4	2762	8.0	690	2.0
2006–07	37599	33275	88.5	865	2.3	2707	7.2	752	2.0
2007–08	40655	36020	88.6	935	2.3	2927	7.2	772	1.9
2008–09	33251	29427	88.5	765	2.3	2560	7.7	499	1.5
2009–10	30807	27295	88.6	739	2.4	2403	7.8	400	1.3
2010–11	35257	31238	88.6	846	2.4	2715	7.7	458	1.3
2011–12	33311	29514	88.6	866	2.6	2498	7.5	433	1.3
2012–13	35059	31168	88.9	876	2.5	2559	7.3	421	1.2
2013–14	35718	31753	88.9	893	2.5	2607	7.3	429	1.2

Source: HMRC (2014).

additional £2.4 billion in private-sector profits.[8] This translates into an additional £10 billion of Gross Value Added (GVA) (current figure £28 billion).

It is apparent, however, that the introduction of a reduction in the rate of CT to 12.5% is not just a binary function of the corresponding level of the block grant. This change in policy is effectively part of a new form of regional industrial policy aimed at transforming the Northern Ireland economy. This centres on the links between greater FDI leveraging investment; growth in output; and subsequent rises in employment. This new environment forms the backcloth of the opportunities arising from corporate tax changes.

In 2011, the Economic Advisory Group (EAG) in Northern Ireland produced a report setting out its estimates of economic benefits from a cut to a 12.5% rate. By 2030, this should produce (EAG, 2011) the following:

- the increase in employment is anticipated to be 58,000 higher by 2030, representing a 6.7% increase from the baseline;
- FDI is forecast to comprise 42% of the net additional jobs;
- GVA per head is forecast to be 13.5% higher than the baseline, implying convergence on living standards in the rest of the United Kingdom;
- average annual GVA is forecast to be around one percentage point higher per year, with the economy 13.8% larger by 2030;
- labour productivity is forecast to be 6.6% higher than the baseline by 2030;
- exporting activity is forecast to be 34% higher than the baseline.

There is danger, however, of seeing reductions in CT in order to stimulate inward FDI as the agency of economic growth. This is reinforced by the discourse about the role of a low rate in the ROI being responsible for its dynamic, albeit volatile, growth performance, as discussed above.

The focus on tax changes, their mechanisms and incentives (for example, those set out in Table 5.5 above) in key targeted sectors is clearly crucial in attempts to embed greater FDI in the economy. An important consideration for Northern Ireland in delivering economic benefits is building upon existing Global Value Chains (GVCs) and developing new ones, as discussed above.

CONCLUSION

It is apparent from the foregoing analysis that the pursuit of devolved powers over setting the rate for Corporation Tax in Northern Ireland is complex and challenging. If the Executive pursues the discourse that this will lead to dynamic economic growth, through increased Foreign Direct Investment, which has become conventional wisdom in its southern neighbour, then this would represent a 'race to the bottom'. That is, substituting CT revenues for central government grant will lead to a net loss of between £300m and £700m with no guarantee of increased FDI. If, however, this change to the business tax regime is part of a more comprehensive policy and framework that targets key sectors that are 'value-additive', then this may be seen to correspond to 'substantive decentralization'. This targeted approach should be seen as part of a regional industrial policy in order to develop and sustain Global Value Chains (GVCs) that may stimulate investment and growth from FDI leading to employment effects and widening of the tax base. There are also the spillovers to related industries, both domestically or internationally based.

In the present uncertain environment, it is clear that Northern Ireland will need transitional funding arrangements so that the projected loss of public revenues can be mitigated if the economy is not to be weakened. If not, there is a danger that the capacity to attract more FDI may be undermined, making the devolution of CT powers irrelevant to sustaining the economy. The election of a Conservative government with a small overall majority and the elevation of the Scottish National Party to national status in the whole of the United Kingdom will change the political landscape. With the Devolution Bill going through Parliament that focuses on England and the controversy over English Votes for English Laws (EVEL), there is a heady brew around the outcomes for an economically devolved and federalized United Kingdom. In this context, the Northern Ireland Executive and Assembly may have a stronger position in negotiating current changes to the welfare budget, which could have a profound effect on an economy that is still vulnerable to negative shocks. By developing a more comprehensive regional industrial policy, in which setting a lower rate of CT is just one instrument, the growing potential of the Northern Ireland economy may be realized. This may also represent the first stage of a form of fiscal federalism for the whole of the United Kingdom, with the English regions looking enviously at their devolved neighbour across the Irish Sea.

NOTES

1. This chapter is based upon a briefing note produced by the author in his role as Special Economic Advisor to the Committee for Enterprise, Trade and Investment of the Northern Ireland Assembly. The views expressed here are entirely my own but I am grateful to the Committee and its Chair of the Committee Patsy Mcglone permission to reproduce part of the note.

2. Silver bullets were ancient solutions to destroying werewolves. In modern times, the cultural radio and TV icon *The Lone Ranger* used silver bullets in a symbol of justice, law and order, and to remind himself and others that life, like silver, has value and is not to be wasted or thrown away.

3. There have been questions as to how sustainable the ROI industrial policy actually is, especially as regards the focus on attracting FDI (Bailey and Lenihan, 2015).

4. MATRIX, the Northern Ireland Science Industry Panel, identified the key sectors in Northern Ireland. Hence, the eponymous term for these sectors.

5. The double Irish loophole allows US companies to reduce their tax bill far below Ireland's 12.5% corporate tax rate by shifting most of their taxable income from an operating company in Ireland to another Irish-registered firm in an offshore tax haven such as Bermuda. The ending of this loophole will be phased over a four-year period.

6. The Azores judgement reaffirmed the EU principle that *the infra-State body not only has powers in the territory within its competence to adopt measures reducing the tax rate, regardless of any considerations related to the conduct of the central State, but that in addition it assumes the political and financial consequences of such a measure.* http://www.reckon.co.uk/item/38dd5bd2.

7. As part of a wider, more holistic approach to industrial policy (see Bailey and Lenihan, 2015).

8. Gerald Holtham was Chair of the *Independent Commission on Funding and Finance for Wales* established to investigate the impact of devolution. The remit of the Commission was to look at the pros and cons of the present formula-based approach to the distribution of public expenditure resources to the Welsh Assembly Government, and identify possible alternative funding mechanisms including the scope for the Welsh Assembly Government to have tax-varying powers as well as greater powers to borrow.

REFERENCES

Adam, S., and Miller, H. (2013). Tax Revenue in England, Scotland, Wales and Northern Ireland, *IFS Observations* Institute for Fiscal Studies: London, http://www.ifs.org.uk/publications/6881 (accessed 23/05/15).

Bailey, D., and De Propris, L. (2014). Manufacturing Reshoring and Its Limits: The UK Automotive Case, *Cambridge Journal of Regions, Economy and Society*, 7, 3: 379–95.

Bailey, D., and Lenihan, L. (2015). A Critical Reflection on Irish Industrial Policy: A Strategic Choice Approach, *International Journal of the Economics of Business*, 22, 1: 47–72.

Belfast Telegraph. (2014). *Northern Ireland's Top 100 Companies 2013 - Moy Park Rules the Roost*, Belfast: Belfast Telegraph. 8/09/14 http://www.belfasttelegraph.co.uk/business/top-100-companies/ (accessed 23/05/15).

Biggs, P. (2007). *Tax Incentives to Attract FDI, Meeting of Experts on FDI, Technology and Competitiveness*, Geneva: UNCTAD, 8–9 March, http://vi.unctad.org/fdiCD/sessions/Session3/Biggs.pdf (accessed 23/05/15).

De Propris, L., and Hamdouch, A. (2013). Editorial: Regions as Knowledge and Innovative Hubs, *Regional Studies*, 47, 7: 997–1000.

Donnelly, D. (2014). *A Review of Literature Regarding the Determinants of Foreign Direct Investment (FDI)*, Research and Information Service Briefing Paper, NIAR 862–14, Belfast: Northern Ireland Assembly.

Economic Advisory Group. (2011). *The Impact of Reducing Corporation Tax on the Northern Ireland Economy*, Belfast: EAG. http://www.eagni.com/fs/doc/publications/impact-of-corporation-tax-on-ni-eag-report-final-report.pdf (accessed 23/05/15).

FDI Intelligence. (2012). *Improving the Quality of Foreign Direct Investment to Northern Ireland*, London: FDI Intelligence.

HMRC. (2014). *A Disaggregation of HMRC Tax Receipts between England, Wales, Scotland & Northern Ireland: Methodology Note*, London: HMRC. https://www.gov.uk/government/uploads/system/uploads/attachment_data/file/359890/disag-method.pdf (accessed 23/05/15).

Independent Commission on Funding and Finance for Wales. (2010). *Fairness and Accountability: A New Funding Settlement for Wales*, Final Report, Cardiff, Independent Commission on Funding and Finance for Wales.

Inland Revenue. (2011). *Briefing for the Incoming Minister of Revenue – 2011: 2. The New Zealand Tax System and How it Compares Internationally*, Wellington: Inland Revenue, New Zealand.

KMPG. (2006). *Competitive Alternatives*, Survey, London: KPMG.

OECD. (2008). *Tax Effects on Foreign Direct Investment. Policy* Brief, OECD Observer, Paris: Organisation of Economic Co-operation and Development, Available at http://www.oecd.org/investment/investment-policy/40152903.pdf (accessed 23/05/15).

ONS. (2014). *Regional Economic Indicators*, London: National Statistics.

PWC NI. (2011). *Corporation Tax: Game Changer or Game Over?*, Available at: http://www.pwc.co.uk/ni/publications/ni-government-futures-corporation-tax.html (accessed 23/05/15).

Lawless, M., McCoy, D., Morgenroth, E., and O'Toole, C. (2014). The Importance of Corporation Tax Policy in the Location Choices of Multinational Firms.

NICEP. (2014). *Outlook Autumn 2014*, Northern Ireland Centre for Economic Policy, Coleraine: Ulster Business School.

Northern Ireland Executive. (2014a). *Northern Ireland Economic Strategy; 2nd Monitoring Report*, Belfast: Northern Ireland Executive: Belfast.

Northern Ireland Executive. (2014b). *Innovate NI: Innovation Strategy for Northern Ireland 2014–2025*, Belfast: Northern Ireland Executive.

Oattes, W. E. (1993). *Fiscal Decentralization and Economic Development*, Working Paper. 93, 4, University of Maryland, Maryland: University of Maryland.

Roper, S. (2006). *Cross-Border and Local Cooperation on the Island of Ireland: an Economic Perspective*, Centre for International Borders Research, Belfast and Dublin: Institute for British-Irish Studies.

Shaxson, N. (2012). *Treasure Islands: Tax Havens and the Men Who Stole the World*, London: Vintage Books.

Thornton, J. (2007). Fiscal Decentralization and Economic Growth Reconsidered, *Journal of Urban Economics*, 6: 64–70.

UNCTAD. (2000). *Tax Incentives and Foreign Direct Investment: A Global Survey*, ASIT Advisory Studies No. 16, Geneva: UNCTAD, Available at http://unctad.org/en/Docs/iteipcmisc3_en.pdf (accessed 23/05/15).

Chapter 6

Commanding Economic Heights?

The Effects of Constitutional Uncertainty on Wales' Fiscal Future

Rebecca Rumbul

INTRODUCTION

The Welsh economic landscape betrays a mixed picture in 2015. Whilst growth has been experienced at a faster rate in Wales than any other part of the United Kingdom in the year 2015 (ONS, 2014a), unemployment remains higher than the UK average at 7% in Wales compared to 5.8% for the United Kingdom as a whole (ONS, 2015), and pay within the private sector remains limited in comparison to other parts of the United Kingdom (ONS, 2014b). Wales has also remained stubbornly within the eligibility bracket for EU Convergence funding, a category reserved for the most deprived regions of the EU and a status that entitles it to significant funding from the EU for economic growth programmes. Politically, much blame for Wales' economic woe has been laid at the feet of the UK government, with the weak devolution dispensation and the 'under-funding' of Wales under the Barnett formula identified as key factors in limiting Wales' potential (Cole and Stafford, 2014). The ongoing constitutional debate in the United Kingdom is, therefore, a significant influence upon Wales' economic future.

It is fair to note that the current constitutional debate in the United Kingdom has primarily been driven by Scottish interests (Trench, 2008), and Westminster responses to these constitutional questions have, in turn, focused upon Scottish concerns as a result. Whilst constitutional concerns also affect Wales and Northern Ireland, albeit in very different forms, the public and private debate on the constitutional future of the United Kingdom has been characterized by bilateral relations between Westminster and Holyrood (Swenden and McEwen, 2014). This bilateral constitutional conversation continues to relegate the interests of Wales to the sidelines, and a lack of public support in Wales for independence, coupled with a significantly less robust economic environment in comparison with Scotland, consolidates this tertiary position of Wales as a lesser voice and a lesser stakeholder in this debate.

The impact of the rise of Scottish nationalism upon Wales and the Welsh economic outlook has been nothing short of significant. The consequences of the Scottish referendum and the resulting political promises made to Scotland by the three leading Westminster parties (Labour, the Conservatives and the Liberal Democrats) locked in an arguably unfair funding system, which provides greater funding per head to Scotland than Wales (or, indeed, England), certainly for the near future. The hastily composed Smith Commission provided a strategy for the provision of significant further devolution to Scotland within seventy days of the Scottish referendum 'no' vote. This was against a backdrop of lethargic Westminster progress towards providing further devolution to Wales based on the recommendations of the Silk Commission. The astonishing performance of the SNP in Scotland in the May 2015 UK General Election supplies an even louder voice for Scottish concerns in Westminster and all but ensures that Scotland is likely to dominate the UK constitutional debate for the duration of the parliament. Whilst Scotland argues for greater devolution and a favourable financial settlement, it is evident from the new Conservative government's statement delaying the promised legislation for Wales to take forward the St David's Day agreement that it is likely that Welsh interests will remain a minor concern in comparison with the continuing dominance of Scottish affairs.

This chapter considers the economic future of Wales through a constitutional lens, proposing that the asymmetrical nature of UK decentralization, the imbalance in the political interests of the Westminster parties between Wales, Scotland and Northern Ireland, and the constitutional uncertainty surrounding an EU referendum form some of the most considerable influences upon Wales' economic future. In the context of the continuing influence of Scottish concerns within Westminster, the enduring inadequacies in the existing Welsh dispensation, the increasing focus upon decentralization in England and the possibility of a UK exit from the EU, it is quite likely that the progress towards a sustainable and coherent devolution dispensation in Wales will lack momentum. Without genuine and quality reform of the fiscal and legislative structures in Wales, and without financial stability, Welsh politicians and policy makers will continue in their attempts to build Welsh policy using outdated tools, and this will likely be to the detriment of the future growth and prosperity of the Welsh economy.

ALWAYS LAGGING BEHIND: A PERENNIALLY
WEAK DISPENSATION FOR WALES

The significant differences in the devolution story between Scotland and Wales have been the subject of much scholarly scrutiny (Bogdanor, 2001; Goodwin, Jones and Jones, 2005; Jeffery and Wincott, 2006; Mooney and Williams, 2006; Trench, 2004; Wyn Jones and Scully, 2006), with consensus that the historic structural and legal environment in Scotland provided more fertile ground for the preparation of devolution following the unsuccessful 1979 devolution referendum, with the constitutional convention specifically cultivating the engagement and support of civil society (Day, 2006; McAllister, 1998). In particular, it is prudent to note that devolution in Wales has historically been distinct from that in Scotland in its relative lack of grass-roots and public support (Day, 2006), and has experienced a much slower pace of devolution as a result of the incoherence of the original devolution dispensation and the originally imposed structure of the Welsh political machinery (Evans, 2014). The birth of the National Assembly in 1999 was the conclusion of a 50.3% 'Yes' vote in a 1997 referendum on a turnout of 50.1%. A second referendum was held in 2011 on proposals to provide the Assembly with primary legislative powers. The result of this referendum, at 65% voting 'yes' in favour of primary legislative powers, is considered to demonstrate that devolution had become the 'settled will' of the Welsh people (Wyn Jones and Scully, 2012); however, it is noteworthy that the turnout was only 35%.

The obscurity of the question and the lack of a real 'no' campaign to balance the cross-party 'yes' campaign failed to capture the public imagination (Wyn Jones and Scully, 2012), and it could be considered that the referendum was an affair by, and for, the Welsh political class. The award of primary legislative powers for Wales provided the Assembly with greater scope for devolved policy making; however, fiscal powers did not form part of this settlement, and in comparison to the Scottish reserved powers model, the Welsh conferred model of powers remained a weaker proposition (Evans, 2014). Following the 2011 referendum and in response to various criticisms of the usability of the Welsh devolution settlement, the coalition UK Government established the Silk Commission to examine the possibility of further devolution for Wales. A wide-ranging brief included the ability to consider the devolution of fiscal powers, the structure of the powers and whether a move to a reserved powers model held any merit, and the possibility of devolution of other policy areas such as policing, transport and justice.

The Silk Commission's mandate was so considerable in scope that it split its reporting into two parts, with the first part examining fiscal responsibilities, and the second part looking broadly at the structure and extent of devolved powers in Wales. The content of the resulting reports provided those in favour of deeper devolution with significant encouragement. The first report on fiscal accountability published in 2012 recommended income-tax-varying powers for up to 10p in the pound, and a range of other small taxes such as landfill tax, Air Passenger Duty and stamp duty.

Limited borrowing powers were also recommended. Notably, however, consideration of the system of funding for Wales, the Barnett formula, was not included within the remit of the Silk Commission, and the subject was not considered within the final reports. The Silk Commission's second report was published in 2013 and recommended significantly that the current 'conferred' model of powers be moved to a reserved model. Recommendations on further devolution of policing, energy and transport were also made, as was a recommendation to increase the number of Assembly Members from the current total of Sixty. These reports provided a comprehensive body of discussion and recommendation with which the UK government could take informed decisions on rationalizing the state of devolution in Wales and the United Kingdom; however, the lack of examination of the Barnett formula restricted the Commission's ability to consider Wales' economic and fiscal future in a rounded and unified manner.

BARNETT: THE FORMULA THAT WOULDN'T DIE

The Barnett formula was introduced in 1979 in Scotland and Northern Ireland, and one year later, in 1980, in Wales. Originally created as a temporary measure, it calculates changes to the 'block grant' provided to each devolved administration based on the expenditure on comparable services in England, and on the size of the devolved nation's population (HM Treasury, 2010). Much criticism has been levelled at the formula, most notably by Lord Barnett himself (McLean and McMillan, 2005), and centres around two fundamental flaws; first, that the formula does not accommodate relative regional spending needs and allows for over- and underfunding per head between the nations, and second, that the funding calculation is based upon departmental expenditure in England and, therefore, vulnerable to the policy decisions taken by a different government. Whilst much support for the abolition of the Barnett formula has been voiced across parties and within academic discourse (Bell and Eiser, 2014; Morgan, 2015; King and Eiser, 2014), the Scottish government and Scottish political parties have been understandably reluctant to see its demise because of the premium per head that Scotland enjoys under the formula (Bell and Eiser, 2014). The continuity of Barnett was affirmed by 'The Vow' provided to Scotland by the leading Westminster parties in the lead-up to the Scottish Independence referendum of 2014.

Faced with polls suggesting a tight contest in which a 'Yes' vote might be possible, the leaders of the Westminster parties guaranteed the endurance of the Barnett formula as part of a package of measures designed to persuade the Scottish people to vote in favour of remaining in the Union. The consequence for Wales of locking-in the Barnett formula is continued underfunding per head relative to need. Whilst the amount of underfunding is no longer considered to be as large as it was at the time of the Holtham Commission (which placed the figure at £300m in 2010), the changing UK economic outlook, a potential withdrawal from the EU and the Conservative government's continued austerity measures will variously place pressure on the amount of funding that the Welsh Government is able to allocate for economic growth and labour-market development.

TOO MUCH OR NOT ENOUGH? THE IMPLICATIONS AND IMPLEMENTATION OF SILK I

The Silk Commission's first report provided the basis for the Wales Act 2014, first tabled as a draft in December 2013. This focused upon devolving further fiscal responsibilities to the Welsh Government, and amongst its provisions were the devolution of partial income tax-varying powers, stamp duty, business rates and landfill tax, and borrowing powers of up to £1 billion. Notably, taxes such as Air Passenger Duty that could instigate competition between Wales and England (specifically between Cardiff and Bristol airports) were left out. In a similar aversion to the creation of competition, in draft form, the Act originally included a 'lock-step' mechanism for income tax that would lock variations in tax bands in tandem, meaning that any rise in the higher rate would be matched by a rise in the lower rate. This mechanism essentially rendered the power unusable, and widespread vocal opposition resulted in the removal of the unpopular mechanism prior to its final stage.

The most significant item in the Wales Act 2014 was the proposed devolution of partial income tax powers; however, the Act also indicated that a referendum may take place to gain public approval prior to this power being devolved. The notion of a referendum has been politically contested, with several political commentators as well as individuals from Welsh Labour, the Conservatives, the Liberal Democrats and Plaid Cymru citing a variety of reasons against such a move. The political debate surrounding such a referendum has significant consequences for the future of Welsh fiscal responsibility.

The rationale for arguing the necessity of a referendum primarily focuses on the issue of constitutional principle. The Lords Select Committee on the Constitution and Referendums in 2009 recommended that referendums only be held on points of fundamental constitutional principle. It is fiercely debated whether the devolution of limited taxation powers is a point of constitutional principle; however, in the case of Wales, the proposition of a referendum also relates to the fact that the people of Wales have never been provided with a question specifically on tax-raising powers being awarded to the Welsh devolved institution (as the Scottish were asked in a second question in the 1997 referendum). Critics of this precedent argue that this 1997 question provided the Scottish Parliament only with the 'option' to exercise tax-variation (a power never utilized), and that this precedent is now outdated as a result of the Scotland Act 2012, which places an obligation upon the Scottish Parliament to take a decision (Wyn Jones, 2014). This was included in the Act for the purposes of making the Scottish Parliament financially accountable, and therefore the argument can be made that if this method of fiscal accountability can be imposed upon the Scottish Parliament without a referendum, why not on the National Assembly for Wales?

In addition to the argument in favour of a referendum resting on the 1997 Scottish 'second question' precedent, it is a consideration that during the campaign for the referendum held in Wales in 2011, commitments were explicitly made by the 'yes' campaign that tax-raising powers would not automatically follow a 'yes' vote. The devolution of tax-varying powers so soon after such campaign pledges were made could render the political class vulnerable to accusations of devolution happening 'via the back door'.

In contrast to these arguments, it is clear why the prospect of a referendum on tax-raising powers is unpalatable to many within this sphere. The detail of such a referendum is unlikely to capture the public imagination, and could possibly result in a very low turnout. The very word 'tax' also catalyses strong emotions in voters, and there is a clear risk that a referendum on such a subject is unwinnable. The very need for a referendum has also been called into question. The principle of the devolution of minor taxes to Wales is supported by the Wales Act 2014, and the further devolution of tax-varying powers can be considered somewhat less significant than a point of constitutional principle. Indeed, it has been described as a point only of technicality (Wyn Jones, 2014) not of great enough significance to warrant a referendum. Individuals from several parties have suggested that the proposals should form part of General Election or National Assembly manifestos, with the manifesto pledges for tax-varying powers to be implemented by the elected government. The imposition of an elected mayor and the devolution of £6 billion in NHS funding to Greater Manchester without such a referendum, a significant structural shift in political responsibility to a devolved level, is considered at odds with the need for a referendum in Wales. The Welsh Labour Leader and First Minister Carwyn Jones has also insisted that any referendum on tax-varying powers should only occur following a change to the Barnett formula, later claiming that any pledges for further funding for Wales should not be linked to a requirement for a referendum. Whilst many of these arguments are political rather than academic, the fundamental question at stake rests on accountability, and whether the fiscal accountability of the Welsh Government should be subject to a popular vote or should be required by law. In the event of a 'no' vote in a tax-varying powers referendum, the Welsh Government arguably continues to govern without the same level of fiscal accountability legally expected of the Scottish Government.

The cumulative effect of such opposition to a referendum and the lack of a political roadmap either for or against one, is to create an environment of continued uncertainty concerning Wales' fiscal future. The further devolution measures proposed in the St David's Day Agreement of 2015, and the delays likely in implementing that agreement, foster further uncertainty still, and with post-general election political attention shifting to the elections to the National Assembly for Wales, Scottish Parliament and Northern Ireland Assembly scheduled for May 2016, and on towards an EU referendum, it is unclear whether meaningful progress in settling Wales' fiscal future could be achieved in the short term.

THE EFFECTS OF SCOTTISH NATIONALISM ON WALES

In order to understand the evolution of the Welsh devolved context, it is necessary to consider the Scottish dimension within UK politics. The story of devolution in the United Kingdom has been one driven by Scottish concerns (Gay, 1997; Trench, 2008), and the rise in popularity of the SNP since devolution in 1997 has provided fertile ground for arguments to enhance the devolved settlement in Scotland. As a confident nation with good economic output and natural resources that currently benefit the whole of the United Kingdom, it is clear to see why Westminster politicians would find a Scottish exit from the Union as undesirable and act to persuade its citizens to remain in the Union. Wales, however, does not benefit from such natural resources (although large-scale renewable energy projects are now being developed), is home to a lower population, has a smaller private sector, and has higher levels of unemployment and health spending. In short, whilst Scotland could conceivably leave the United Kingdom and maintain its 'lifestyle', Wales would likely have to make significant cuts to services and/or implement large tax increases to live within its means as an independent nation. Most importantly, support for Welsh independence is incredibly low at only 6% (BBC/ICM, 2015). Wales, therefore, does not provide the credible threat to the future of the Union that Scotland does, and as such, commands far less influence in any discussion about the future of devolution.

One of the key moments influencing the extent of further devolution in the United Kingdom came in the negotiations of the Edinburgh Agreement, during which the SNP lobbied hard for a 'second question' on an undetermined form of 'Devo-Max', which was eventually dropped in favour of a single Yes/ No question. The decision not to back a second question was championed by Prime Minister David Cameron, as well as the other Westminster parties, who were at the time confident that a 'no' vote would be secured and that the status quo would be maintained following the vote. This essentially left much meaningful debate on practical steps towards further devolution across the United Kingdom as a whole in limbo. Once the Edinburgh Agreement setting out the timetable and question for the referendum was signed in October 2012, the cases for 'yes' and 'no' immediately sprang to life, and the campaigns built into increasing and fevered zeal as the 18th of September 2014 inched closer. As political attention was diverted to the campaign, the fate of Welsh devolution was put to one side. Although the Wales Bill continued through Parliament during 2014, it contained significant limits on potential fiscal powers that represented a knee-jerk reaction to events in Scotland. The second report of the Silk Commission setting out broad recommendations for the enhancement of the Welsh dispensation was seemingly left to one side whilst the parties focused upon developments in Scotland.

As the frequency of polling increased, it became clear that a 'yes' vote was not outside the realms of possibility. The lack of a coherent and progressive offer of further powers from Westminster provided the SNP with yet another argument for independence. Pro-Union politicians recognized, almost too late, the possibility of a 'yes' vote, and the Westminster parties scrambled to offer incentives to Scotland to remain within the United Kingdom, culminating in 'The Vow' agreed to by the party leaders and published only days before the referendum on the front page of the *Daily Record*. The promises enshrined in 'The Vow' included extensive further devolution of powers, and the preservation of the Barnett formula in calculating the funding to Scotland.

The package seemed to have been put together without any consideration of the implications for devolution in the United Kingdom as a whole, and the preservation of the Barnett formula fundamentally preserved the funding disadvantage experienced in Wales. Reflecting on these last-minute concessions, it is interesting to reflect on the original negotiations for the Edinburgh Agreement. If that second question had been included in the vote, would the swing towards 'yes' have been so convincing? And if so, would this have prevented the last-minute panic and reactionary offer of further powers to Scotland? While we can never know what would have happened if that second question had been approved and asked, in a survey of 1001 voters on 12th September 2014, 25% of individuals responded that they would have voted for greater devolution without independence, with 30% opting for the status quo (Daily Mirror/Survation, 2014). It is quite possible that a second question on Devo-Max would have enhanced the quality of debate and clarified the parameters of future devolution. This may ultimately have dampened the 'yes' surge and facilitated a more structured and less reactive approach to further Scottish devolution that took into account devolution across the United Kingdom as a whole, and provided a more stable and sustainable dispensation for each nation. As it stands, 'The Vow' has facilitated greater fiscal autonomy for Scotland, which, once again, goes further and deeper than that provided to Wales.

DIVERGING DEVOLUTION: THE SMITH COMMISSION AND THE ST DAVID'S DAY AGREEMENT COMPARED

The progress of Welsh devolution in comparison to Scotland's experience has been slow and characterized by difficulties in the structure and quality of powers (McAllister, 2015; Rawlings, 2003). The failure of many quality-enhancing recommendations to be implemented served to lock-in that structural deficit, and the often frosty relations between Cardiff Bay and Westminster frustrated attempts to move devolution forward. Between 2010 and 2014, the Conservative Secretaries of State for Wales (Cheryl Gillan MP, later replaced by David Jones MP) had been reluctant to engage with issues of further devolution, and David Jones MP had exacerbated relations with the devolved Assembly by referring the first and second pieces of primary legislation passed in Wales to the Supreme Court for review. The recommendations of the Richard Commission in Wales in 2004 had long failed to be fully implemented, and many of the recommendations of the Silk Commission made almost ten years later appeared to be heading for the same fate, so overlooked had they been in the midst of the Scottish referendum campaign. Indeed, the recommendations of the Silk Commission's second report were at risk of becoming irrelevant given the pace of devolution in Scotland. What was clear, however, was that regardless of the outcome, Scottish concerns would continue to occupy those within Westminster with the will and expertise to address devolved matters.

'The Vow' promised 'extensive' new devolved structures, and following the 'no' vote, and in the face of creating even greater asymmetry in the UK's devolved framework, an opportunity existed to conduct a meaningful and UK-wide conversation on the extent and structures of devolution in the United Kingdom. Many voices, particularly from Wales, including First Minister Carwyn Jones, called for a Constitutional Convention to ensure that further changes were rational, fair and proportionate for all of the UK's nations, including England. However, the pace and focus of debate following the referendum continued to be directed toward Scotland. On September 19, 2014, the Smith Commission was announced, chaired by Lord Smith of Kelvin and populated by members of each significant party in Scotland. The remit was to 'convene cross-party talks and facilitate an inclusive engagement process across Scotland to produce, by 30 November 2014, Heads of Agreement with recommendations for further devolution of powers to the Scottish Parliament' (Smith Commission, 2014). On the same day, Prime Minister David Cameron announced that further powers for Wales, too, would be considered.

A small positive step towards a better settlement for Wales had come in the Cabinet reshuffle of May 2014. Secretary of State for Wales David Jones MP was replaced by Stephen Crabb MP, Member for Pembrokeshire and Preseli. Crabb presented a more collaborative and less combative approach to demands for Welsh devolution. On 17th November 2014, Crabb announced plans to conduct cross-party talks with the aim of presenting a roadmap for further devolution to Wales by 1st March 2015 (St David's Day). In his speech, he specifically acknowledged the parallel work being conducted in Scotland under the Smith Commission, but made clear that no intention existed for parity of powers to be devolved:

> It will be important that we identify the proposals arising from the Smith Commission that warrant further consideration and analysis for Wales . . . I am certainly not saying that what is right for Scotland will necessarily be right for Wales. Far from it. I believe it is important for each of the devolved settlements to have the right set of powers for that particular nation. (Stephen Crabb MP, 2014)

This assertion that the comparative powers of the nations would continue to be asymmetrical was eventually borne out in the final 'St David's Day Agreement' command paper, released on 27th February 2015 (HM Government, 2015). This roadmap responded to key 'asks' such as the intention to move Wales from a conferred to a reserved model of powers, and in a similar vein to the new Scotland Bill, matters relating to the elections to, operation of, and ultimate permanence of the National Assembly for Wales. Law, justice and policing, historically devolved in Scotland and Northern Ireland, were missing from the new proposals. In financial terms at least, the St David's Day Agreement would move Wales to a position of parity with Scotland *prior* to the recommendations of the Smith Commission, which, given the further progress of Scottish devolution and the Prime Minister's claim that the new Scotland Bill 'would make Scotland the most powerful devolved assembly anywhere in the world' (HM Government, 2015), confirms the impression that Wales remains in a significantly less powerful position than Scotland in terms of its devolution settlement.

The Scotland Bill, introduced following the Smith Commission's recommendations, provides for a level of devolution much more substantial than that outlined in the St David's Day Agreement, and was the product of deeper and broader consideration and negotiation than that conducted for the St David's Day Agreement. Whereas standard intergovernmental channels considered the Welsh dispensation, the Smith Commission was led by a business heavyweight with a staff of fifteen and the scope to draw 18,000 consultation responses from across the public and private sphere. The new proposals for Scotland move that nation further towards fiscal responsibility and autonomy, which contrasts with the limitations and political uncertainty surrounding such responsibilities in Wales.

AN AMBIVALENT CITIZENRY: PUBLIC ATTITUDES IN WALES

An important, if often overlooked, influence in driving forward devolution in the United Kingdom is public attitude. Whilst devolution in 1997 was the product more of political than public design (McAllister, 2015), the progress of devolution in Wales and in Scotland has been characterized by political decisions taken in part on the basis of public opinion polling. In Wales, public engagement with politics and political decision making is slightly lower than in Scotland, and polling therefore provides a clearer (although not infallible) indicator of public attitudes. The wafer-thin 0.3% majority that approved Welsh devolution in 1997 increased to 65% in the 2011 referendum on primary legislative powers, but on a far lower turnout (36%). Indeed, turnouts in elections in Wales are generally lower than in Scotland, with the 2015 general election turnout at 65.7% in Wales, and 71.1% in Scotland, and turnouts of 42.2% in Wales compared to 50% in Scotland in the devolved elections of 2011.

Adding to this relatively low level of public engagement with political and constitutional concerns, the Welsh have shown far greater ambivalence towards issues such as devolution and membership of the EU. Welsh attitudes to EU membership have fluctuated, with polls from 2013 showing that a slim majority would vote to leave (37%–29%, 40%–39% and 40%–38%, (Scully, 2015a)), against polling from 2015 showing that a growing majority would vote to stay (44%–36% and 43%–36%, (Scully, 2015a)).

With regard to further devolution, recent polling in the wake of the Smith Commission and St David's Day Agreement shows that 42% of people in Wales agreed with the proposition that the National Assembly of Wales should have the same powers as the Scottish Parliament. This is compared to 43% agreeing that the Assembly should *not* have the same powers, and instead believing that devolved powers should be tailored to the circumstances of each nation (Parry et al., 2015). When asked whether the National Assembly for Wales should have tax-varying powers, support is again balanced on a knife-edge, with the two 2015 polls putting those in favour at 37% in both polls, and with 39% (January) and later 36% (March) against (Scully, 2015b). Possibly one of the least encouraging figures for supporters of devolution is a poll from 2014, in which just 34% of people believed that devolution had led to an improvement in the way Wales is governed, with 46% saying it had 'not made much difference' (BBC Wales, 2014).

What is interesting about each of these figures is the volume of 'don't knows' and 'would not votes', demonstrating that a significant number of individuals in Wales are ambivalent or uninterested in constitutional considerations. The lack of very clear majorities in many of these figures is also interesting, evidencing a clear divide in public opinion that provides much fuel for political debate, but does little to convince the UK government of the necessity of structural change. In Scotland, the significant support for the 'yes' campaign in the independence referendum, the ensuing surge in membership of the SNP, and the overwhelming success of the SNP in the 2015 General Election demonstrates a clear will of the Scottish people to have a greater say in their own affairs. The same cannot be said for Wales. The divide in public opinion could, in part, be attributed to a level of ignorance about the Welsh political structures.

In 2014, only 48% of individuals in Wales understood that health was a devolved issue, against a backdrop of popular media coverage of Prime Minister David Cameron using the Labour NHS record in Wales as a reason to vote Conservative. A majority in the same poll understood that education was devolved (61%), but 42% wrongly thought that policing was also devolved (BBC Wales, 2014). This lack of clarity in the public's knowledge adds to the picture of an ambivalent electorate, and provides the Westminster parties with the latitude to sculpt the devolution dispensation without significant public interest or opposition. If the people of Wales are not clearly united in demanding a change to the devolution dispensation, if the people of Wales are not in favour of independence, and if the people of Wales continue to feel they should get a bigger share of UK funding, then they present little threat to the union, and command little weight with which to negotiate.

A FINANCIALLY WEAK FUTURE FOR WALES?

The scope for the Welsh economy to grow and to foster innovation is inextricably linked to Wales' political and constitutional stability. Without clarity of power, without appropriate levels of agreed funding and without sustainable structures to legislate within, the Welsh Government lacks the economic tools and political power to implement effective measures, and the credibility to provide environmental certainty to business and citizens alike. Similarly, without clearly defined fiscal responsibilities, and a public understanding of devolved policy areas, the Welsh Government is unable to demonstrate true accountability to the electorate. The quality of the Welsh devolution dispensation has been poor, and the incremental tweaks to the Government of Wales Acts 1998 and 2006 did very little to provide a more stable settlement. The bilateral focus of the UK devolution debate, driven by a more engaged, united and vocal Scottish public, had the effect of sidelining Welsh interests and delaying meaningful change. Whilst substantial change to the Welsh devolved structure has now been promised through the St David's Day Agreement, the Scottish referendum and the subsequent offer of further devolution born out of 'The Vow' places Scotland once again in the most powerful devolved position in the United Kingdom.

The presence of fifty-six SNP MPs in Parliament following the 2015 General Election ensures that the passage of the Scotland Bill will be accompanied by SNP arguments that the Bill is not substantial enough in certain areas, and this will continue to monopolize the debate on devolution in the United Kingdom. Whilst the SNP and Scottish people continue to drive the devolution debate, Wales will continue to be underfunded under the Barnett formula, and remain in limbo whilst the decision on whether to hold a referendum on tax-varying powers is left unmade. The lack of a strong political narrative on Welsh devolution and the divide and uncertainty exhibited by the Welsh public with regard to further or broader powers reinforces the ability of the parties to avoid substantial constitutional change in Wales. The combination of these factors results in a Wales stunted by its structural environment and cowed by its limited fiscal abilities, in which the Welsh Government can shelter behind arguments of underfunding and spending, without responsibility for raising its income. Each time there is a change in the dispensation, claims are made that this will finally create a stable and enduring settlement under which Wales can flourish; however, these claims have been so frequent as to have lost any sense of real promise (Parry et al., 2015). The Wales Bill 2014 and the legislation to implement the St David's Day Agreement will certainly address some of the structural issues that have thus far throttled Wales' economic potential; however, without fiscal responsibility, and against a backdrop of constitutional change across the United Kingdom, involving devolution within England as well as further devolution within Scotland and uncertainty in Europe, it seems likely that Welsh devolution will limp along in the same neglected fashion it has for the last fifteen years.

REFERENCES

BBC Wales, and ICM. (2014). Fewer than Half the Population know Who Runs Welsh NHS, "Says Poll", Available at http://www.bbc.co.uk/news/uk-wales-politics-27739205 (accessed 27/05/2015).

BBC Wales, and ICM. (2015). St. David's Day Poll 2015, Available at http://blogs.cardiff.ac.uk/electionsinwales/wp-content/uploads/sites/100/2013/07/BBCICM-St-Davids-Day-2015.pdf (accessed 27/05/2015).

Bell, D., and Eiser, D. (2014). Scotland's Fiscal Future in the UK, Available at http://www.storre.stir.ac.uk/bitstream/1893/21180/1/Scotlands%20Fiscal%20Future%20in%20UK%20Sep%202014.pdf (accessed 27/05/2015).

Bogdanor, V. (2001). *Devolution in the United Kingdom*. Oxford: Oxford University Press.

Cole, A., and Stafford, I. (2014). *Devolution and Governance: Wales between Capacity and Constraint*. Basingstoke: Palgrave Macmillan.

Daily, Mirror, and Survation. (2014). Scottish Referendum Issues Poll, Available at http://survation.com/wp-content/uploads/2014/09/Mirror-Full-Tables.pdf (accessed 27/05/2015).

Day, G. (2006). Chasing the Dragon? Devolution and the Ambiguities of Civil Society in Wales, *Critical Social Policy*, 26, 3: 642–55.

Evans, A. (2014). A House of Cards? The Failure to Find a Stable Devolution Settlement in Wales, *Renewal: a Journal of Labour Politics* 22, 1–2: 47–57.

Gay, O. (1997). *Wales and devolution*. House of Commons Library. Available at http://www.parliament.uk/briefing-papers/RP97-60.pdf (accessed 27/05/2015).

Goodwin, M., Jones, M., and Jones, R. (2005). Devolution, Constitutional Change and Economic Development: Explaining and Understanding the New Institutional Geographies of the British State, *Regional Studies*, 39, 4: 421–36.

HM Government. (2015). *PM Visit to Scotland: May 2015*, Available at https://www.gov.uk/government/news/pm-visit-to-scotland-may-2015 (accessed 27/05/2015).

HM Government. (2015). *Powers for a Purpose: Towards a Lasting Devolution Settlement for Wales*, Available at https://www.gov.uk/government/uploads/system/uploads/attachment_data/file/408587/47683_CM9020_ENGLISH.pdf (accessed 27/05/2015).

HM Treasury. (2010). *Funding the Scottish Parliament, Welsh Assembly Government, and Northern Ireland Assembly: Statement of Funding Policy*. London: HM Treasury.

Jeffery, C., and Wincott, D. (2006). Devolution in the United Kingdom: Statehood and Citizenship in Transition. *Publius: The Journal of Federalism*, 36, 1: 3–18.

King, D., and Eiser, D. (2014). Reform of the Barnett Formula with Needs Assessment: Can the Challenges be Overcome? *Regional Studies*, Available at http://dx.doi.org/10.1080/00343404.2014.93379 (accessed 27/05/2015).

McAllister, L. (1998). The Welsh Devolution Referendum: Definitely, Maybe?, *Parliamentary Affairs*, 51, 2: 149–65.

McAllister, M. (2015). Immature Relationships in the New Multi-Level United Kingdom: Perspectives from Wales, *Public Money & Management*, 35, 1: 31–38.

McLean, I., and McMillan, A. (2005). 1. The Fiscal Crisis of the United Kingdom, Available at http://citeseerx.ist.psu.edu/viewdoc/summary?doi=10.1.1.203.5769 (accessed 27/05/2015).

Mooney, G., and Williams, C. (2006). Forging New 'Ways of Life'? Social Policy and Nation Building in Devolved Scotland and Wales, *Critical Social Policy*, 26, 3: 608–29.

Morgan, K. O. (2015). The Welsh Referendum and Territoriality in British Politics, Available at http://revuesshs.u-bourgogne.fr/individu&nation/document. php?id=746 (accessed 27/05/2015).

Office for National Statistics. (2014b). *Public and Private Sector Pay, November 2014*, Available at http://www.ons.gov.uk/ons/dcp171776_383355.pdf (accessed 27/05/2015).

Office for National Statistics. (2014a). *Regional Gross Value Added (Income Approach), December 2014*, Available at http://www.ons.gov.uk/ons/dcp171778_388340.pdf (accessed 27/05/2015).

Office for National Statistics. (2015). *Labour Market Statistics, January 2015*, Available at http://www.ons.gov.uk/ons/rel/lms/labour-market-statistics/january-2015/index.html (accessed 27/05/2015).

HM Government. (2014). *Secretary of State for Wales Sets Out Long-Term Vision on Devolution*, Available at https://www.gov.uk/government/speeches/secretary-of-state-stephen-crabb-sets-out-long-term-vision-on-devolution (accessed 27/05/2015).

Parry, R., Eichhorn, J., Kenealy, D., Paterson, L., and Remond, A. (2015). Elite and Mass Attitudes on How the UK and Its Parts are Governed – Wales and the Process of Constitutional Change, Available at http://www.aog.ed.ac.uk/__data/assets/pdf_file/0010/171559/Briefing_-_Wales_and_the_Process_of_Constitutional_Change. pdf (accessed 27/05/2015).

Rawlings, R. (2003). *Delineating Wales: Constitutional, Legal and Administrative Aspects of National Devolution*, Cardiff: University of Wales Press.

Scully, R. (2015a). Wales, EU Referendum Polls, Available at http://blogs.cardiff.ac.uk/electionsinwales/wp- content/uploads/sites/100/2013/07/Wales22.pdf (accessed 27/05/2015).

Scully, R. (2015b). The Latest Figures on Referendum Voting Intentions, [Online]. Available at http://blogs.cardiff.ac.uk/electionsinwales/2015/03/16/the-latest-figures-on-referendum-voting-intentions/ (accessed 27/05/2015).

Smith Commission. (2014) *About*, Available at https://www.smith-commission.scot/about/ (accessed 27/05/2015).

Swenden, W., and McEwen, N. (2014). UK Devolution in the Shadow of Hierarchy & Quest; Intergovernmental Relations and Party Politics. *Comparative European Politics*, 12, 4: 488–509.

Trench, A. (2008). Finding a Voice for Wales. Assessing Three Phases of Constitutional Development in Wales. In *Rennes: Paper presented at the ECPR Joint Sessions of Workshops*.

Trench, A. (Ed.) (2004). *Has Devolution Made a Difference? The State of the Nations 2004*, London: Imprint Academic.

Trench, A. (2011). Referendum Result: Wales Said Yes, Available at https://devolutionmatters.wordpress.com/2011/03/04/referendum-result-wales-said-yes/ (accessed 27/05/2015).

Rebecca Rumbul

Wyn Jones, R. W., and Scully, R. (2006). Devolution and Electoral Politics in Scotland and Wales, *Publius: The Journal of Federalism*, 36, 1: 115–34.

Wyn Jones, and Scully R. (2012). *Wales Says Yes: Devolution and the 2011 Welsh Referendum*, Cardiff: University of Wales Press.

Wyn Jones, R. (2014). Policy Response to: House of Commons Welsh Affairs Select Committee on the Draft Wales Bill, Available at http://sites.cardiff.ac.uk/wgc/files/2014/02/Written-Evidence-to-Welsh-Affairs-Select-Committee-on-Draft-Wales-Bill-RWJ-Feb-2014.pdf (accessed 27/05/2015).

Chapter 7

Securing Economic and Social Success

The Local Double Dividend[1]

Neil McInroy and Matthew Jackson

INTRODUCTION

It is well known that long-standing problems of inequality, disadvantage and poverty persist even in times of economic growth. Whilst a recent return to some national economic health has occurred, it is already evident that growth is geographically and socially skewed and uneven. Long-standing issues of de-industrialization, worklessness, low skills and underinvestment remain in many areas. So, even with a return to economic growth for the nation as a whole, a positive economic and social future for some local areas – and the people that live in them – is not assured. Indeed, some of the recent thinking around agglomeration theory advocated by the so-called New Economic Geography school (e.g., the World Bank, 2009) purports that government should effectively abandon efforts to rebalance the economy and let market forces determine the economic and social landscape (see Bailey et al. in this volume).[2] Under this laissez-faire approach, the prosperity of the United Kingdom should be shaped by where spatial agglomeration is greatest and productivity rewards are highest – namely in London, and the other major cities. Other places, as a result, would be losers and become more reliant on the success of 'super-cities'.

In contrast to the argument that policy should focus solely on economic success where there is already significant critical mass, this chapter advocates an approach to local prosperity whereby an enabled local state seeks to ensure that local communities enjoy the fruits of any growth (Carnegie UK Trust, 2014). As a counterpoint to spatial agglomeration, the argument for fairer and sustainable growth appreciates that spatial imbalances are wasteful and socially destabilizing (Martin et al., 2013). Economic efficiency is an important policy goal, but this chapter asserts that social equity and fairness are of equal importance. The devolution of powers and resources to local government and cities could facilitate this localized approach. Indeed, freed from the tramlines of central government, there could be a significant social dividend in the development of forms of economic growth that fit more securely with local characteristics and social need.

Up until recently, the community benefits of growth have been mostly piecemeal and confined to planning gain and particular policy initiatives, such as Business Improvement Districts or funding tools such as Tax Incremental Financing and planning gain on new housing developments. The ideas set out in this chapter take the concept of community benefit and social equity further, with greater stress on how social investment complements and actively supports economic growth. This concept of a double dividend is already happening, as the case studies shown later in the chapter demonstrate.

However, in many instances, the examples lack momentum and cultural will and are "resource lite." The challenge facing policy makers is how to raise awareness, enhance capability and scale up best practice. Against the backdrop of continued fiscal austerity, many areas will soon have no other option than maximizing the resources and assets they have. The prospect of doing nothing will merely fuel existing spatial social and economic inequalities. As we argue throughout the chapter, making the most of social capacity must be a much bigger part of the solution to achieving sustainable local growth – in areas of both disadvantage and places of opportunity.

AN UNEQUAL AND DIVERGENT ECONOMY

The last thirty years of economic development policy and regeneration activity has had its successes, but has broadly failed to end regional economic divides and the long-standing disparities of economic and social disadvantage. There is still a looming economic gap between London and the rest (London and the South East now account for 36 per cent of total GVA in England). Furthermore, the regional divide is widening and at a faster pace than elsewhere in Europe (Martin et al., 2013). According to the Smith Institute, over the past twenty years, relative growth has risen steadily in London (and relatively faster during the recession); remained more or less static in the East and South East of England; and fallen in the Midlands and each of the three Northern regions (Ward, 2011).

Part of the argument about why the imbalances remain so ingrained rests in the way tax and spend is divided between local and central government. Central government's share of public spending in the United Kingdom, for example, is 72 per cent, compared with only 19 per cent in Federal Germany.

Yet, the economic divide between the German Lander is much less than between the UK regions. The economic geography of England's cities shows a similar pattern of central control. Research from New Economy (2014) shows that of the £23bn of public funds spent in Greater Manchester, central government controls how £16bn is spent and has a significant say over the rest. The disparity on the tax side is equally pronounced. According to the London Finance Commission (2013), only 7 per cent of all the tax paid by London residents and businesses is retained by the mayor and the London boroughs. The figure is even less in other cities, although it should be noted that most of the major cities outside of London run a large tax and spend deficit. The deficit between public spending and tax generated in Greater Manchester, for example, is nearly £5bn a year.

Successive governments (dating back to the inter-war years) have struggled with rebalancing the economy. Under the last Labour government, the focus in England was on supporting regional economies through nine Regional Development Agencies (RDAs), established as business-led non-departmental bodies and coined by ministers as 'economic powerhouses'. Funding for the RDAs from across Whitehall was increased from £1.7bn a year to £2.2bn over the period 2006–2010 and was complemented by targeted area-based regeneration and housing programmes, such as the Housing Market Renewal Pathfinders Programme and the Growth Areas initiative. Despite these efforts (which were supported by a regional government office network, EU regional funding and improved regional spatial planning), economic rebalancing remained an uphill task. Indeed, by the time of the 2010 election, the economic position of the regions had stayed virtually the same since the 1980s. It could, of course, be argued that the gap (within and between regions) would have been wider without active interventions.

The previous Labour government did experiment with locally led economic initiatives (such as the Neighbourhood Renewal Programme) and initiated the policies for combined authorities and city-regions. However, the pre-recession years of growth were also characterized by Whitehall-led housing, skills and transport programmes (such as the multi-billion 'Decent Homes' programme). In retrospect, the pace of English devolution outside of London over the period 2000–2010 seemed painfully slow. As Sir Michael Lyons commented: 'The history of the last 30 years is marked by a series of well-intentioned devolution initiatives, which have often evolved into subtle instruments of control' (Lyons, 2007). The story was different in London, Wales, Scotland and Northern Ireland, which have retained much of the regional institutional architecture lost to areas in England.

One of the principal failings of past policy approaches in England was not that they were just 'top down', but that wealth creation which often came with inequality and investment often failed to 'trickle down' to communities as anticipated. Places that failed to succeed became trapped in a vicious spiral, where weak performance led to fewer opportunities and a loss of capability. The introduction of a more stakeholder approach to regeneration funding and the insistence of partnership working and more joined-up policy making (such as Labour's flagship £2bn New Deal for Communities programme) was seen as a means of combating this, sometimes successfully. However, policy support for disadvantaged areas was often discretionary and piecemeal, with the measurements and metrics for local programmes set centrally. Local projects were often time limited, ring fenced and detached from each other. Some programmes would be locally based (social housing) and others (skills and transport) would remain national. Much of the emphasis was also on securing private finance and leveraging public funding.

The incoming Coalition Government abolished the RDAs, which ministers claimed were remote, expensive and ineffective. They were gradually replaced with thirty-nine private sector-led Local Enterprise Partnerships (LEPs), which vary in size and status. Previous RDA single funding pots have been partly replaced by a mix of government-controlled funding regimes, such as the Regional Growth Fund. Needless to say, the overall funding for local growth (including grant funding for transport, housing and skills training) have been significantly cut back. Whilst there has been some delegation of funding to city-regions and combined authorities, much of the regeneration/ local business support funding is now channelled through a competitive bidding process. There has also been a sweeping away of the area-based initiatives and a new mix of policies that support local philanthropy and incentivize particular types of growth programmes, such as the New Homes Bonus, which rewards councils for building new homes.

Whilst these changes are significant, they have had much less of an effect on local government than the overall spending cuts, which have led to the closure of many community-based projects. According to the LGA, local government will have suffered a 42 per cent real terms reduction in funding over the period 2010–2015, leaving a financial black hole going forward of around £2.1bn per year. Central government funding for 2015/2016 is meanwhile forecast to fall by an average of 8.8 per cent. Renewing local economies against such a backdrop of continued austerity poses an enormous challenge to local government.

CITY DEVOLUTION AND NATIONAL REDISTRIBUTION

A recent body of reports has ramped up the push for devolution, including work by Lord Heseltine, Lord Adonis, the London Mayor, the Core Cities Group and the RSA's City Growth Commission (Heseltine, 2012; IPPR

North, 2014; IPPR North and Northern Economic Futures Commission, 2012; RSA, 2014). Impetus has been gained following the Scottish independence referendum and the Smith Commission report. More than twenty City Deal schemes have been announced since 2012, and last year, Liverpool, the Greater Manchester Combined Authority (HM Treasury, 2014) and Sheffield City Region (Deputy Prime Minister's Office, 2014) struck groundbreaking City Region Growth Deals with central government (with the Leeds City Region expected to follow soon).

Despite some division of opinion around city-region governance structures, there is a cross-party recognition that local economic growth is best served when it comes with some local control. It is also widely acknowledged (although far from universally accepted in Westminster) that devolved decisions on housing, transport, skills, business support etc. are best made by town halls and combinations of local authorities, working with businesses, local communities and local economic bodies (such as the Local Enterprise Partnerships) rather than Whitehall departments. With this comes an acceptance that social need and demand on public services can be better addressed by coordinating spending across local authorities and local agencies.

However, the political consensus breaks down on the topic of funding priorities and local fiscal freedoms, and around the balance between local autonomy and the equalization of funding. One of the main concerns among local councils in disadvantaged areas is that hypothecated funding (such as full retention of business rates) could reward the already wealthy and lead to a significant depletion of common funding pots. This concern is brought into sharp focus when applied to some of London's richest boroughs. The borough of Westminster, for example, has an income from business rates worth nearly as much as the eight largest English cities combined.

The agenda for change is mostly centred on economic growth in cities, with less attention on areas beyond the cities or concern about inequalities within and between places. This is, as already mentioned, in part a factor of the government's preoccupation with agglomeration economics. Therefore, the focus is on the larger cities, as this is where there is a greater likelihood of cost reductions and increases in productivity, and where the potential for profit attracts the most investment capital. In areas with no new devolved powers (and in some outlying city areas), there is less opportunity, much lower values and difficult issues around transport, skills and housing. The retention of inequality within regions and across the country is probable, if growth prospects in these 'less advantageous' places are overlooked.

Agglomeration can, of course, create greater levels of economic growth and jobs. Furthermore there could be a virtuous 'trickle outwards' toward the outlying suburbs and neighbouring towns. We also know that any economic growth within the city region and city centre creates 'problems of success', such as an increase in land and property prices, and rents and other associated 'downsides' such as congestion. These 'problems' may be good for outlying and poorer areas as investment and businesses would start to look to cheaper locations beyond the city centre and city region. However, agglomeration without a general context of national economic growth extracts economic activity and energy from elsewhere. We also must question how a singular focus on city agglomeration can solve city or national inequality, without dealing with the arguably bigger questions of national and intra-city redistribution. Failure to do so will heighten the stakes between winners and losers, which in turn will make coordinating public investment for transport and industry between places all the more protracted. There surely needs to be greater sensitivity not just to connecting places and integrating policies to achieve that, but also to the social dimension – to how narrowing inequalities within places can itself promote economic growth.

The city devolution agenda in this sense needs reconfiguring, with less emphasis on Treasury-backed agglomeration policies and more on social investment and addressing city-wide inequalities. It cannot be a mere spatial reshuffling of the existing haves and have-nots. The change that precedes an economy for all and greater levels of social inclusion would require national (and local) government to recognize that inequality is socially and economically destabilizing (Piketty, 2014), and that an innovative state can tackle inequality (Mazzucato, 2013). As the most recent OECD research has shown, more equal societies do better economically in terms of innovation and social mobility (Cingano, 2014; Wilkinson and Pickett, 2009). Growing income inequality becomes a constraint on growth, not least (as the OECD research documents demonstrate), in large part because poorer members of a community are less able to invest in their education and skills.

Tackling inequality can make our societies fairer and our economies stronger, and that includes addressing inequalities both between and within places.

Maximizing opportunity is, of course, important and there are few policy makers who would argue that the devolution or local growth agenda should move at the pace of the slowest in the convoy. Some places are better equipped and more able to embrace change than others, which may not necessarily be a factor of their economic readiness or attractiveness to investors. However, the future needs a central (and local) government that acknowledges that the poorer areas require more of a hand up than wealthier areas. Local economic development is often hampered in these areas because of poor skills and weak investment propositions. A failure to balance incentives between places of need and places of opportunity is therefore critical. Focusing growth policies and resources for community support on rewarding just the winners and punishing losers will only further deter investors and widen inequalities.

London and the core cities are leading the argument for the devolution of more fiscal powers as a means of addressing some of these local social issues, harnessing any accrued wealth for limited forms of local distribution (Core Cities, 2013).

This is not without problems. First, as public spending pressures are greatest in poorer areas, it is unlikely that the development of a local tax base alone will be able to support any improvement – indeed, reliance on a dwindling local tax base creates greater reliance on central government subsidy. Second, in the present tax system, London is a net contributor to the public purse (Oxford Economics, 2012) – it gives more to the public purse than it takes. In contrast, all core cities (bar Bristol) are net beneficiaries. Any fiscal devolution to core cities and London would mean cities retaining more of the tax they generate. Under this scenario, there could be even more pressure on national budgets and potentially less money for national public services and services in those non-city areas with no fiscal powers.

Although in the first instance, retention of local tax revenues (net additions) would be offset by reduced central government grant, over time that may change and the collective pot could shrink. This is not an argument against greater fiscal devolution, but a warning that an over-reliance on local taxes may exacerbate the problems facing some local communities – especially in places that face disproportionate demands on welfare services (e.g., higher unemployment, ageing population, lower health and educational achievements).

ENABLING LOCAL ECONOMIC DEVELOPMENT

To date, the local economic growth agenda has followed a well-trodden path, which assumes that once investment capital is enticed and landed, the supply chain will benefit and local jobs will be secured. Unfortunately, that pathway is often not guaranteed or voracious enough. Local growth does not necessarily come with significant new employment, the poorest do not always benefit, gains made are sometimes short term and dissipate, and are lost once sweeteners are gone, and a historically weakened local economy does not always have the 'local' supply chains. As it stands, the promise of a city devolution approach, predicated on agglomeration economics, is unlikely to address social issues. There is a possibility that a local state, emboldened with new powers and tram-lined by a new order of orthodoxies, merely replicates past local economic development policies or simply implements a version of the national treasury economic model, which has failed to deliver on tackling income inequality. Indeed, there is academic evidence to suggest that the economic benefits from this type of devolution are very limited or highly variable, and over-ridden by the role of national economic growth (Pike et al., 2010a).

To be socially inclusive, plans and activity need to be embraced by a deeper sense of national fairness and redistribution and, in turn, be more enabling, securing the local links between growth and the improvement in the fortunes of its citizens and businesses. An alternative approach is needed that seeks to actively secure social outcomes by working to ensure that the system, networks and relationships across an area are at the heart of the policy-making process (Pike et al., 2010b; Vale and Campanella, 2005). In order to create social benefits, social objectives must be embedded in the policy framework. Such an enabling economic development model views the economy through a 'whole place economic' lens (Hildreth and Bailey, 2014; and Bailey et al. in this volume). It is, therefore, through developing social and economic growth in tandem that we can have socially inclusive economies. Local economic policy then can absorb the qualitative aspects of place development, accommodating the breadth of social, cultural, economic and environmental facets that are part of the whole networked system within a locality (Pike et al., 2007).

The Centre for Local Economic Strategies (CLES) has shown that systems within local economic development are often characterized in two ways: there are those with a small number of key actors perhaps involving the local state and significant business players who play a major role, making the key decisions that affect a range of people and institutions. And there are those with a wide range of connected actors from a range of sectors (across public, social and commercial) who play important facilitation and brokerage roles, connecting a wide range of assets and resources (Arnold et al., 2009). Improving the quality of the multitude of such relationships within a local economy is the critical ingredient to securing the double dividend.

A DOUBLE DIVIDEND STRATEGY

The basis of the double dividend approach is that any economic benefits accrued through local devolution delivers a social dividend. This borrows from system thinking regarding how activity operates in a network and produces positive outcomes. Perhaps the most fundamental element of a good system is that it is not about independent elements of a singular actor or activity, but about the connections and collaborations. For example, in nature, a typical ecosystem includes air, water, flora and fauna – what is important is how it all works together as a system, not how it works in isolation. This is the same for local economies. Similarly, the success of advanced manufacturing growth requires a series of relationships for success, including inputs of capital, land and labour as well as links with higher education, public agencies and commerce. Growth that delivers a high level of social benefit is not just about growth itself, but it is about the inputs to growth and how it links with the social and economic context and social need.

Historically, local economic policy was always a pragmatic mixed bag. However, in recent times, a somewhat neo-liberal take on local economic policy has meant that social outcomes are not equally planned for and developed alongside economic growth, competition and productivity. At best, social dimensions are reduced to outcomes of an often overstated 'rising tide' of growth. At worst, improved social outcomes are viewed as a barrier to growth, with low wages seen as a price worth paying for greater competitiveness.

A double dividend strategy embraces the need to focus on developing local communities as an intrinsic and fundamental part of economic success. So, rather than seeing local communities, people and society as mere downstream recipients of economic success via trickle down, we should see them as active upstream parts of a system that creates success in the first place. This locally driven growth idea sees social success in the form of more jobs, decent wages and a general local rising standard of living, not just as an end of the line outcome, but also as an input. Social success in this instance is less a mere consequence of economic development action, but something that feeds into, sustains and creates a virtuous economy for all. To achieve this, we must have a deliberative and conscious set of policies that support business growth and private gain alongside actions to strengthen the local economic infrastructure and build enduring social and civic institutions.

SOCIAL CAPITAL AND NETWORKS

Some communities can provide the social capital that gets people through tough times, as others can also be so depleted of resource that they are powerless in the face of global change. . . . We need to pay exquisite attention to what is really going on. We risk ignoring it at our peril (Joseph Rowntree Foundation, 2012).

There is increasing recognition that strong links between social capital and economic prosperity are important (Kenworthy, 1997; Christoforou, 2001). Inputs to a successful economy are not simply about physical and financial capital, but also about human and social capital (Cohen and Prusak, 2001; Crudelia, 2006). Location decisions for people and businesses can be influenced significantly by how somewhere is perceived in terms of attractiveness as a place to live and viability as a stable business environment (Christoforou,

2001; Cohen and Prusak, 2001). Places where communities work well and have good levels of social capital are more attractive to potential residents (Grant and Kronstal, 2010). Therefore, social capital is an important link in the chain of prosperity and the activities undertaken by the social sector are central to developing local economies.

Social networks (often overlooked in traditional approaches to economic development) are formed through social capital acting as a mechanism for joining people together in socially and economically productive ways (Coleman, 1988). Such networks are important to supporting economic success. The ties between people, groups and local organizations engender confidence and allow knowledge transfer. Furthermore, happiness, health and prosperity all grow when communities and organizations collaborate to support each other, form relationships and work together towards shared goals. These social networks can act as the basis upon which economic activity is forged, a conduit for allowing ideas and innovation to flow, and the basis of well-being in individuals (making them potentially more productive workers). The point to stress here is that local economies are not simply an isolated silo of private sector activity that can be switched on and off. As CLES research has shown, they are made up of networks of social, public and commercial economic activity (McInroy and Longlands, 2011). These aspects are interconnected and dependent upon one another.

PROMOTING BUSINESS CITIZENSHIP AND LOCAL INVESTMENT

There is a mutual reliance between the private and social sectors to ensure that the local economy functions for all. Private businesses rely on an effective workforce and an economy that can support their operations. Communities rely on sustainable employment to provide financial and personal stability. This reciprocal relationship is of key importance.

With the public sector being impacted by deep spending cuts, the social and private sectors will increasingly need to be at the centre of stewardship of communities. In order for this to be successful, there is a need to forge stronger links between the two sectors. At present these are often weak – reflecting a pattern across much of the country.

The emphasis should be on a move away from corporate social responsibility (CSR) and towards ingrained behavioural change within both businesses and social sector organizations where the social is not perceived as a 'bolt on', but is rather incorporated into corporate attitudes and approaches. To achieve this, cross-sector narratives need to be established and developed - not least around the economic and community benefits of business citizenship.

As small businesses are most closely associated with local communities, there is potential for employers' organizations, Chambers of Commerce and the Federation for Small Businesses (and other localized business networks) to enhance their existing engagement with social organizations to scope out potential for local collaborative working, and schemes for bringing the two sectors closer together.

The public sector has a key role to play in providing the space to allow these relationships to take root and grow. Examples of this might include providing small-scale seed grants to organizations that take on roles of organizing formal relationships between social and private sector organizations in local areas, and acting in a wider brokerage role between the sectors. See Boxes 7.1 and 7.2 for examples.

The LGA has long argued the case for more effective use of local authority pension schemes for regeneration and housing purposes. Although the levels of these so-called local 'impact investments' have so far been fairly low (in part because of restrictions on local authorities investing in their own areas and because of the perception that local projects are much less viable than passive, conventional investments) (Smith Institute et al., 2012), there have been some recent encouraging changes in behaviour. For example, West

Box 7.1   Forever Manchester

FM are the Community Foundation for Greater Manchester, supporting over 1,300 community groups and projects annually. Through a business citizenship approach, the charity is seeking to alter and tap into business CSR and philanthropy. It is offering new ways in which businesses can get involved in local communities, such as running community building workshops focused on skills and assets within a neighbourhood, rather than focusing on what is lacking. FM says that this type of work seeks to reduce the distance between the business and community and 'helps local people discover and share the talents and resources that they already have to make long-term improvements to their community'. The relationships between the public/social and private sectors can extend to investment issues, such as directing more (public and private) pension fund investments into supporting local growth. Whilst local private firms may be cautious about intervening even from afar about where their employees' pensions are invested, local authority schemes are overseen by local trustees who may be more attracted to the idea of investing funds locally (albeit within the legal requirements on what local government can put into local assets). In principle, there is nothing to stop the pension funds or local anchor institutions, like hospitals and housing associations, encouraging their funds to invest more locally.

Box 7.2 Be Involved, Bradford

The Be Involved business brokerage service was delivered by Bradford Chamber of Commerce. At the heart of the programme was the transfer of skills from the private sector to social sector organizations through a combination of skills sharing, mentoring, volunteering and pro bono work, in particular supporting local enterprises operating in the most deprived areas or who have customers/beneficiaries living within the most deprived areas. Support to participants in the programme comprised one or more of the following elements:

Mentoring – The main activity of the project was to promote a mentoring scheme, using business brokers to promote links between established local employers and social sector organizations looking to become more entrepreneurial, providing benefit to both organizations.

Volunteering – Be Involved has helped place volunteers from business in activities that allow them to share and develop skills, and support community and voluntary sector organizations. These opportunities ranged from board membership to individual placements.

Pro bono work – Supporting professional firms to offer their services free of charge to community and voluntary projects is an excellent way of helping small organizations develop big plans. Be Involved matched participating businesses and third sector organizations on projects that meet the identified needs of both partners and the wider needs of people in deprived communities.

The team at the Chamber worked as brokers for ensuring that the skills needs of the social sector organizations, particularly with regards to volunteering and pro bono work, were met through their understanding of the expertise of interested businesses. This 'matching' process minimized the risk of bringing organizations and volunteers together where specific needs were not met.

Midlands, Greater Manchester, West Yorkshire, Merseyside and East Riding have recently launched a combined £152m fund for tailored local investment. Similar initiatives have been taken by some London councils.

THE POWER OF PROCUREMENT

The public sector spends around £240bn a year for buying goods and services, with local government procurement in England alone totalling some £45bn.

The process of undertaking this spend (procurement) can enable a double dividend if undertaken in a way that recognizes and values the local benefits.

In recent years, social clauses have begun to be embedded in procurement language. Local government has realized that procurement can and should bring wider benefits to communities beyond the provision of a service. Indeed, these benefits can include direct spend in areas of deprivation, the creation of jobs and apprenticeships, the development and sustainability of small business and social enterprise, and environmental mitigation.

Despite fiscal austerity and downward pressure on tender pricing, government policies (such as the Duty of Best value and the Public Services (Social Value) Act permit councils to procure goods and services according to criteria other than simply the lowest price. The Social Value Act (2012) actually requires councils to consider social value in managing procurement. These are welcome developments (supported by recent EU procurement regulations), which can help councils secure the double dividend.[3]

However, if procurement is to be used to best effect, there needs to be a greater understanding of and influence over local supply chains (Jackson, 2010). For example, targeting procurement spend in deprived areas can deliver growth benefits as it can lead to a multiplication of spend in that community. However, the commissioning body will also need to take into account the extent to which local suppliers may seek to import labour from outside the area. Some councils are alive to this and have developed more sophisticated procurement through the use of checklists identifying social benefits. In recent years, some councils have also begun to use social clauses in contracts linked to paying the living wage and to local recruitment and apprenticeship schemes.

There is clearly potential to use the power of procurement to encourage more employers to pay a living wage to their staff. However, the Smith Institute's recent report on 'making work better' showed that local authority procurement officers and legal advisers were often overly cautious about inserting wage clauses (The Smith Institute, 2014). Nevertheless, the case for a more progressive approach to procurement, including the wider use of wage clauses, is gaining ground – in part encouraged by the greater clarity on the legality of such clauses. See Box 7.3 for a recent example.

Procurement can support the development of voluntary and community sector organizations, particularly in the buying of services that are public facing, such as adult social care and services targeted at individuals living in poverty (e.g., debt advice services). Similar principles of capacity building and developmental activity in relation to procurement also apply to the small business sector and small- to medium-sized enterprises (SMEs).

According to the National Association for Voluntary & Community Action, the new procurement rules allow for certain contracts, mainly in the social and health sectors, to be 'reserved', so that competition is restricted

Box 7.3   West Midlands Procurement Framework for Jobs and Skills

The West Midlands Economic Inclusion Panel (launched in 2010) has produced a framework for how public sector organizations can increase access to jobs and skills opportunities through procurement exercises. The framework, aimed at reducing worklessness, is based around four approaches:

Charters, where public sector organizations share their strategic priorities to address worklessness with current and prospective contractors.

Voluntary agreements, where public sector organizations work with existing contractors to secure informal commitments to achieving jobs and skills outcomes.

Contract clauses, where public sector organizations include contractually binding jobs and skills clauses within specific procurement exercises.

Strategic application of contract clauses, where public authorities monitor performance against skills and employment commitments through monitoring.

Box 7.4   Manchester City Council – Maximizing the Supply Chain

CLES has undertaken a range of work seeking to understand procurement spend, shift cultures in local government and influence the behaviour of suppliers. Work with Manchester City Council focused on spend with the top 300 suppliers (spend of £357 million). In 2008–2009, the study found that 51.5 per cent was spent with suppliers and contractors based in the Manchester City Council boundary, and that suppliers re-spent 25p in every £1 back in the Manchester economy.

The impact of the study resulted in procurement officers thinking about where their procurement spend was going, and how procurement linked to wider economic and social priorities. As a result, Manchester City Council has undertaken a range of strategic activities designed to promote their procurement practices and influence the behaviour of the supply chain. This has included the development of cross-departmental procurement working groups, supplier networks, gap analysis, influencing activities with suppliers based in areas of deprivation (those suppliers with a base in neighbourhoods in Manchester in the 10 per cent most deprived nationally), and the development of an outcomes framework for monitoring suppliers against wider economic and social indicators.

In terms of the procurement process, spend and re-spend in the local economy has increased, as has spending in areas of deprivation: 65 per cent of spend in 2012–2013 was with suppliers and contractors based in the Manchester City Council boundary (increasing from 51.5 per cent); the proportion of spend with Manchester-based businesses in areas of deprivation had increased to 53.1 per cent (from 47.6 per cent); and suppliers re-spent 47 pence in every £1 in the Manchester economy (from 25 pence in every £1).

only to local not-for-profit organizations. Potential bidders can also become involved in the planning and pre-procurement process, provided it does not result in any unfair advantage.

Procurement can be used as the means through which public authorities indirectly influence the behaviour of suppliers, particularly in terms of their practices around recruitment and their own procurement policies. Councils can also influence the behaviour of suppliers by making them aware of the challenges facing their locality, such as worklessness and skills shortages – see Box 7.4 for an example.

LOCAL LABOUR MARKETS

A sufficient stock and flow of basic, intermediate and higher level skills are crucial to the successful development of a local area and to the prosperity of its people. However, the skills of the resident workforce have lagged behind in many communities, threatening recovery and long-term growth. The lack of basic skills and lack of employability for large cohorts of the population reduces the available workforce, constrains economic output levels and reinforces concentrations of deprivation.[4] It also leads to a shortfall of 'good' employment for residents where wages and terms and conditions are at acceptable levels. There is a need to focus on promoting occupational mobility and opportunity, particularly within deprived communities. The social sector can play an important role here, not least in raising aspirations and providing training and employability skills that employers need.

In-work poverty (with 1m workers paid the National Minimum Wage and some 5m workers paid below the Living wage), the recent 2015 Budget announcement notwithstanding, is an issue of increasing concern for local communities, especially those that are already struggling with welfare cuts. As the Centre for Cities work shows, there has been a disproportionate growth in low-paid work in disadvantaged areas. Many of the poorest areas have also experienced large public sector job losses, with new private sector work often available only on a part-time basis and on lower pay rates. If low-paid jobs serviced by those with basic skills do not pay a living wage and/or have poor terms and conditions, then employment will make less of a difference for people and communities. There is a need for major employers with local organizations to improve access to skills training and higher quality and better-paid jobs.

The local public sector could develop principles of good employment practice to be applied for local government/NHS, contracting authorities and suppliers, as highlighted for instance by the Cabinet Office guide on good employment principles (Cabinet Office, 2010). This could, as already mentioned, mean higher weighting within procurement assessments around ensuring that employees are paid a living wage (Jackson, 2014), although many councils struggle to pay both in-house and contracted staff the living wage.

Some areas are now witnessing the emergence of a two-tier workforce, driven by the growth in low-skill, low-wage employment (and in many areas of stronger growth by skills underutilization). According to the Smith Institute, a failure to invest in high-end goods and services will lead to a worsening of skills utilization, persistent underemployment and continued job insecurity. This path could further encourage the development of a two-tier workforce, with secure and well-remunerated employment at the top and more insecure, low-paid work at the bottom. It could also widen the divide in labour standards between the public, private and voluntary sectors (The Smith Institute, 2014). Temporary and agency work is becoming a major concern in local areas, especially casual work (mainly work that is mostly in insecure, and sometimes on zero hours, contracts). Although not all temporary or agency work is per se bad work, there is a worry that a failure to raise local labour standards will generate a 'race to the bottom' in local pay and conditions, with detrimental effects not only on productivity but also on local growth and social cohesion. Some Councils, like Corby, Salford and Islington, are taking steps to tackle this problem by forming alliances with local employers and employment agencies in order to set higher standards; see Box 7.5.

A range of interlinked measures rather than one defining action will be needed to improve local labour standards, including a role for councils to enforce compliance with the National Minimum Wage, a wider use of living wage clauses in public procurement, and greater social partnership between councils, trade unions and local employers. There is also a desperate need for more of a local focus on achieving the right local balance between the supply and demand for skills. Such locally led, bespoke schemes, could focus more on raising aspirations of local residents to return to or join the labour market as well as support greater third sector involvement, especially in engaging the 'hard to reach' learners.[5] See Boxes 7.6 and 7.7.

Box 7.5   Corby Employment Agency Code of Conduct

Corby has a large number of employment agencies, some of which were found to be exploiting workers and adding to the climate of job insecurity in the town. In 2013, HMRC visited local employment agencies and discovered that £100,000 was owed to 3,000 workers in the area. In an effort to combat the problem, the local MP, Andy Sawford, and the borough council recently established the Corby Employment Agencies Forum, which sets common, high standards for the town's businesses. The forum, which involves employers, unions, workers, employment agencies and trade associations, has adopted a Code of Practice for Employment Agencies, Client Companies and Temporary Workers, which includes a commitment by employment agencies to operate in a lawful and ethical way and by employers to:

- avoid the replacement of permanent jobs with temporary employment through effective workforce planning;
- carry out regular reviews with their agencies to establish that the management of temporary workers on-site is carried out effectively and professionally; and
- contract only with agencies that sign up to the code of conduct.

The forum has signed up eleven of the town's employment agencies and employers, including TATA Steel and RS Components.

Source: Smith Institute (2014).

Box 7.6   London Borough of Islington's Employment Commission

The Commission brought together local employers, public services, the voluntary sector and residents to focus on solutions to unemployment in the area. The Commission's report (published in November 2014) concluded that a radical change is needed in how the system works, not least to provide targeted employment support, based on a coaching and mentoring approach for the people who need it most. It also called on employers to commit to creating good-quality, flexible jobs that pay the London Living Wage; to respect employment rights and make them available to local people; and to create change for the next generation and improve a careers education and employability offer that just isn't consistently good enough at the moment.

(Continued)

Box 7.6   London Borough of Islington's Employment Commission *(Continued)*

The report concluded that 'we need to enable employers to recruit better locally by engaging with and supporting their local community. We need to create one place where employers can get the help they need to recruit flexibly and we need dynamic businesses who can get involved and make real change happen for the local area'.

The Commission stated that 'these are ambitious aims and we all need to work together to make them happen. It will require some change at a national level, to allow local communities to do what is best for people who live locally, but mostly it is about working together to create a culture of employment for Islington and to help people to get, keep and ultimately enjoy their job'.

Box 7.7   Salford's Employment Charter

The Salford City Mayor's Charter for Employment Standards is designed to help raise employment standards for employees and businesses across the city.

The Charter contains a suite of pledges, grouped in three categories:

- Putting Salford first: creating training and employment opportunities for Salford people, particularly those facing the greatest disadvantage
- Buying in Salford: looking to purchase Salford goods and services at every practicable opportunity
- Setting the standard: promoting the adoption of the best possible working practices and conditions, such as working towards the introduction of a living wage, a commitment to eradicating the illegal practice of blacklisting and opposing the use of zero-hour contracts.

There are a number of benefits for business, including entitlement to use the Charter Supporter or Charter Mark recognition on websites and company literature, and the logo appearing on the Council's website so that prospective employees, commissioners and customers can easily see who supports the Salford City Mayor's Charter.

Employers working in the city are encouraged to voluntarily sign up to the charter. The city council and its partners support businesses interested in achieving this Charter Mark and offer assistance with local recruitment and selection, training and workforce development needs, access to the local supply chain and other business support services.

COMMUNITY WEALTH BUILDING

The Centre for Research on Socio-Cultural Change (CRESC) has been at the forefront of new thinking around community wealth building (Williams et al., 2013). They have suggested that rather than attempting to redistribute wealth via a return to significantly higher levels of taxation, which is unlikely to garner wide support, we should, instead, seek to reorganize our local economy. They argue for the 'grounded city', which places an emphasis on the distribution of goods and services essential for civilized life, rather than the pursuit of growth, which may be unattainable in some areas (Bowman et al., 2014).

The grounded city is one that structures social innovation in a way that meets the needs of the local circumstances. Rather than cities and places competing, they advocate a focus on developing the internal capacity of the places, people and businesses to provide some of the goods and services that are the local focus for social life. In essence, this means more local and plural production and ownership of energy, care and food. The 'Grounded City Manifesto' also stresses that 'it is time to think radically about delivering fairness not by redistributing income or reforming schools, but by reorganizing sectors of the economy'. See Box 7.8 by way of example.

Box 7.8   The Deep Place Approach

The recent report by CREW Regeneration Wales, 'Toward a New Settlement: A Deep Place Approach to Equitable and Sustainable Places' (Adamson and Lang, 2014) offers an alternative approach to revitalizing post-industrial communities. The report adopts a 'Deep Place' approach to tackling poverty and deprivation in the former industrial town of Tredegar in South Wales. The report argues that a focus on place is an effective mechanism for addressing two major interconnected social policy problems: how to overcome the inequitable distribution of wealth and the levels of poverty in post-industrial communities; and how to effectively adjust to a more environmentally sustainable model of the economy. Although the report does not suggest that the economy of communities like Tredegar should exist in isolation from wider economic activity, it does call for more localized supply chains and patterns of employment across four key areas: food; energy conservation and generation; the care sector; and, e-commerce and employment.

The report concludes: 'Our (current) policies are failing to address the contemporary problems we face, whilst building new problems for the future. We need to radically imagine the future rather than our collective tendency to re-invent the past'. The authors call for an alternative approach:

(Continued)

Box 7.8   The Deep Place Approach *(Continued)*

Here, localities are managed as unified spaces, with conscious forward planning that meshes with regional and national objectives.

- There will be a subsidiarity of decision making that engages with local people to energize and empower them.
- There will be a strong economy, promoting patterns of local economic circulation and associated multiplier effects.
- Residents are well educated, skilled and engaged with the economic realities of the day.
- The foundational economy will be strong and embedded in the delivery of public services.
- The population will not suffer from preventable illnesses and where life expectancy and well-life expectancy reach national norms.
- Our patterns of production and consumption are sustainable and protect the environment for future generations.

DEVELOPING THE ROLE OF ANCHOR INSTITUTIONS

The term 'anchor institutions' is commonly used to refer to organizations that have an important presence in a place, usually through a combination of being large-scale employers, one of the largest purchasers of goods and services in the locality, controllers of large areas of land and owners of relatively fixed assets (Netter Centre for Community Partnerships, 2008). Examples include local authorities, NHS trusts, universities, trade unions, local businesses and housing associations. Interest in the role of anchor institutions has risen in recent years as a result of their potential to generate economic growth and bring improvements to the local community and environment. Anchors have a large stake in the local area because, due to their activities, they cannot easily relocate. For example, while many corporations may be able to move, an airport or a hospital probably will not.

While the primary objective of anchors may not always be local regeneration, the scale of these institutions, their fixed assets and activities and their links to the local community mean that they are 'sticky capital' on which local development strategies can be based. According to The Work Foundation:

> Making the most of existing assets like anchor institutions will be vital for towns and cities across the UK. Capitalising on these assets represents an opportunity to mitigate the impacts of recession and do better in recovery. (The Work Foundation, 2010)

The influence of anchor institutions on the local area varies according to the anchor's history, resources, activities and partnerships as well as the socioeconomic situation in the place and its political landscape. There are, therefore, a range of ways in which different anchor institutions can leverage their assets and revenue to benefit the local area. In terms of economic development, anchors can act as purchasers, using local suppliers and producers; as employers, recruiting locally; and as incubators, supporting start-up businesses and community organizations. For example, universities can provide technological innovation and research expertise for local businesses and support the economy through student spending, and housing and hospitals can support local businesses through purchasing local goods and services, such as food, bed linen and information technology.

Although during a recession, anchor institutions may be more inward-facing and less willing to engage in community support, it is difficult to imagine how towns and cities can recover without support from these powerful engines. The question is, therefore, how local government can engage with anchor institutions, aligning their objectives with goals for local social, environmental and economic development. This will require close collaboration between local government and anchor institutions and could involve local government forming an 'anchor network' or encouraging partnerships between anchors and public sector bodies, local businesses and community sector organizations. See Box 9 for an example.

There are more ways in which local authorities and other anchor institutions can enable community wealth. These include through municipal entrepreneurship in the form of local energy schemes or utilizing derelict assets for new forms of service delivery or local authority-enabled businesses. See Box 7.10 on the use of local authority assets.

Housing providers have become key anchor organizations. They have long-term investments and an in-built social purpose, and a community presence. As such, they have the potential to influence the lives of some of the most vulnerable in society. Indeed, a growing number of housing associations see social development as both their role and responsibility – working with local authorities, businesses, the third sector and others to bring about sustainable improvement and create opportunities for the locality as a whole (Macauley, 2014). As such, many have branched out into wider neighbourhood work, whether it is tackling worklessness, promoting enterprise or supporting health initiatives. Some have also entered into new collaborative agreements with local authorities. According to the National Housing Federation: 'Regeneration is literally in the DNA of many urban housing associations. If they don't do regeneration, they have lost their social purpose. However, there are risks that we need to be realistic about but there are also opportunities. Many housing associations are thinking creatively bringing their development pipeline,

Box 7.9   Preston's Anchor Partnership

CLES has been working with Preston City Council to explore how anchor institutions based in the City can bring benefits for the local economy and community. Our starting point has been procurement spend and seeking to create a collective vision across institutions for undertaking procurement in a way that benefits the local economy. The supply chains of each of the anchor institutions (worth £750m pa) have been analysed with a view to identifying particular sectors where there are gaps in expenditure in the local economy and where there is scope to influence that spend in the future. Other initiatives include the following:

- Living Wage – Preston City Council has been a Living Wage employer since 2009. It seeks to ensure that other organizations across the public, commercial and social economies pay their own employees. The principle of the activity links to community wealth in that it seeks to provide a fair level of pay for Preston residents and also ensure the circulation of income within the local economy.
- Move Your Money – In recognition of the need to create a better financial system, Preston City Council has become part of the Move Your Money campaign. This seeks to encourage communities to bank in a more ethical way. The Council has also helped establish a new credit union ('Guildmoney').
- Guild Cooperative Network – The council and its Social Forum supports worker-led cooperatives and encourages other anchor institutions to utilize local cooperatives, most of which are engaged in front line provision around catering and building cleaning, for example.

Box 7.10   The Use of Local Authority Assets

CLES and APSE conducted case study research (Jackson, 2013) on the role that local authority buildings as anchors played in four localities: Ballymena; West Dunbartonshire; Southampton; and Neath Port Talbot. The work found that the use of local authority buildings offers significant potential to support better networking and closer working between different stakeholders in the local economy.

This work identified five key roles:

- Strategic. Local authority buildings are essential spaces for the provision of shared services between providers in the public sector, such as local government and the health service.

They also bring providers together in a single space to reduce duplication in delivery and also reduce building management costs for the authority and partners.

- Place. Heritage is vital to our identity and to the local image as buildings such as town halls and galleries may have archaeological, architectural, artistic or historic significance, contributing to the richness of local places and providing economic, social and environmental benefits.
- Economic. Local growth assets have an economic role as regards providing jobs and growth, creating business hubs and helping stimulate investment through private sector relationships.
- Social. Recognizing the social value of local authority assets is important. These assets have a significant social role in town centres in that they provide cultural venues that enhance visitor numbers and they can be used by the voluntary and community sector. Local authority assets can be used as facilitators of new forms of ownership or community management, spaces for voluntary and community sector organizations, and spaces for 'meanwhile' use.
- Environmental. The environmental role of local authority assets must not be overlooked. They can be the basis for public realm improvements and new energy schemes. The size and scale of public sector assets mean that they can be used as sites for new energy schemes, for example renewable energies such as solar or wind. In addition to creating renewable sources of energy, this can also bring economic benefit in the form of local supply chains and employment opportunity.

Box 7.11 Oldham's Neighbourhood Agreement with REGENDA

An ambitious plan to revitalize an Oldham estate has seen a pioneering agreement between Oldham Council and the housing provider Regenda.

Regenda has been working on a ten-year, £5m vision for a small estate in Limehurst Village, Oldham, for almost a year, looking at ways to deliver on residents' wishes to improve the environment, housing, recreation and employment opportunities.

A Neighbourhood Cooperative Agreement between the Oldham Council and Regenda was signed to agree shared ambitions for improvement and success. It includes looking at key ways to work together to:

- find innovative ways to improve quality of life and opportunities for local people,
- make a real contribution to Get Oldham Working through innovative employment and enterprise action,

(Continued)

Box 7.11   Oldham's Neighbourhood Agreement with REGENDA *(Continued)*

- focus on well-being and health through working together with health partners and local residents.

A series of key themes have been identified that will support the development of Limehurst and neighbouring Hollinwood, including the following:

- Collaborating on bringing new opportunities for work and training to Limehurst, via the Get Oldham Working project around enterprise, employment and new business creation,
- Jointly developing an active sports and well-being programme in the village,
- Unlocking the potential to develop land in Limehurst that is owned by the council.

asset management and community investment into a more joined up, and viable regeneration programme that can deliver a greater social return on investment.' See Box 7.11 for an example.

CONCLUSION

This chapter has provided an overview of recent approaches to local and regional economic development (good and bad) and offered a critique of some of the problems surrounding the current fashion for market-led approaches based on agglomeration in 'cities of growth'. It has also discussed some of the key issues concerning the push for devolution and what the next phase may mean for local economies, not least in regard to places having the resources and capability to deliver new delegated functions and services.

The contemporary debate around devolution presents local government with a key opportunity on two counts. First, it provides an opportunity to obtain sources of power and resource from central government. With this will come the ability to shape and frame key local activities around housing, skills and transport, for example, and subsequently grow local economies. Second, and more important, it provides local government with a key opportunity to challenge the orthodoxy of the way in which local economic development has been undertaken over the last thirty years and develop approaches that bring a double dividend in economic and social terms.

In this chapter, we argue that the trickle-down economic approach of successive governments and the current Coalition Government have not brought the degree of economic and social benefit that they should have done. Looking all the way back to the Urban Development Corporations of the 1980s through to the RDAs in the 2000s, and the contemporary LEPs, we can see that wealth creation has come at the expense of inequality. As a nation, we continue to have problems around worklessness, low skills levels, low productivity and worryingly entrenched poverty and deprivation.

Against a backdrop of continued austerity and deep-rooted socio-economic inequalities between and within places, the chapter has tried to place the spotlight on the often overlooked social dimension to prosperity. Whilst recognizing the importance of boosting local productivity and improving economic efficiency, and acknowledging the huge influence of macro-economic trends on local growth, the chapter highlights the value of social investment, social capital and social networks. Indeed, we argue that social factors are key to economic success and that local communities should be aiming for a double dividend, not merely higher local GVA per capita. The chapter offers a prospectus for an enabled local state to advance such a double dividend, embracing both economic and social success. In this way, it highlights the importance of both a redistributive central state and an enabled and more socially active local set of policies and actions.

In this we suggest there are six key components to an approach that enables a double dividend to be achieved:

- Utilizing social capital and the existing public, commercial and social sector networks that places already have in place;
- Promoting business citizenship and investment;
- Harnessing the potential of procurement spend;
- Stimulating the local labour markets;
- Utilizing the internal capacity of place and enabling community wealth; and
- Realizing the role and power of anchor institutions with a significant stake in place.

There is, of course, much work still to be done in enabling local government to act differently with other public, social and commercial players. At the centre of this is appreciating that local communities, people and society are not just downstream recipients of economic success but active upstream participants of a system that creates success in the first place. Social success, in this instance, is less a mere consequence of economic development action, but something that feeds into, sustains and creates a virtuous economy for all.

NOTES

1. An earlier version of this chapter was published as a Smith Institute 'Policy in the Making' discussion paper (McInroy and Jackson, 2014). We are grateful to the Carnegie UK Trust for supporting the work in this chapter.

2. Agglomeration economies are where the benefits of proximity and concentrated networks of policy makers, companies, consumers and workers stimulate economic growth. Therefore the focus is on the larger cities, as this is where there is greater likelihood of smaller supply chains, cost reductions and increases in productivity taking place and where the potential for profit attracts ever more investment capital.

3. It should be noted that smaller value public contracts are outside the scope of the Social Value Act and EU regulations. The government is currently reviewing the Social Value Act to see how it might be extended in a way that continues to support small businesses and voluntary, charity and social enterprise organizations to bid for public contracts.

4. The UK Commission for Employment and Skills states that one in five vacancies is down to a poor skills base.

5. The BIS (2013) report on 'Third sector engagement' noted that 'the third sector has a valuable ability to take a holistic approach to delivery and is often critical in engaging 'hard to reach' learners.

REFERENCES

Adamson, D., and Lang, M. (2014). Toward a New Settlement: A Deep Place Approach to Equitable and Sustainable Places, Cardiff: CREW.

Arnold, J., Longlands, S., McInroy, N., and Smith, J. (2009). *Toward a New Wave of Local Economic Activism: The Future for Economic Strategies*, Manchester: Centre for Local Economic Strategies.

Department for Business Innovation & Skills. (2013). *Third Sector Engagement,* London: Department for Business Innovation & Skills.

Bowman, A., Froud, J., Johal, S., Law, J., Leaver, A., Moran, M., and Williams, K. (2014). *The End of the Experiment: From Competition to the Foundational Economy.* Manchester: Manchester University Press.

Cabinet Office. (2010). *Principles of Good Employment.* London UK Cabinet Office.

Carnegie UK Trust. (2014). *The Enabling State. A New Relationship between Government and People,* Available at http://www.carnegieuktrust.org.uk/changing-minds/people---place/enabling-state (accessed 21st July 2015).

Christoforou, A. (2001). *Social Capital and Economic Growth: The Case of Greece*: Florence: European Institute.

Cingano, F. (2014). Trends in Income Inequality and its Impact on Economic Growth, *OECD Social, Employment and Migration Working Papers*, 163, OECD Publishing.

Cohen, D., and Prusak, L. (2001). *In Good Company. How Social Capital Makes Organizations Work*, Boston: Harvard Business School Press.

Coleman, J. S. (1988). Social Capital in the Creation of Human Capital, *American Journal of Sociology* 94, *Supplement: Organizations and Institutions: Sociological and Economic Approaches to the Analysis of Social Structure*, 95–120.

Core Cities. (2013). *London and England's Largest Cities Join to Call for Greater Devolution to Drive Economic Growth*, Available at http://corecities.

com/news-events/london-and- englands-largest-cities-join-call-greater-devolution-drive- economic-growth (accessed 20/01/15).

Crudelia, L. (2006). Social Capital and Economic Opportunities, *Journal of Socio-Economics*, 35, 5: 913–27.

Deputy Prime Minister's Office. (2014). *'Oyster-Style' Cards for Sheffield as Deputy PM Agrees to Devolution Deal*, Available at https://www.gov.uk/government/news/oyster-style-cards- for-sheffield-as-deputy-pm-agrees-devolution-deal (accessed 2001/15).

Gardiner, B., Martin, R., and Tyler, P. (2010). Does Spatial Agglomeration Increase National Growth? *Journal of Economic Geography*, 1–28.

Grant, J. L., and Kronstal, K. (2010). The Social Dynamics of Attracting Talent in Halifax, *The Canadian Geographer*, 54, 3: 347–65.

Heseltine, M. (2012). *No Stone Unturned: In Pursuit of Growth*, London: Department of Business, Innovation and Skills.

Hildreth, P., and Bailey, D. (2014). Place Based Economic Development in England: Filling the Missing Space, *Local Economy*, 29, 4–5: 363–77.

HM Treasury. (2014). *Devolution to the Greater Manchester Combined Authority and Transition to a Directly Elected Mayor*. London: HM Treasury.

IPPR North. (2014). *Decentralisation Decade: A Plan for Economic Prosperity, Public Service Transformation and Democratic Renewal in England*, Newcastle Upon Tyne, Institute for Public Policy Research.

IPPR North and Northern Economic Futures Commission. (2012). *Northern Prosperity is National Prosperity: A Strategy for Revitalising the UK Economy*, Newcastle Upon Tyne, Institute for Public Policy Research.

Jackson, M. (2010). *The Power of Procurement*, Manchester: Centre for Local Economic Strategies.

Jackson, M. (2013). CLES Findings: Enhancing the Value of Local Authority Assets in Town Centres, Manchester: Centre for Local Economic Strategies.

Jackson, M. (2014). *Living Wage and the Role of Local Government*, Manchester: Centre for Local Economic Strategies and The Greater Manchester Living Wage Campaign.

Joseph Rowntree Foundation. (2012). *A Lecture by Julia Unwin – What Future for a Devolved Approach to Opposing Poverty? Some Reflections from Research and from Experience*. York: Joseph Rowntree Foundation.

Kenworthy, L. (1997). Civic Engagement, Social Capital, and Economic Cooperation, *American Behavioural Scientist*, 40, 645–56.

Lyons, M. (2007). *Lyons Inquiry into Local Government. Place-Shaping: A Shared Ambition for the Future of Local Government: Executive Summary*. London: TSO.

Macauley, A. (2014). Should Housing Associations Build Homes or Neighbourhoods?, *New Start Magazine*, March 2014.

Martin, R., Gardiner, B., Sunley, P., and Tyler, P. (2013). *Britain's Spatially Unbalanced Economy is Both Wasteful and Unstable. The Solution Requires Much More than Small-Scale Measures*. London: London School of Economics.

Mazzucato, M. (2013). *The Entrepreneurial State: Debunking Public vs. Private Sector Myths*. London: Anthem Press.

McInroy, N., and Longlands, S. (2011). *Productive Local Economies Creating Resilient Places*, Manchester: Centre for Local Economic Strategies.

McInroy, N., and Jackson, M. (2014). *The Local Double Dividend. Securing Economic and Social Success.* London: The Smith Instiutute.

Netter Centre for Community Partnerships. (2008). *Anchor Institutions Toolkit: A Guide for Neighbourhood Revitalisation*, Philadelphia: University of Pennsylvania.

Oxford Economics. (2012). *London's Finances and Revenues, City of London Corporation*, London: City of London.

Pike, A., Rodríguez-Pose, A., and Tomaney, J. (2007). What Kind of Local and Regional Development and for Whom?, *Regional Studies*, 41, 9: 1253–69.

Pike, A., Rodríguez-Pose, A., Tomaney, J., Torrisi, G., and Tselios, V. (2010). *In Search of the 'Economic Dividend' of Devolution: Spatial Disparities, Spatial Economic Policy and Decentralisation in the UK*, London: Spatial Economics Research Centre.

Pike, A., Dawley, S., and Tomaney, J. (2010). Resilience, Adaptation and Adaptability, *Cambridge Journal of Regions, Economy and Society*, 3, 1: 59–70.

Piketty, T. (2014). *Capital in the Twenty-First Century.* Cambridge, MA: Belknap Press.

Royal Society of Arts. (2014). City *Growth Commission. Unleashing Metro Growth*, London: Royal Society of Arts.

The Smith Institute. (2014). *Making Work Better: An Agenda for Government*, London: The Smith Institute.

The Smith Institute, the Centre for Local Economic Strategies (CLES), Pensions Investment Research Consultants (PIRC) and the Local Authority Pension Fund Forum (LAPFF). (2012). *Local Authority Pension Funds: Investing for Growth*, London: The Smith Institute.

Vale, L. J., and Campanella, T. H. (2005). *The Resilient City: How Modern Cities Recover from Disaster.* New York: Oxford University Press.

Ward, M. (2011). *Rebalancing the Economy: Prospects for the North*, London: The Smith Institute.

Wilkinson, R., Pickett, K. (2009). *The Spirit Level: Why More Equal Societies Almost Always Do Better.* London: Allen Lane.

Williams, K. et al. (2013). *Manifesto for the Foundational Economy*, Manchester: CRESC.

The Work Foundation. (2010). *Anchoring Growth: The Role of 'Anchor Institutions' in the Regeneration of UK Cities: UK, Regeneration Movement.*

World Bank. (2009). *World Development Report 2009: Reshaping Economic Geography.* Washington, DC: World Bank.

Chapter 8

Beyond 'Localism'?

Place-Based Industrial and Regional Policy and the 'Missing Space' in England[1]

David Bailey, Paul Hildreth, and Lisa De Propris

INTRODUCTION

A range of recent contributions (e.g., OECD, 2012; Parkinson and Meegan, 2013) suggest that strong growth is possible in all types of regions, from capital cities to less developed towns and rural areas. Whilst a relatively small number of key centres (such as London) account for a disproportionate share of economic growth, even less developed regions make a vital contribution to national growth, accounting for 43% of aggregate OECD growth between 1995–2007 (OECD, 2012). Far from 'weighing down' national economic performance, less well performing regions, such as in the North of England, should rather be viewed as important sources of potential growth. To realize that potential, however, requires a new approach moving away from traditional policies. In particular, this chapter along with other contributions (e.g., Barca, 2009; OECD, 2009a, 2009b, and 2012) explores the foundations for 'place-based'[2] approaches to sub-national economic development policy. These offer the possibility to realize new opportunities in developing the potential of currently less well performing places. But in doing so, they raise questions about the framework that has been adopted by the 2010–2015 UK Coalition Government toward sub-national economic growth, in the English context at least.

This chapter considers the implications of a 'place-based' framework in the UK (or English) context, focusing on two key issues: the role of '(national and local) institutions' and the role of 'knowledge'. The chapter is organized around the following sections to address the question: What would a genuinely 'place-based' strategy mean in the English context? Section two draws an analogy with the humble pizza in terms of understanding regional policy, before section three outlines the basic foundations of 'place-based' policy approaches drawing on the international literature.

It draws out in particular the two key features of a 'place-based' approach, particularly as they relate to 'institutions' and to 'knowledge', recognizing that a more comprehensive coverage of the foundations of 'place-based' policy are offered elsewhere (e.g., see Hildreth and Bailey, 2013 and 2014; Barca et al., 2012). Section four examines more closely the role played by 'national' and 'local' institutions. It introduces key concepts in the 'place-based' policy literature, such as 'communities of interest' and 'capital city and local elites' and shows how they might be interpreted in a UK policy context. It also demonstrates that whilst Whitehall has ostensibly been focused on the performance of the 'local', whilst simultaneously either centralizing functions or imposing a 'conditional' form of localism (Hildreth, 2011), it may be that reform of the Centre is more critical to a 'place-based' framework. Section five introduces a 'place-based' approach towards an understanding of the role of knowledge. In doing so, it shows why there is an important 'missing space' in the last government's local growth agenda between the 'national' and the 'local' and how that space might be filled through appropriate institutions and policy responses going forward. The chapter's final section reaches conclusions on what a 'place-based' approach might mean in terms of:

• Whitehall, in changing its approach towards sub-national places;
• Local places, in seeking to realize their own potential;
• What the 'missing space' is and how it might be filled; and
• What a 'place-based' sub-national economic strategy might address.

THE 'POLICY PIZZA': RHETORIC, POLICY AND BASE IN REGIONAL POLICY

Back in May 2010, the coalition government claimed to offer a 'new approach to local growth' (HMG, 2010) that would shift power away from central government to local communities. At the centre of this approach, Local Enterprise Partnerships (LEPs) were created through a relatively 'bottom-up' process across England largely reflecting local partners' perceptions of the natural economy of their area (or the real politics of local cooperation). A first round of City Deals was then negotiated with the eight English Core Cities,[3] followed by a second round of City Deals, and more recently, the formation of Combined Authorities. Claims are made by the government that this approach was 'place based'. The intention was to create 'a more balanced economy' that 'recognises that places have specific geographic, historic, environmental circumstances that help to determine the prospects for growth and the most suitable approach to support the private sector and residents' opportunities' (HMG, 2010, page 7).

But was policy 'place based' in practice? It may appear to be somewhat of an oversimplification to compare British policy making in Whitehall with making a pizza. Nevertheless, there are useful parallels that can be drawn to illustrate an examination of the economics behind the 2010–2015 Coalition Government's local growth and creation of Local Enterprise Partnerships (LEPs) (see Hildreth and Bailey, 2013). In particular, three basic layers can be identified in both. A pizza is often completed by a scattering of cheese, which goes on top of the chosen topping, which is layered onto the base. On a visit to a restaurant, we may take time to choose our favoured topping. However, in practice, it is not the topping that marks an outstanding pizza, but the quality of the cooking of its base.

Similarly, it could be argued that at a basic level, UK policy making in Whitehall involves three key elements (see Figure 8.1). The top layer is the presentation of the political and policy case ('rhetoric') that accompanies policy making, which is reflected in Ministerial speeches and statements and in the phrasing of the supporting policy documents. The purpose is to communicate (and sell) to a public or professional audience the direction of travel and intended policy outcomes. Supporting the 'rhetoric' are the policy initiatives ('policies') that are designed to deliver the intended outcomes. The temptation is to focus almost exclusively on the complex menu, variations and synergies (or none) between these top two layers. This is particularly so as there are often inconsistencies. For example, in their 'rhetoric', the Labour governments of 1997–2010 emphasized their devolution and decentralization credentials (e.g., HMT et al., 2004). Whilst there was significant devolution to Scotland, Wales and London early on, Labour's approach towards localism became increasingly 'conditional' upon meeting Whitehall's policy priorities, and Regional Development Agencies (RDAs) were constrained in terms of what they could do and what targets they had to meet (Hildreth, 2011).

To focus on the first two layers almost exclusively can result in missing an important lesson from the humble pizza. In parallel to the pizza base, the economic framework ('base') is the frequently neglected but crucial element that fundamentally underpins both the 'rhetoric' and the 'policies'. Whilst the 'rhetoric' and the 'policies' are constantly changing, the 'base' remains remarkably constant (Richards, 2001). Indeed, until recently, since the end of World War II, there have arguably been only three dominant paradigms in UK economic policy (Balls et al., 2006; Hildreth, 2009): Neo-Keynesian (post-1945 to the late 1970s); neo-classical (exogenous growth) (late 1970s to the mid-1990s); and the new regional policy (mid-1990s to 2010), which saw its roots in endogenous growth theory (ibid). To follow our analogy, did the 'base' change again under the 2010–2015 Government's *Local Growth* agenda? And whether it has or has not, does the 'base' of economic ideas that underpins local growth fit consistently with the 'rhetoric' by which it is presented or the 'policies' by which it is operated?

In addressing this, first, there may be limitations in taking the 'rhetoric' (what Ministers and government publications say that a policy is all about) and even the 'policies' at face value (Hildreth and Bailey, 2013). The 'rhetoric', the 'policy' (the policy initiatives themselves) and the 'base' (the underlying framework of ideas from which the policies are derived or influenced) may be connected or disconnected in practice. Claims were made by both the Coalition and previous Labour government that their sub-national policies were 'place-based', for example, in seeking to realize the potential of all places (e.g., HMG, 2010; HM-Treasury et al., 2007) or 're-balancing the economy' (HMG, 2010), the validity of which should be carefully examined (Hildreth and Bailey, 2013, 2012; Froud et al., 2011a; Hildreth, 2009).

Second, if *Local Growth* was not, in fact, really 'place-based', then what is the alternative for the new Conservative government elected in 2015? In the UK (and particularly English) context, the contrast has been made with 'people-centred' (or also referred to as 'space-neutral') approaches. In domestic sub-national policy, the distinction between 'place-based' and 'people-centred' approaches has been framed narrowly as about appropriate policy solutions; is it better to prioritize investment in place ('place-based') or invest in people ('people-based') (e.g., Crowley et al., 2012)? The issue came to a head after more than a decade of active urban and regional policy under Labour, with investment into the English regions through Regional Development Agencies (RDAs) and spatially targeted programmes, such as the New Deal for Communities.[4] Commentators questioned how effective this spending was in practice (Crowley et al., 2012; Overman and Gibbons, 2011), and in doing so highlighted what they perceive as the limitations of 'place-based' investments.

Pizza layer	Layers of policy	Examples		
1. Scattering of cheese	Rhetoric	e.g. "create a fairer and more balanced economy"; "cities are engines of growth		
2. Topping	Policy initiatives	e.g. LEPs; RGF; EZs; TIF etc		
3. Base		Economic and conceptual framework		
		When	**Dominant**	**Influence**
		1945 to mid 1970s	Neo-Keynesian	
		Mid-1970s to mid 1990s	Neo-Classical	Exogenous growth
		Mid 1990s - 2010	Neo-Classical	Endogenous growth
		2010 onwards	Neo-Classical	New Economic Geography, Place based approaches

Figure 8.1   The UK 'Policy Model'

At the same time, economic and social disparities, which have been a long-standing feature of the regional and local geography of the United Kingdom, have widened further (Gardiner et al., 2013; Martin et al., 2015). Despite this, the case for a more 'people-centred' approach has been arguably more vocal in the United Kingdom than the case for any 'place-based' alternative. This is despite the acknowledged risk of (already considerable) spatial disparities in England widening still further, by centring economic activity and people even more in already successful places (Overman and Gibbons, 2011; Gill, 2010). In England, this would concentrate growth yet further on London and the Greater South East (GSE), and potentially some Core Cities.[5]

Nevertheless, arguments in favour of a case for 'place-based' approaches have been articulated in a UK context (e.g., Heseltine, 2012; IPPR, 2012; Martin et al., 2015).

These have focused on alternative approaches towards realizing economic and social potential more broadly across places in the United Kingdom (and England) and raised some key questions about 'institutions' and 'knowledge'. However, even then, such arguments risked the retort of being more appropriate to the past than for today's circumstances:

> The Heseltine report isn't all bad. But it is hard to shake the feeling that Mr Heseltine is arguing for a return to policies, many of them not particularly successful, that were developed in different times, to tackle different challenges. (Overman, 2012)

There is the question, at least in the UK context, as to whether there is some confusion around what 'place-based' really means in practice and whether it really matters. Part of the problem is the remarkably narrow way in which the debate has been framed nationally. As already indicated, this contrasts markedly with the international debate. Indeed, it is surprising that the lively debate (e.g., see Gill, 2010; Barca and McCann, 2010) outside the United Kingdom between proponents of 'place-based' and 'people-based' (or 'space-neutral') policy approaches, has been largely ignored in the United Kingdom. This is especially surprising given that the next round of EU Cohesion Policy from 2014 is largely shaped around a 'place-based' framework (Barca, 2009) and, as already indicated, is central to OECD policy toward 'regions' (OECD, 2009a, 2009b and 2012). Furthermore, with the last and current UK governments seeking to restore economic growth and reduce the budget deficit in a context of austerity, how limited resources are spent to maximum impact becomes increasingly important. This includes, critically, the contribution that places outside London and the South East can make to national economic prosperity, an approach in line with the international 'place-based' debates and approaches.[6] Hence the suggestion that it may indeed be time for the broader issues raised by this literature to be given appropriate focus in the UK context.

However, this represents a challenge in the English context for three reasons. First, as already noted, governments (both past Coalition and former Labour ones) use the 'rhetoric' of 'place-based' policy, even when their 'policies' and 'base' may not really fit them in practice (Hildreth and Bailey, 2013 and 2014). Loose 'rhetoric' like 'rebalancing the economy' (HMG, 2010) has been used by Ministers without any real substance behind it (Hildreth and Bailey, 2013; Froud et al., 2011a). Second, differences across approaches are open to misunderstanding (Barca, 2011). Both place-based and spatially blind approaches start from a primary concern for the welfare of the people, although they then diverge around different underlying assumptions, as detailed in Figure 8.2. Also, both are founded on logical economic principles, and both recognize spatial agglomeration as a reality. However, in practice, there are significant points of divergence between the two approaches that are somewhat different from those that have been explored so far, at least, in the UK literature. Third, some of the differences between the two approaches are not entirely straightforward to comprehend. In particular, the 'place-based' approach draws on its own distinctive language (e.g., 'communities of interest' and 'local and capital city elites') that requires further explanation before being understood in a UK (or English) context, and to which we now turn.

	Space-blind (e.g. WDR 2009)	Place-based (e.g. Barca Report, OECD 2009a, b)
Purpose	Facilitate agglomerations , migration and specialization for development	Realize growth potential in all regions, focusing on urban system as a whole
Urban system	Homogenous (in relation to city size)	Heterogeneous (not city size dependent) Agglomerations are not all natural
Geographical and historical context	Regions and localities follow standard development path	Regions and localities follow multiple development paths varied by their economic, social, cultural, historical and institutional characteristics
Institutions	Invest in provision of space-blind 'universal' public services (e.g. education, social services)	Design appropriate institutional structures and governance in context.
Solutions	Standardised: 1st order: spatially-blind institutions 2nd order: infrastructure to connect across distance 3rd order: sparingly spatially-targeted interventions	Design appropriate public good interventions and institutional frameworks in context of place
Knowledge	Predictable	Uncertain, embedded in locality and needs to be uncovered through bottom-up participatory processes to build consensus and trust
Role of central state	Design and provision of spatially-blind public services and appropriate infrastructure	Lacks 'sense of community', may support investments promoted by 'capital city elites'

Figure 8.2 Contrasting 'Space-Blind' and 'Place-Based' Policy Approaches

THE FOUNDATIONS OF 'PLACE-BASED' POLICY

Several recent influential publications advocate 'place-based' approaches towards sub-national economic policy (Barca, 2009; OECD, 2009a, 2009b, 2012; Barca et al., 2012). Two contrasting images might be used as a basic introduction to distinguish between 'placed-based' and 'space-neutral' approaches. First, the 'space-neutral' world is one where spatial adjustments occur relatively smoothly between levels of equilibrium in response to market-based price and cost signals in an urban system that is both homogenous and predictable. In pictorial terms, it might be thought of as being like a smooth free-flowing river system.[7] The alternative, a 'place-based' world is somewhat different. It is one where the combination of geography, history, culture and institutions create unpredictability, heterogeneity and uncertainty in the urban system and market outcomes. Pictorially, it is more like a river system with big boulders and rapids that cause many disruptions to the natural flow of the market system. In summary, distinctions between the two approaches are as described below:

> In essence, the differences between the space-neutral and the place-based approaches centre on the question of whether the territorial systems in evidence today are the result of a unique first-best solution to efficiency and space or rather of path dependency, sunk costs, and institutional issues. As such, the two approaches represent a different reading of the relationships between economic history and economic geography, giving rise to fundamentally different approaches. (Barca, 2011, Barca, McCann and Rodríguez-Pose, 2012: 141)

However, as Barca (2011) points out, it is necessary to go beyond this to identify the essence of the case around 'place-based' policy approaches. Barca (ibid) identifies five different approaches taken towards development policy, to distinguish what is both common and divergent amongst them.[8] From this analysis, important lessons can be learnt that are of relevance for understanding what 'place-based' approaches might mean in a UK/English context.

First, the case for 'people-based' (or 'space-neutral') approaches is not always framed in the same way. As Barca points out, a classic report that presents a 'space-neutral' approach based on a particular reading of the New Economic Geography (NEG) framework is the 2009 World Development Report (World Bank, 2009). This draws on a mix of three of the five approaches: a particular emphasis on the role of 'unique' institutions, agglomeration driven development, and a market-led approach towards economic redistribution. In a UK context, the case for 'people-based' approaches (e.g., Overman and Gibbons, 2011), puts a stronger emphasis on the role of efficient markets in promoting agglomeration within a NEG-type framework (what Barca calls an 'agglomeration driven approach') and a significantly lesser emphasis on 'unique' institutions'.

Second, it becomes apparent that the distinction between 'people-based' and 'place-based' approaches is not after all centred on choices between investing in people or places. As Barca states: "Any attempt to read the current debates if some approaches were concerned with persons and others were concerned places is preposterous" (Barca, 2011, page 221). Both approaches are actually concerned with both people and place. What distinguishes the 'place-based' approach is that it puts greater emphasis on arguing that ". . . the well-being of each person, given its individual characteristics, also depends on the context in which he/she lives." (Ibid, page 221).

Third, Barca goes on to identify the core of the argument around 'place-based' approaches. In effect, it boils down to two key hypotheses concerning the role of 'knowledge' and 'local (and national) elites' in institutions that arise out of the significance of the impact of geography, history, culture and institutions on development:

> First, the 'place-based' approach argues that no actor knows in advance 'what should be done'. It posits that sensible and reasonable decisions can emerge as the innovative result of a process of interaction and even conflict between endogenous and exogenous forces i.e., between the knowledge embedded in a place and external knowledge. In conjunction with this assumption, it also stresses the role played in producing under-development by the failure of the part of local elites, even when democratically elected, and their innate tendency to seek rents from public interventions. For these two reasons, the place-based approach . . . assigns a much greater role of exogenous institutions – their knowledge, preferences and values – and therefore advocates multi-level governance. (Barca, 2011, 223)

Of course, there is more to the 'place-based' framework (on this see Barca, 2009; OECD, 2009a, 2009b, and 2012; Barca et al., 2012). However, for the purpose of this chapter, the two key issues of 'institutions' and 'knowledge' are explored further below to offer an illustration of how a 'place-based' framework might begin to challenge the present policy paradigm.

THE NATIONAL AND THE LOCAL: THE ROLE OF INSTITUTIONS

We now focus on institutional issues relating to the national and the local dimensions of 'place-based' policy making.

National

A good place to start is to consider whether the State itself may be part of the problem as well as part of the solution. A 'place-based' framework identifies two potential institutional weaknesses in the National government (the 'national') as it conducts sub-national economic policy. The first is that the 'national' has a tendency to lack both an understanding and knowledge of local places – it lacks a 'sense of community'. In the literature, this is identified as a form of social capital that understands the local institutional context in which development takes place (Tabellini, 2010; Barca, McCann and Rodríguez-Pose, 2012). It is argued that the 'national' has a consequent weakness in its capacity both to adapt its approach towards local places and to mediate local consensus and trust between local actors, as well as mobilize local resources effectively (Rodríguez-Pose and Storper, 2006). If this is not appropriately understood, or adapted to, it might become a serious problem undermining the 'national' design and conduct of sub-national policy. The second argument is that the 'national' is also prone to the influence of 'capital city' elites in policy making, favouring infrastructure, innovation and sectoral investment for the capital city over other sub-national places (Barca, McCann and Rodríguez-Pose, 2012). As a result, national policy decisions may divert resources to promote unnatural agglomerations, as well as support natural ones.

How might this be relevant to UK government departments in London (Whitehall)? It appears that there are key reasons why, as Heseltine (2012) noted, Whitehall might have a built-in tendency towards addressing economic issues in a 'place-less' or 'space-blind' context. This is despite its active use of 'place-based' language. Some key reasons why this might be a problem are summarized as follows:

First, there is a long-standing culture of centralism (Heseltine, 2012). England is one of the most centralized countries in the Western world. Arguably, despite the 2010–2015 government's 'rhetoric' of localism, very little actually changed in substance of the distribution of powers between the 'national' and 'local' under the Coalition government. Furthermore, historically, at the first sign of trouble or when the opportunity so arises, powers tend to be taken back into Whitehall, illustrated by the recentralization of RDA functions back into the Department of Business and Innovation, following their abolition.

Second, there is an entrenched culture of 'conditional localism' (Hildreth, 2011). This is a model where the 'national' approach to decentralization is conditional on the 'local' supporting the national policy objectives and/ or performance priorities and standards. This can be compared with the 'representative' localism model, which is much closer to a Western European approach based on strong local leadership and a clear separation of responsibilities between the 'national' and the 'local'. Arguably, England has shifted from a 'conditional' model enforced through top-down inspection and performance regimes put upon the 'local' by Whitehall under Labour, to one enforced through increasing austerity in local resources (Featherstone et al., 2012) – in terms of both cuts in government grant and imposing constraints on the ability of local authorities to raise levels of council tax. It is also seen in the language of Whitehall reports. For example, it is reflected in the 'conditional' language of 'Cities', where cities, rather than Whitehall, are seen as the potential barrier to effecting change (HMG, 2011). Furthermore, localism in practice has also sometimes meant bypassing the elected local institutions of local government, particularly in areas of neighbourhood planning and education policy.

Third, Whitehall lacks a holistic perspective of 'place' (Heseltine, 2012; Marvin and May, 2003). Whitehall is organized around themed policy departments, which in turn are shaped around functions and largely 'space-blind' initiatives that focus on policy specifics. As Heseltine pointed out, with this fragmentation, no one is tasked to look holistically at the full range of issues facing particular places (Heseltine, 2012). This culture is reflected in the National Policy Planning Framework (DCLG, 2011), which unusually for a Western European country offers a largely un-spatial approach to spatial planning.

Fourth, Whitehall operates around short-term policy cycles. Policy is geared, in place development terms, around 'short-term' electoral cycles of up to five years. These are subject to frequent institutional and policy changes reflecting the policy priorities of the current administration. The 2010–2015 elected Coalition Government swept away regional institutions with little regard for how institutional learning, knowledge and experience in regions had been developed and how it could be retained. No apparent consideration was given to the longer time scales involved in the economic transition of places and the requirement to embed institutional learning, investment and development over the longer term. This possibly reflected Whitehall's blindness to this being an important real issue in the development of places.

Fifth, institutional memory is absent in Whitehall. This point is related to the previous one. In view of the nature of the 'national' political cycle, Whitehall puts particular value on general policy-making expertise in response to the immediate political requirements of the governing administration, with frequent movement between roles. This is valued over embedding institutional memory. This may have an adverse impact in Whitehall undervaluing why it is critically important in a local context.

Sixth, the 'national' is subject to a process of 'hollowing out'. A longer-term process of 'hollowing-out' of the 'national' is reinforced by austerity cuts on departments – both under the 2010–2015 government and post-2015.

However, it is a weakness that when resources are scarce, proposals to reform the Civil Service fail to address how the 'national' might engage more strategically with sub-national places with more limited resources or devolve responsibilities to the 'local' (HMG, 2012).

Seventh, the 'national' economic framework is largely un-spatial. In government, the long-standing neo-classical economic framework reinforces the dominance of a 'space-neutral' perspective that is clouded in an apparently 'place-based' 'rhetoric' (Hildreth, 2009; Hildreth and Bailey, 2013; Froud et al., 2011a). It also constrains Whitehall's openness to new evidence; challenging its validity if it does not conform to the parameters of its favoured framework.

Eighth, London is given undue influence in policy and resource allocation. London (and the Greater South East (GSE) and its banking and financial sector) is prioritized at all costs, against other places and sectors. As a result, institutional and investment decisions are London/GSE-centric (spatially and sectorally), with London provided with a unique model of government in England not on offer elsewhere. As a result, statements regarding the spatial and sectoral 're-balancing' of the economy become empty 'rhetoric' without any real substance behind them (Froud et al., 2011a).

For these reasons, a barrier to realizing the potential of currently weaker places – such as the Northern economy – may lie not in the North but in Whitehall itself. A 'place-based' approach predicts:

> It is wholly unrealistic to expect that central government decision-makers have either the knowledge or expertise regarding North East Local Enterprise Partnership area issues – of a technological, skills-related, or institutional nature – in order to make sound judgments appropriate to context. (McCann, 2013, 4)

Part of the problem is that Whitehall is presently largely failing to both understand and do something about it. When the 'national' prioritized 'place-based' initiatives, for example in City Deals, it did so by establishing a special unit outside the usual departmental structure to do so, but which was then left fighting its corner between other departments and the 'local'. The reform of the 'national' is therefore key to a 'place-based' approach. But this needs to go alongside changes in the 'local', to which we now turn.

Local

A 'place-based' perspective does not just raise questions about the Centre. It also acknowledges that there are potential weaknesses that relate to the 'local' that need to be addressed. In particular, the possibility of 'under-development traps' occurring is highlighted that may inhibit the growth potential of regions and localities or perpetuate the presence of social exclusion (Barca, 2009; Barca, McCann and Rodríguez-Pose, 2012). A 'place-based' approach argues that this may not just be a consequence of the market. Rather, it may also relate to a failure by 'local elites' to act effectively, or to local institutional weaknesses (Barca, 2009).

There may be two sets of problems. Each may arise out of different understandings of 'place'. 'Place' is a dynamic concept. It is the subject of an extensive literature offering a diverse range of meanings (e.g., see Hubbard and Kitchins, 2011). A challenge for economic geography is that places do not stand still. Places are not islands, but interact both within and with other places around them through the market-influenced behaviours of their key foundational elements of people and firms (Hildreth, 2007). They are shaped by history, their geographical and social setting and their institutional characteristics, making each place distinctive and different (Barca et al., 2012). As noted, a key difference between a 'place-based' and a 'people-centred' approach is whether this really matters in the design of policy.

The first set of problems might relate to an understanding of place that relates *to 'how we are governed'*. This relates to the area administered by the (city or town) local authority. It is important, because it is usually associated with the civic, cultural and historical identity of the 'place', which is shaped by events and transitions over long periods of time (Hildreth, 2007). This concept of 'place' had significance within the 2010–2015 Coalition Government's localism agenda (Hildreth, 2011).

These may impact on the effectiveness of 'local elites' (local authorities and their partners) both within 'places' and across neighbouring 'places' to enable effective change. This has implications about how the city sees itself and its relationships with other places around it, for example, politically in matters of 'trust', 'control' and respect of its neighbours (Tabellini, 2010). Key issues are, therefore, the following:

First, there may be a lack of trust – There may be long-standing historical rivalries between 'places' that lie within the same 'natural economy' that are acted out by political leaderships through lack of effective cooperation across boundaries. This may occur, for example, 1. within a single local authority; 2. across two (or more) local authorities within a 'natural economy', or 3. between two overlapping authorities in a two-tier situation.

Second, serious underbounding may impact on capacity – Where a city is seriously underbounded in relation to its physical footprint, it may constrain its capacity to act strategically in relation to its economic area, particularly if there is an absence of 'trust' between neighbouring authorities. A few English city local authorities are so well bounded as to capture part of their economic area, beyond the physical footprint of the city. Leeds is one example (see Figure 8.3). However, many are well underbounded. The physical city

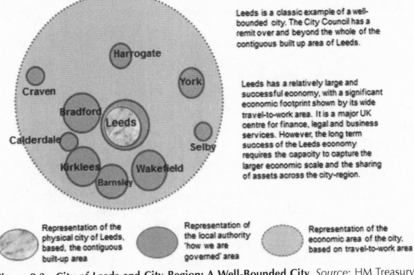

Leeds is a classic example of a well-bounded city. The City Council has a remit over and beyond the whole of the contiguous built up area of Leeds.

Leeds has a relatively large and successful economy, with a significant economic footprint shown by its wide travel-to-work area. It is a major UK centre for finance, legal and business services. However, the long term success of the Leeds economy requires the capacity to capture the larger economic scale and the sharing of assets across the city-region.

Representation of the physical city of Leeds, based, the contiguous built-up area

Representation of the local authority 'how we are governed' area

Representation of the economic area of the city, based on travel-to-work area

Figure 8.3 City of Leeds and City Region: A Well-Bounded City. *Source*: HM Treasury et al., 2006.

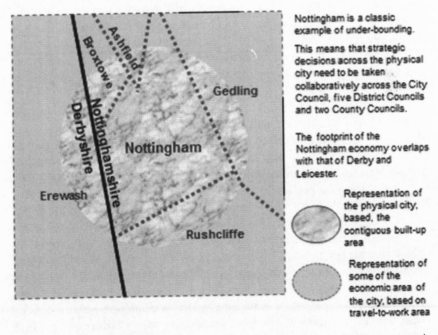

Nottingham is a classic example of under-bounding.

This means that strategic decisions across the physical city need to be taken collaboratively across the City Council, five District Councils and two County Councils.

The footprint of the Nottingham economy overlaps with that of Derby and Leicester.

Representation of the physical city, based, the contiguous built-up area

Representation of some of the economic area of the city, based on travel-to-work area

Figure 8.4 City of Nottingham: An Under-Bounded City. *Source*: HM Treasury et al., 2006.

of Nottingham, for example, is crossed by the boundaries of five district councils and two county councils, as well as by the City Council itself (see Figure 8.4).

Third, a culture of 'conditional localism' – In the context of a dominant culture of 'conditional localism', there is constant pressure on the 'local' to conform to the demands and priorities of the Centre over local needs and priorities. This may stifle local innovation and lead to the misappropriation of allocation of local resources in relation to local development needs (Hildreth, 2011).

The second issue relates to an economic understanding of 'place', which is defined by *'how we live and work',* by the ways in which people and firms operate their lives between the city and towns and villages that surround it. It might be referred to as the 'natural economic area' (HMG, 2010), or sub-region, or in appropriate cases, city region. It is a dynamic concept expressed in terms of the connections and flows from home to work, home to shop, home to home in housing moves, and home to cultural entertainment as well as the way that businesses relate to their customers and suppliers (Harding, Marvin and Robson, 2006; Hildreth, 2007b). This was central to the 2010–2015 Coalition Government's case for the establishment of LEPs as 'natural economic areas' (HMG, 2010).

'How we live and work' is a loosely defined or fuzzy concept. There are different ways of understanding a 'natural economic area' (HMG, 2010). The most common is to relate it to the containment of labour markets, beyond the boundary of a city into its surrounding area. This might be interpreted in a narrow sense, such as in a functional urban region (FUR) (e.g., Centre for Cities, 2013), or more widely, within the context of a city region as expressed in the POLYNET study, which identified fifty FURs within the London Mega-City-Region (Hall and Pain, 2006). In most cases, the concept of an LEP has been interpreted more narrowly rather than broadly. A total of thirty-nine LEPs have been created, some based on limited sub-regional geographies, sometimes influenced by who partners get on with or not, rather than any systematic economic analysis of spatial economies. The 'Greater Birmingham and Solihull' LEP, for example, omits the Black Country, which in reality clearly forms part of the city-region footprint (see Figure 8.5). Also, the idea of a 'natural economy' based on labour markets has limitations outside the bigger city agglomerations. It works well for Manchester and Leeds, where there clearly is a city-regional geography. But for 'gateway' cities like Hull, and 'industrial' cities like Blackburn and Burnley (Hildreth, 2007a), the geography of their labour markets is contained within a limited space and their economies 'isolated' in relation to other places (e.g., see Work Foundation, SURF and Centre for Cities, 2009, 2010). This undermines the value of a 'natural economy', as a loosely used concept. To an extent, the

LEP boundaries for these cities do acknowledge this. However, the question is, do they go far enough? Further, the geography of firms, for example, in supply chain relationships or broader cluster relations may go far wider than that captured by travel to work areas. The relevant 'economic' scale for the automotive cluster, for instance, covers at least five English regions (the East Midlands, North West, South East, South West and the West Midlands) (Hildreth and Bailey, 2013; Amison and Bailey, 2014).

The consequential outcome is likely to be a widening institutional capacity gap between places in responding to the challenges of their local economies.[9] As an example, Leeds and its partners have been building city-regional capacity since the early 2000s. Progress has been gradual, rather than spectacular, but the city region was able to absorb the most 'useful' features of the new LEP (such as gaining the input of able private sector leaders new to working with the public sector) and to carry on building on an existing capacity-building trajectory. Contrast this with the North East LEP. Despite the encouragement of the 2006 OECD Territorial Review to form effective city-regional collaboration (OECD, 2006), local authority partners found it difficult to maintain progress because of lack of trust, particularly, but not wholly, between Newcastle and Sunderland. Efforts to establish a Tyne & Wear city region foundered following the abolition of the RDA, and the new North East LEP was started with limited resources almost from scratch and was left having to work very hard to try to catch

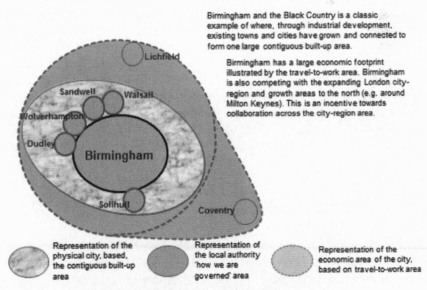

Figure 8.5   Birmingham, the Black Country and Coventry

up, although the more recent moves to form a 'combined authority' show that progress can be made.

The issue of trust does not arise just because of the factors outlined above relating to *'how we are governed'*. Also, crucially, they relate to the impact of economic linkages between places, which may operate in a way that is either 'complementary' or 'less complementary'. (Lucci and Hildreth, 2008; Work Foundation et al., 2009; Overman, Rice, and Venables, 2010) In other words, if one city grows, its neighbour within the same 'natural economy' may not benefit (Ibid). Locally understood perceptions of this are likely to impact on the willingness or otherwise to collaboratively effectively, which can be seen as a problem of collective action in economic terms.

It can, therefore, be seen that in a 'place-based' framework, institutional weaknesses might be identified in both the 'national' and the 'local', which potentially act as barriers to the successful realization of the potential of different places. Part of the answer in a 'place-based' framework is to develop a multi-level governance (MLG) framework to bridge the 'national' and the 'local'. For the 'national', it is about recognizing its weaknesses – in particular its inability to make sound judgements appropriate to local context and having no ability to foster the engagement of the local stakeholders (public or private) to drive economic development (McCann, 2013). On the other hand, it has an important role to foster trust between the 'national' and 'local', in the design of devolution of responsibilities and resources to maximum effect, and to incentivize collaborative behaviours. For the 'local', it is about seeking an exogenous input to support locally based collaboration to enable the targeting of places with appropriate bundles of public good investments and overcoming issues of 'trust'.

However, as already indicated, the spatial gap between the 'local' (including the LEP) is wide, not just in geography, but also in 'trust'. In addition, this is not just about the public sector. The significance of the MLG approach is not that it is just public to public, but rather recognizing that in a 'place-based' framework, different actors – public and private – interdependently contribute towards the success of the sub-national economy. In that context, much of the action and collaboration may take place in what we have termed the 'missing space'. It is to this that our attention now turns.

THE 'MISSING SPACE' IN POLICY

As a result, there is a 'missing space' or gap between the 'national' and the 'local', which, we argue, present policy (in England at least) does not fully address, either in the sense of spatial scale or that of institutional arrangements. On the scale aspect, it is argued here that this 'missing space' occurs for at least three reasons, particularly outside the larger city regions (such as Manchester and Leeds). First, because the 'local' (including the LEP) often lacks sufficient scope, depth and capacity to be effective. Linked to this, there is the risk that local elites may capture policy and funding for their own benefit, so exogenous challenge is required (this is a point picked up in international policy debates and which also links to the need for a multi-level governance framework). Second, outside the larger city regions, LEPs commonly lack appropriate geography, being fragmented and effectively incomplete (see Heseltine, 2012, on the need to review LEP boundaries).[10] Third, there remains the absence of effective MLG from the 'national' to the 'local' based on the key principles of 'trust' and 'respect'. Labour sought to fill this 'missing space' in a top-down way with administrative regions and regional institutions, particularly RDAs. Few might argue for going back to that top-down administrative geography. However, given the fragmentation and significant capacity variation in the subsequent LEPs, which were created in a bottom-up way, the critical question is this: Is there a 'missing space' that present policy does not fill and does it matter? This, in fact, relates to a long-standing debate in industrial policy design as to the appropriateness of 'top-down' versus 'bottom-up' designed interventions and institutions (see for example, De Bandt, 1999).

Under a 'space-neutral' framework, none of this would seem to matter as such industrial and regional policy interventions are anyway of limited value and may be seen as counter-productive. Rather, under a 'space-neutral' approach, key elements of policy should, instead, focus on, first, supporting disadvantaged people to achieve better individual outcomes, through education, skills and welfare policy, regardless of where they live; second, enabling greater geographic mobility to make it easier for people to move to growing areas; and, third, reducing the barriers to the expansion of economically successful places (Overman and Gibbons, 2011; Crowley et al., 2012).

The basic argument presented is that left to themselves, markets will adjust if the barriers preventing them from doing so are addressed. Hence, it is more important to focus on universal spatially blind universal institutional solutions, rather than seeking to fill a 'missing space' with institutionally based or related solutions. However, giving local authorities greater local discretion is supported to some extent, because it does facilitate experimentalism and innovation. Nevertheless, in terms of industrial and economic development, the view taken is that it is better to allow the market to work by itself, rather than for the State to actively intervene in any way, for example through an industrial policy. Indeed, a smaller public sector is seen as potentially creating more space for the private sector to grow (Faggio and Overman, 2012) and hence is seen as beneficial. The spatially blind approach is, in fact, highly critical of anything more than a limited market-failure role for state intervention, seeing industrial and regional policies and their accompanying institutions as ineffective (Overman, 2012).

A 'place-based' approach sees things rather differently. In part, this is because, as noted earlier, under such a perspective, knowledge is seen as critical for effective policy development (Barca, McCann and Rodríguez-Pose, 2012, Barca, 2011). Yet, within this perspective, it is recognized that such knowledge is not already known by the state, firms or local stakeholders. As a result, there is a positive role for policy in aiming to stimulate new knowledge and ideas through interactions between local groups (endogenously) and external actors (exogenously) (ibid). Linked to this, the 'smart specialization' approach has been closely linked with place-based approaches to regional development policy, at least in how they have been developed in the European Union (Barca, 2009: European Commission, 2011).[11] In particular, in terms of regional policy, it has been used to emphasize the need to exploit related variety, build regional embeddedness and enable strategic diversification (McCann and Ortega-Argilés, 2011). In so doing, it stresses the need for regional actors (government, firms, universities, research institutions) to collaborate, recognizing the current starting point for the region in terms of skills, technologies and institutional governance and then to build on these capabilities, rather than trying to start 'from scratch' (Wolfe, 2011).

This approach thus sees the capacity of territories to root their economic activity into the local institutional fabric as being at the heart of their economic success, through the generation, acquisition and exchange of knowledge. Yet, such knowledge is, in turn, uncertain, and is embedded in localities and needs to be uncovered through participatory and bottom-up processes to build consensus and trust (Barca et al., 2012). Indeed, as noted earlier, the tendency of the 'state' is to lack both an understanding and knowledge of local places (it lacks a 'sense of community' (e.g., Barca, McCann and Rodríguez-Pose, 2012), with a consequent weakness in its capacity to adapt its approach towards local places and mediate local consensus and trust between local actors, as well as to mobilize local resources effectively.

This place-based smart specialization approach has strong parallels with Rodrik's (2004, 2008) perspective of industrial policy as a *process* of discovery requiring strategic collaboration between the private sector and state in unlocking growth opportunities, but set within a framework of multilevel governance so as to enable a process of local collaboration and discovery, while enabling external challenge to local elites engaging in rent-seeking behaviour. So, industrial and regional policies that facilitate this process of discovery through strategic collaboration are seen as relevant under place-based/smart specialization perspectives and require appropriate institutions to engender this.

In fact, this is largely how modern, intelligent industrial policy design is conceived of in contemporary debates (see Rodrik, 2004 and 2008; Bailey et al., 2015b), with industrial policy ideally having the quality of 'embedded autonomy', whereby it is not captured by firms and sectors, but where, as noted, it focuses on the discovery process, where firms and the state learn about underlying costs and opportunities and engage in strategic coordination. So, for example, in the context of reshoring possibilities for UK manufacturing, it might mean government working with industry to identify key fractures in the supply chain and how to address them (Bailey and De Propris, 2014).[12] This is no longer about 'picking winners' or propping up failing firms or industries, but rather, as the IPPR and Northern Economic Futures Commission (2012; page 9) note, about 'seeking to identify and support the elements of comparative advantage within the economy that enable innovation and new technologies to take root and companies to grow'.

In this regard, there is an institutional and capacity failure inherent at the national level in terms of the lack of resources to design industrial policy interventions. As Froud et al. (2011b; page 20)[13] note, on industrial policy there is a

large gap between the old interventionism of 'picking winners' on the one hand, and the generic neo-liberal enterprise policies that have failed us for the last thirty years. But this is a gap that urgently needs to be bridged. It's an area of ignorance, a knowledge space that needs to be fashioned, if the UK is to start to create the successful industrial policies needed for regeneration.

In this sense, given the lack of resources at a national level to develop such policies, and given the capacity constraints of many LEPs outside of major cities, there would appear to be a role for an intermediate tier in bringing 'place' and 'sectors' together in terms of industrial and regional policy development, a point that has been highlighted by the IPPR and Northern Economic Futures Commission (2012). This has examined what a 'northern' industrial strategy might look like, identifying sectoral trends, analysing emerging strengths and opportunities identified by LEPs, and carrying out analysis of the export potential of key sectors in which the North already holds emergent strengths and which can be built on in a 'smart specialization' sense. Indeed, as the report notes, the results of this analysis offer some cause for optimism: despite an ongoing decline in traditional sectors such as manufacturing and extraction, new sectoral strengths are seen as emerging in related fields such as advanced manufacturing, pharmaceuticals and biohealth. The report goes on to note that LEPs and local authorities need to continue to develop their intelligence on key sub-sectors that are seen as having potential locally, but that between the LEP level and the national level there is scope (or space in our terms) for 'a clear northern innovation agenda that is based on a small number of priorities and strategic assets and which addresses some of the North's cross-cutting innovation challenges' (ibid, 9).

The wider point is that filling this missing space requires regionally based industrial development strategies promoting 'related diversification'. Such strategies need to recognize (i) the need to bring together different but related activities in a region and (ii) the differing potentials of regions to diversify, resulting from different industrial, knowledge and institutional structures linked to specific regional historical trajectories. Rather than 'starting from scratch' or applying 'one size fits all policies', regional industrial strategies require tailor-made policy actions embedded in, and linked to, the specific needs and available resources of regions, starting with the existing knowledge and institutional base in that region. These need to capitalize on region-specific assets, rather than attempting to replicate and apply policies that may have worked in quite different places.

This 'missing space' can also be seen in terms of the industrial policy capacity that has been lost with the abolition of the RDAs. In particular, the removal of RDAs has effectively removed a tier of governance that was – in some cases at least – engaged in attempts to exploit related variety, build regional embeddedness and enable strategic diversification. As one leader of a combined authority stated to us: 'LEPs talk place but BIS talks sectors'.

In essence, the subsequent policy 'base' here is 'space-neutral', emphasizing the importance of London and the GSE (Hildreth and Bailey, 2013). It is difficult to see how this shift to a policy of 'centralized localism' will actually help, for example, clusters in mature industrial regions like the West Midlands (or the North) to compete in the high-skill and high-technology niches that they increasingly occupy (Bentley et al., 2010). Indeed, it is in the areas of cluster and innovation policy that there may be particular challenges (Centre for Cities, 2013).

Part of the problem is that what remains of industrial policy post-RDAs is centralized in London, where civil servants are removed from events on the ground and – as noted – they generally lack the capacity to develop appropriate industrial policies for the reconstruction of the manufacturing base (Froud et al., 2011a; 2011b). The key point here is that RDAs were often better positioned to make sound judgements about how best to offer support and to which clusters (and/or technologies) as they had a superior information base than central government. By way of example, the RDA Advantage West Midlands supported the Niche Vehicles Network, comprising a network of stakeholders across the region, which collaborates on the application of new technologies in low-volume vehicle production. This classic open-innovation-type approach (MacNeill and Bailey, 2010) is too fine-tuned in scale to have visibility and relevance in Whitehall, yet offers much opportunity for this region's automotive cluster in shifting from low-value volume work to niche high-value low-carbon activities. Here, regional-level industrial policy was critical to helping to develop a 'phoenix industry' linked to trends in open innovation, and which might be seen as a good example of place-based 'smart specialization' in operation (Amison and Bailey, 2014).[14]

An important lesson is that there remains a key role for the coordination of LEPs' economic and cluster strategies, most obviously via some sort of intermediate-tier infrastructure. The need for joint LEP working can also be evidenced in the regional data and intelligence legacy of the RDAs. Whilst this is being retained in core cities such as Birmingham and Manchester after the abolition of RDAs, it is not clear whether other parts of their regions will have access to such data and intelligence. The key point is that if smart specialization is an important element of place-based approaches, then questions remain as to whether LEPs have the powers, resources and governance arrangements necessary to deliver such an approach. This is especially pertinent if, as Barca et al. (2012) suggest, 'place-based' development strategies require mechanisms that build on local capabilities and promote innovative ideas through the interaction of local and general knowledge and of endogenous and exogenous actors.

An interesting question is to what extent Whitehall responded to the recommendations of the Heseltine (2012) report and was actually prepared to change so as to allow this 'missing space' to be filled.[15] While the 2010–2015 Government announced that they were 'accepting in full, or in part, 81 of Heseltine's 89 recommendations', the reality was less encouraging, as a detailed examination of Annex A of the government response (HM Treasury, 2013) indicates. Marlow (2013), for example, noted that of the fifteen Heseltine proposals relating to 'local growth deals', the government accepted just nine of them. Furthermore, Marlow (2013) noted that, as regards local leadership of innovation, 'even "accept" means, de facto, enduring top down control of this vital agenda'. Marlow goes on to highlight that the inability of LEPs and (local authorities) to position innovation and knowledge-economy at the centre of local growth strategies in cities and areas seeking to be globally competitive will leave a massive hole which no amount of single local growth fund is likely to fill. Similarly, the response points to continued top-down control of innovation funding (HM Treasury, 2013; page 43, para 2.26) even though no justification is offered for this stance.[16]

City Deals, whilst welcome as a positive way forward for the national to engage with the cities in mediating locally based solutions, nevertheless, contain their own weaknesses. The outcomes have often been opaque and complicated, and it is a challenge to resolve what was actually agreed upon in terms of decentralization and resource allocations. In its focus on a 'northern powerhouse', it is replicating in part a London-type solution in Greater Manchester, as an alternative Northern-based agglomeration – although it should be stressed that the most substantive resources, particularly for infrastructure investment have still gone to London, as the UK's global city; the practical outcome remains one of privileging of the economy of one 'region' of the United Kingdom, namely London and the South East, over all other places, with some second-tier cities, and particularly Greater Manchester, coming some distance behind.

It could be argued that the formation of combined authorities may go some way to filling this missing space. However, there are question marks as to how far city deals and combined authorities actually go in devolving power and responsibilities. In the context of Manchester, for example, Moran and Williams (2015) argue that it is unlikely that the devolution currently on offer will give Manchester the resources, capability and policy tools to tackle its structural problems:

> We could argue about what needs to be done. But the fundamental point is that 'devo Manc' is not doing enough if it only offers bits of money and devolved authority to an elected mayor whose role will be to manage more cuts and preside over unsolved structural problems. Centralisation has certainly disappointed, but this kind of 'devo Manc' decentralisation is bound to fail.

CONCLUSIONS: FILLING THE MISSING SPACE?

Given that 'the "place-based" approach is the "new paradigm" of regional policy' (Barca, 2011, 225), this chapter has sought to answer the following question: What might a genuinely place-based approach in England look like? Having highlighted the basic foundations and key concepts of 'place-based' policy approaches, this chapter has interpreted and applied them in an English context. Using this analysis adds value to policy debates as it highlights that in a 'place-based' framework, institutional weaknesses can be identified in *both* the 'national' and the 'local', which potentially act as barriers to the successful realization of the potential of different places. Indeed, part of the policy solution in a 'place-based' framework is to develop a multi-level governance framework to bridge the 'national' and the 'local'.

For the 'national', it is about recognizing its weaknesses – in particular, its inability to make sound judgements appropriate to the local context and having no or limited ability to foster the engagement of local stakeholders (public or private) to drive economic development. Yet, it also has an important role to foster trust between the 'national' and 'local', in the design of the devolution of responsibilities and resources to maximum effect, and to incentivize collaborative behaviours. For the 'local', it is about seeking an exogenous input to support locally based collaboration to enable the targeting of places with appropriate bundles of public good investments and overcoming issues of 'trust'.

The significance of the multilevel governance approach is not that it is just public to public, but, rather, recognizing that in a 'place-based' framework, different actors – public and private – interdependently contribute toward the success of the sub-national economy. In that context, much of the action and collaboration may take place in what we perceive as the 'missing space', between the 'national' and the 'local', which present policy (in England at least) does not fully address, either in the sense of spatial scale or that of institutional arrangements.

Filling this 'missing space' or 'governance gap' requires regionally based industrial development strategies that bring place and sectors together and which recognize (i) the need to bring together different but related activities in a region and (ii) the differing potentials of regions to diversify, resulting from different industrial knowledge and institutional structures linked to specific regional historical trajectories. Such an approach also calls for the recognition that knowledge is not already known either by the state or by firms, or by local stakeholders. As a result, there is a positive role for policy in aiming to stimulate new knowledge and ideas through interactions between local groups (endogenously) and external actors (exogenously) (ibid). This has similarities with modern conceptions of industrial policy whereby the latter is perceived of as a *process* of discovery requiring strategic collaboration between the private sector and state in unlocking growth opportunities. Rather than 'starting from scratch' or applying 'one size fits all policies', regional industrial strategies require tailor-made policy actions embedded in, and linked to, the specific needs and available resources of regions, starting with the existing knowledge and institutional base in that region. These need to capitalize on region-specific assets, rather than attempting to apply policies that may have worked in quite different places.

In summary, the 'missing space' in the English context has a number of dimensions. In the 'boulder strewn' river of sub-national geography, the design of institutions and interventions at appropriate spatial levels matters. Moreover, such 'place-based' institutions and interventions need to overcome potential weaknesses that operate at and between both the 'national' and 'local', which constitute barriers to the realization of enterprise, innovation and potential across the economic system as a whole. This, we argue, has yet to be realized properly in policy debates over devolution and industrial and regional policy in the English context.

NOTES

1. This chapter develops and updates Bailey et al. (2015a).

2. A 'place-based policy' is a long-term strategy aimed at tackling persistent underutilisation of potential and producing persistent social exclusion in specific places through external interventions and multilevel governance. It promotes the

supply of integrated goods and services tailored to contexts, and it triggers institutional change. (Barca, 2009, page VII).

3. Birmingham, Bristol, Leeds, Liverpool, Manchester, Newcastle, Nottingham and Sheffield.

4. Despite these regional institutions and a regional system of planning, there was much about Labour's approach that was, in fact, relatively space-neutral. A major criticism of RDAs was that they were effectively imposed top down and in an arbitrary way. They were seen as bearing little relationship with functional economic geography and were not accountable to localities.

5. On media coverage of this, see for example 'London's Precarious Brilliance' in *The Economist*, 30/06/2012, which argues that 'anything that jeopardises London endangers the country'.

6. On this, see for example ESPON (2013) on the role of second-tier cities in growth, which notes that 'there are many concerns about the dominance of capital cities, especially the costs and negative externalities of agglomeration' (page 2). See also the IPPR and Northern Economic Futures Commission (2012), which notes that in spite of the strongest growth being in London, some '57 per cent of net aggregate growth in the UK was generated by its lagging regions in the decade to 2008' (Garcilazo 2010 in IPPR/Northern Economic Futures Commission, 2012; p. 6).

7. The authors would like to thank Professor Philip McCann for this metaphor of a river system to illustrate the differences in approach between a 'place-based' and 'space-blind' economic system.

8. The five approaches Barca (2011) identifies are (1) Perfect institutions – that good institutions (e.g., education, labour markets etc.) are a primary driver of growth and that the state knows best what they are and their effectiveness is not context (or place) dependent; (2) Agglomeration – that agglomeration is a primary driver of growth, and the recognition that development requires appropriate institutions and investment suited to what set of unique optimal set of agglomerations that market forces may uncover; (3) Redistributive – that agglomeration not only brings efficiency but also social exclusion, and the response is either a market-oriented approach by those who are constrained in approaches toward redistribution through belief in an optimal set of agglomeration outcomes, or a softer redistributive approach by those who believe on the contrary that the world is flat; (4) Communitarian – that local awareness of their own knowledge and preferences is the primary driver of development and that development is the result of a local deliberative process; and (5) Place-based approaches. Barca argues that there are both intersections and divergences in these different approaches.

9. In a similar vein, see Bailey and De Propris (2001) on the 1988 reform of the EU Structural Funds, which gave EU regions an *entitlement* to participate in the design and implementation of regional policy. They found that some of the weakest regions lacked the institutional capacity to access and implement the structural funds allocated to them, and as a result regional inequalities initially increased and only later started to narrow. Only after a process of institutional capacity building and learning were some regions able to interact with the European Commission and national governments on regional policy issues, and only then were member states allowed it.

10. As noted, major criticisms of the 'old' RDAs were that they were imposed in a top-down manner, bore little relationship with functional economic geographies, and were not accountable to localities. RDAs had the 'wrong geography', it was argued. In contrast, the creation of LEPs was very much a bottom-up process, and while potentially helpful in terms of accountability, there was no guarantee that the resulting configuration of LEPs had the 'right geography' either. In fact, the configuration of LEPs had just as severe problems over scale and boundaries as the old RDAs, albeit in a different form (see Hildreth and Bailey, 2013; Townsend, 2012).

11. See Barca (2009, p. XVII):

> Place-based interventions, building on the strengths and taking account of the weaknesses of previous experience as regards cohesion policy in this area, could complement policies aimed at developing a European Research Area, by selecting in each region a limited number of sectors in which innovation can most readily occur and a knowledge base built up. Through such an approach – defined in the current policy debate as 'smart specialisation' – the most could be made of the present diversity of industrial agglomerations and networks, while their 'openness' beyond regional or national boundaries would be promoted.

12. The latter has been identified as a key weakness of the UK's manufacturing base. Froud et al. (2011a), for example, note that in the UK's largely foreign-owned branch assembly plants, broken supply chains effectively undermine high British content and limit domestic backward linkages.

13. Froud et al. (2011b, page 18) see the Bombardier case as

> an exemplary instance of how things go wrong in the absence of industrial policy. Generic pro-enterprise policies plus neglect of sectoral specifics about demand management and ownership has decimated British manufacturing capacity in key sectors, destroyed the supply chains that sustain successful industries, and deskilled core sections of the labour force. In the aggregate, neglect has thrown hundreds of thousands out of work, and undermined the economies of the ex-industrial regions whose service-based private sectors are clients of the state.

14. An opposing challenge may also be evident, in that excessive decentralization may see an 'all hands in the pork barrel' approach, with a fragmentation of RDAs into much smaller LEPs leading to limited public resources effectively being wasted on a myriad of micro-scale and uncoordinated projects. For example, as Swinney et al. (2010) note, only a small number of cities will actually be able to develop specialist clusters in sectors identified as 'high-growth' industries, and they identified a serious 'reality gap' in policy. The danger is that many such projects are likely to fail as they will not actually be building on natural historical bases with genuine skill sets that can be re-orientated toward new growth or 'phoenix' clusters (ibid) in a smart specialization sense.

15. In as far as Heseltine (2012) actually proposes filling this space. His review can anyway be criticized, for example in terms of a failure to embrace multilevel governance and hence a genuine place-based smart-specialization approach, or for really proposing an industrial policy for the regions (on the latter see Williams, 2012 for a critique).

16. The government response (HM Treasury, 2013; page 43, para 2.26) on innovation does state that 'where local areas make the case that they can deliver better results if funding was devolved, then government will listen'. Listening is one thing, doing something is quite different.

REFERENCES

Amison, P., and Bailey, D. (2014). Phoenix Industries and Open Innovation? The Midlands Advanced Automotive Manufacturing and Engineering Industry, *Cambridge Journal of Regions, Economy and Society*, 7, 3: 397–412.

Bailey, D., and De Propris, L. (2001). The 1988 Reform of the Structural Funds: Entitlement or Empowerment? *Journal of European Public Policy*, 9, 3: 408–28.

Bailey, D., and De Propris, L. (2014). Manufacturing Reshoring and Its Limits: The UK Automotive Case, *Cambridge Journal of Regions, Economy and Society*, 7, 3: 379–98.

Bailey, D., Hildreth, P., and De Propris, L. (2015a). Mind the Gap! What Might a Place-Based Industrial and Regional Policy Look Like? in Bailey, D., Cowling, K., and Tomlinson, P. (Eds.), *New Perspectives on Industrial Policy for a Modern Britain*. Oxford: OUP.

Bailey, D., Cowling, K., and Tomlinson, P. (2015b). Introduction: New Perspectives on Industrial Policy for a Modern Britain, in D. Bailey, K. Cowling, and P. Tomlinson, (Eds.), *New Perspectives on Industrial Policy for a Modern Britain*. Oxford: OUP.

Balls, E., Healey, J., and Leslie, C. (2006). *Evolution and Devolution in England: How Regions Strengthen Our Towns and Cities*, London: New Local Government Network.

Barca, F. (2009). *An Agenda for a Reformed Cohesion Policy: A Place Based Approach to Meeting European Union Challenges and Expectations*, DG Regio, Available at http://www.interact-eu.net/downloads/1224/An_Agenda_for_a_Reformed_Cohesion_Policy.pdf

Barca, F. (2011). Alternative Approaches to Development Policy: Intersections and Divergences, in OECD, *OECD Regional Outlook 2011*, 215–25, Paris: OECD Publishing.

Barca, F., and McCann, P. (2010). *The Place-based Approach: A Response to Mr Gill*, VoxEU.org, 9th October, Available at http://www.voxeu.org/article/regional-development-policies-place-based-or-people-centred . (accessed on 25/04/2014).

Barca, F., McCann, P., and Rodríguez, P. (2012). The Case for Regional Development Intervention: Place-Based Versus Place-Neutral Approaches, *Journal of Regional Science*, vol. 52, no. 1, pp. 134–52.

Bentley, G., Bailey, D., and Shutt, J. (2010). From RDAs to LEPs: A New Localism? Case Examples of West Midlands and Yorkshire, *Local Economy*, 25, 7: 535–57.

Centre for Cities. (2013). *Industrial Revolutions: Capturing the Growth Potential.* London: Centre for Cities/McKinsey.

Crowley, L., Balaram, Band Lee, N. (2012). *People or Place? Urban Policy in the Age of Austerity*. London: The Work Foundation.

De Bandt, J. (1999). Practical Issue of Networking and Cooperation, in K. Cowling, (Ed.), *Industrial Policy in Europe. Theoretical Perspectives and Practical Approaches*. London: Routledge.

Department for Communities and Local Government (DCLG). (2011). *National Planning Framework*, Available at http://www.communities.gov.uk/publications/planningandbuilding/nppf . (Accessed on 25/04/2014).

The Economist. (2012). 'London's Precarious Brilliance', 30th June 2012.

European Commission. (2011). Regional Policy for smart growth in Europe 2020 Brussels: European Commission, Directorate-General for Regional Policy.

ESPON. (2013). *SGPTD Second Tier Cities and Territorial Development in Europe: Performance, Policies and Prospects*, Available at http://www.espon.eu/export/sites/default/Documents/Projects/AppliedResearch/SGPTD/SGPTD_Final_Report_-_Final_Version_27.09.12.pdf (accessed 25/04/2014).

Faggio, G., and Overman, H. (2012). The Effect of Public Sector Employment, LSE Research Laboratory, Available at http://www.spatialeconomics.ac.uk/textonly/serc/publications/download/sercdp0111.pdf. (accessed 25/04/2014).

Featherstone, D., Ince, A., Mackinnon, D., Strauss, K., and Cumbers, A. (2012). Progressive Localism and the Construction of Political Alternatives, *Transactions of the Institute of British Geographers*, 37, 2: 77–182.

Froud, J., Johal, S., Law, J., Leaver, A., and Williams, K. (2011a). *Rebalancing the Economy (or buyer's remorse)*, CRESC Working Paper no. 87, CRESC, Manchester University, Available at http://www.cresc.ac.uk/publications/rebalancing-the-economy-or-buyers-remorse (accessed 25/04/2014).

Froud, J., Johal, S., Law, J., Leaver, A., and Williams, K. (2011b). *Knowing What to Do? How Not to Build Trains*. CRESC Research Report. CRESC, Manchester University, Available at http://www.cresc.ac.uk/sites/default/files/Knowing%20what%20to%20do.pdf (accessed 25/04/2014).

Gardiner, B., Martin, R., and Tyler, P. (2013). Spatially Unbalanced Growth in the British Economy, *Journal of Economic Geography*. doi: 10.1093/jeg/lbt003.

Gill, I. (2010). *Regional Development Policies: Place-Based or People-centred?*, VoxEU.org, 9th October, Available at http://www.voxeu.org/article/regional-development-policies-place-based-or-people-centred (last accessed 25/04/2014).

Hall, P., and Pain, K. (2006). *The Polycentric Metropolis: Learning from Mega-City Regions*. London: Earthscan.

Harding, A., Mavrin, S., and Robson, B. (2006). A Framework for City-Regions: Reserch Report, London: Office of the Deputy Prime Minister.

Heseltine, M. (2012). *No Stone Unturned in the Pursuit of Growth*, BIS, London, Available at https://www.gov.uk/government/uploads/system/uploads/attachment_data/file/34648/12-1213-no-stone-unturned-in-pursuit-of-growth.pdf (accessed 25/04/2014).

Hildreth, P. A. (2007a). Understanding Medium-Sized Cities, *Town & Country Planning*, 76, 5: 163–67.

Hildreth, P. A. (2007b). The Dynamics of 'Place-Shaping': The Changing Rationale for Urban Regeneration, *Journal of Urban Regeneration and Renewal*, 1, 3: 227–39.

Hildreth, P. A. (2009). Understanding 'New Regional Policy': What Is Behind the Government's Sub-National Economic and Regeneration Policy for England? *Journal of Urban Regeneration and Renewal*, 2, 4: 318–36.

Hildreth, P. (2011). What Is Localism, and What Implications Do Different Models Have for Managing the Local Economy? *Local Economy* 26, 8: 702–14.

Hildreth, P., and Bailey, D. (2012). What Are the Economics Behind the Move to LEPs, in M. Ward, and S. Hardy, (Eds.), *Changing Gear. Is Localism the New Regionalism?* London: Smith Institute and Regional Studies Association, 25–34.

Hildreth, P., and Bailey, D. (2013). The Economics Behind the Move to 'Localism' in England, *Cambridge Journal of Regions, Economy and Society*, 6, 2: 233–49.

Hildreth, P., and Bailey, D. (2014). Place-Based Economic Development Strategy in England: Filling the Missing Space, *Local Economy*, 29, 4–5: 363–77.

HM Government (HMG). (2010). *Local Growth: Realising Every Place's Potential*, Cm 7961, London: Department of Business Innovation and Skills.

HM Government (HMG). (2011). *Unlocking Growth in Cities*, Available at http://www.dpm.cabinetoffice.gov.uk/sites/default/files_dpm/resources/CO_Unlocking%20GrowthCities_acc.pdf (accessed 25/04/2014).

HMG. (2012). *The Civil Service Reform Plan*, London: Civil Service, Available at http://www.civilservice.gov.uk/wp-content/uploads/2012/06/Civil-Service-Reform-Plan-acc-final.pdf (accessed 25/04/2014).

HM-Treasury. (2013). *Government's Response to the Heseltine Review*. London: HM-Treasury. Cm8587, Available at http://www.hm-treasury.gov.uk/d/PU1465_Govt_response_to_Heseltine_review.pdf (accessed 25/04/2014).

HM-Treasury. (HMT). Department of Trade and Industry (DTI), and Office of the Deputy Prime Minister (ODPM). (2004). *Devolving Decision Making: 2 – Meeting the Regional Challenge: Increasing Regional and Local Flexibility*, London: HM-Treasury.

HM-Treasury, DTI, and ODPM. (2006). *Devolving Decision Making: 3 – Meeting the Regional Economic Challenge: The Importance of Cities to Regional Growth*, London: HM-Treasury.

HM-Treasury, BERR, and CLG. (2007). *Review of Sub-National Economic Development and Regeneration*, London: HM-Treasury.

IPPR, and The Northern Economic Futures Commission. (2012). *Northern Prosperity Is National Prosperity: A Strategy for Revitalising the UK Economy*, Institute for Public Policy Research, Available at http://www.ippr.org/images/media/files/publication/2012/12/northern-prosperity_NEFC-final_Nov2012_9949.pdf (accessed 25/04/2014).

Lucci, P., and Hildreth, P. (2008). *City Links: Integration and Isolation*. London: Centre for Cities, Available at http://www.centreforcities.org/citylinks (accessed 25/04/2014).

MacNeill, S., and Bailey, D. (2010). Changing Policies for the Automotive Industry in an 'Old' Industrial Region: An Open Innovation Model for the UK West Midlands? *International Journal of Automotive Technology and Management*, 10, 2–3: 128–44.

Marlow, D. (2013). Is There a Big Hole in the Innovation 'Stone' in the Government's Response to Heseltine? *Regeneration & Renewal*, 25/03/2013, Available at http://davidmarlow.regen.net/2013/03/25/is-there-a-big-hole-beneath-the-innovation-stone-in-governments-response-to-the-heseltine-review/ (accessed: 25/03/2013).

Martin, R., Pike, A., Tyler, P., and Gardiner, B. (2015). *Spatially Rebalancing the UK Economy: The Need for a New Policy Model*. Seaford: Regional Studies Association.

Marvin, S., and May, T. (2003). City futures: Views from the centre *CITY* 7(2), 213–25.

McCann, P. (2013). *The North East (NELEP) Area in the Context of the Global Economy*, Available at http://www.nelep.co.uk/media/2636/nelep-report-philip-mccann.pdf (accessed 25/04/2014).

McCann, P., and Ortega-Argilés, R. (2011). Smart specialisation, regional growth and applications to EU cohesion policy. *Working Papers 2011/14, Institut d'Economia de Barcelona (IEB)*.

Moran, M., and Williams, K. (2015). 'Devo Manc': 'Northern Powerhouse' or 'Northern Poorhouse'? *speri.comment: The Political Economy Blog*, 7th April 2015, Available at http://speri.dept.shef.ac.uk/2015/04/07/devo-manc-northern-powerhouse-northern-poorhouse/ (last accessed 25/04/2014).

OECD. (2009a). *How Regions Grow: Trends and Analysis*, Paris: OECD.

OECD. (2009b). *Regions Matter: Economic Recovery, Innovation and Sustainable Growth*. Paris: OECD.

OECD. (2012). *Promoting Growth in All Regions*. OECD: Paris.

Overman, H. G., Rice, P., and Venables, A. J. (2010). Economic Linkages Across Space, *Regional Studies*, 44, 1: 17–33.

Overman, H. G., and Gibbons, S. (2011). Unequal Britain: How Real Are Regional Disparities? *CentrePiece*, 16, 2: 3–25, Available at http://cep.lse.ac.uk/pubs/download/cp353.pdf (last accessed 25/04/2014).

Overman, H. (2012). Heseltine's Report Is a Return to the Unsuccessful, *Financial Times*, 31 October 2012.

Parkinson, M., and Meegan, R. (2013). Economic Place Making: Policy Messages for European Cities, *Policy Studies*, 34, 2: 377–400.

Richards, S. (2001). Four Types of Joined-Up Government and the Problem of Accountability, in *National Audit Office, Joining Up to Improve Public Services*, HC 383, Session 2001–2002, London: The Stationary Office.

Rodríguez-Pose, A., and Storper, M. (2006). Better Rules or Stronger Communities? On the Social Foundations of Institutional Change and its Economic Effects, *Economic Geography*, 82, 1: 1–25.

Rodrik, D. (2004). *Industrial Policy for the 21st Century*. Cambridge, MA: John F Kennedy School of Government.

Rodrik, D. (2008). *One Economics, Many Recipes: Globalization, Institutions, and Economic Growth*. Princeton: Princeton University Press.

Swinney, P., Larkin, K., and Webber, C. (2010), *Firm Intentions: Cities, Private Sector Jobs and the Coalition*. London: Centre for Cities.

Tabellini, G. (2010). Culture and Institutions: Economic Development in the Regions of Europe, *Journal of the European Economic Association*, 8, 677–716.

Townsend, A. (2012). The Functionality of LEPs – Are They Based on Travel to Work? in M. Ward, and S. Hardy, (Eds.), *Changing Gears. Is Localism the New Regionalism?* London: The Smith Institute/Regional Studies Association, 2012.

Williams, K. (2012). What Lord Heseltine Doesn't Say About the Regions, *The Guardian*, 31/10/2012, Available at http://www.guardian.co.uk/commentisfree/2012/oct/31/lord-heseltine-britain-ex-industrial-regions (accessed 25/03/2013).

Wolfe, D. A. (2011). *Regional Resilience and Place-Based Development Policy: Implications for Canada*, Paper Presented to the Canadian Political Science Association, Wilfred Laurier University, Waterloo, Ontario.

Work Foundation, SURF, and Centre for Cities. (2009 and 2010). *City Relationships: Economic Linkages in Northern City Regions*, Available at http://www.centreforcities.org/cityrelationships.html (accessed 25/04/2014).

World Bank. (2009). *World Development Report 2009: Reshaping Economic Geography*. Washington, DC: World Bank.

Chapter 9

Prospects for Devolution to England's Small and Medium Cities[1]

Zach Wilcox

The United Kingdom is one of the most centralized countries in the OECD, with central government grant accounting for almost 74 per cent of local authority budgets (London Finance Commission, 2013). It is not surprising, then, that local governments in the United Kingdom have been calling for more control over their policies and spending. In recent years, political focus has centred on national devolution to Scotland, accelerated by the Scottish Nationalist Party's commitment to hold a referendum on independence. But some of the United Kingdom's cities, particularly those in England, have been calling loudly for freedoms as well.

In England, London leads the way in devolution with its powers passed down initially in the GLA Act in 1999, and the capital has gained incremental powers from the Homes and Communities Agency and for Transport for London over time. Manchester has recently followed in its wake, building off years of co-working between the Greater Manchester councils and the combined authority established in 2010.

Under the Coalition Government, Scotland and England's larger cities have gained more powers over local policies and programmes, and a set of national legislations, like the Local Government Finance Bill, have brought about some more funds and policy levers for local government in England and Wales. But the more dynamic small- and medium-sized cities have struggled to match the larger devolution deals struck between Government and Manchester.

This chapter first analyses the devolution policies under the Coalition Government; then it examines the potential for further devolution to England's small and medium cities. It highlights the importance of filling the governance gap between 'national' and 'local' and for creating a platform for cities to coordinate their transport, economic development and strategic planning strategies to a geography that reflects the scale at which each city operates. Finally, it lays out a blueprint for how to devolve powers to small and medium cities in the current political context, including the requirement for metro mayors and how to rationalize the relationship with Local Enterprise Partnerships.

DEVOLUTION UNDER THE COALITION GOVERNMENT: 2010–2015

The United Kingdom is one of the most centralized countries in the OECD, as central government exerts hard and soft controls over local policy and budgets. In 2013–2014, local taxes accounted for only 18 per cent of local government budgets (Wilcox and Sarling, 2013). Pressures from councils have been mounting for years to transfer policy and fiscal powers from central government down to local councils who argue that they could make decisions that better reflect the needs of their place.

The Coalition Government introduced changes to the governance structure in the United Kingdom that – while not initially radical or sweeping – set in motion something much larger for devolution of powers from Whitehall to local government.

Three major changes to the political economy have led to the largest devolution of power since the Greater London Authority Act (1999) – austerity, governance gap and localism. It started with the Coalition's commitment to reducing the deficit – a program of austerity that dramatically reduced spending in the Department for Communities and Local Government and local authorities. Local government funding from central government fell 36.3 per cent over the course of the Coalition, and their spending power fell over 20 per cent in real terms. These cuts put pressure to change the way councils can work to be more efficient (Innes and Tetlow, 2015).

Alongside austerity, the second change was a deficit in sub-national governance. The Coalition dismantled the Regional Development Agencies at the start of their term and instituted the new public-private sub-national bodes: Local Enterprise Partnerships (LEPs). As LEPs are not statutory bodies, it became increasingly clear that there was a spatial gap for strategy and policy between the local authority and the national levels.

Lastly, a more comprehensive devolution programme has slowly taken shape with the evolution of piecemeal localism policies. Reforms to the business rates tax system, institution of the New Homes Bonus and changes to the National Planning Policy Framework, including neighbourhood plans, put more control at the local level or incentivized councils to be pro-growth. In addition, the Local Government Bill (2011) offered councils the 'General

Power of Competence,' which allows them to do anything any citizen can do, provided it is not prohibited by other legislation. This power was quite an important change to local government powers, but the vague language of the Bill and entrenched ways of working have held back councils from invoking it in a widespread manner (Local Government Association, 2013).

These three movements – austerity, regionalism and localism – built the momentum and pressure for central government to devolve powers in a more comprehensive way.

However, Whitehall and politicians wanted to make sure that any devolution was going to lead to something different and more efficient and would significantly contribute to national economic growth. In addition, Government also had to manage risk. They could not give control and responsibility to councils while still being held culpable for their outcomes. Government needed a new governing body they could devolve to that would assume accountability and promote economic growth.

What transpired from these parallel pressures was a quid pro quo approach to devolution: Government would continue austerity, but they would also loosen the reins to allow councils to adapt to new ways of working. Importantly, Government signalled that they would loosen the reins more for places that could be considered more capable and accountable.

A DEAL-BASED APPROACH TO DEVOLUTION

Looking back, it seems inevitable that devolution would have come about in a deal-based approach. Each side had something to gain and something to lose. Government had to manage risks, but offer enough localism to support councils to deal with budget cuts. Councils, on the other hand, needed more power over their policies and finances to invest in growing their economies, but they had to offer Government some certainty that they were capable of managing these new powers.

This transaction-based approach to devolution led to a process of what the Government coined 'City Deals.' City Deals are agreements between government and a city that give the city more control over how they grow their economy and spend their money in exchange for strengthening their governance arrangements. Crucially, city deals did not offer cities new ways of taxing or financing their growth; the Chancellor was clear that a deficit reduction programme could not go hand in hand with giving local government new tax and spend powers.

The Localism Act 2011 introduced the Core Cities Amendment, which allows councils to make the case for being given new powers to promote economic growth and set their own distinct policies (HM Government,

2015). The first city deals (Wave 1) came about in 2012 (launched in 2011) and were originally offered to the Core Cities – the eight largest cities in the United Kingdom outside of London. This was enabled through the Core Cities Amendment in the Localism Act (2011), which allowed local authorities to make the case for being given new powers to promote economic growth and set policies (HM Government, 2011).

Working with the core cities gave Government more visibility and impact, because any outcomes from these deals would be larger and more observable in these big cities. Ministers also had better working relationships with the larger cities, emphasizing the importance of existing connections and personality in the political process. Lastly, working with a group of eight large cities gave the Government an opportunity to trial the Deals process, without having to offer deals to every city in the country.

Central government had the power, and the onus was on local government to prove they could handle new responsibilities. Government was ultimately culpable for the success of City Deals, and they had to be measured in their devolving of power. To secure a deal with government, each city had to show in its proposals for growth that:

- it could prove how it would take greater responsibility and leadership with decisions affecting its local economy.
- it would use the advice, expertise and resources of the private sector.
- it was dedicated and ready to put resources into the deal.
- it would plan on using public money wisely.
- it would improve its area by following the government's strategy of lowering regulation, boosting private sector growth and making it easier for businesses to grow (HM Government, 2015).

The first City Deals were a politically and administratively challenging process, but they were overall considered a good first step by giving cities some specific freedoms in choosing projects and programmes that suited their needs (ibid).

Some Deals were significant locally, but they were piecemeal overall. Greater Manchester's Earn Back scheme is the most radical, which allowed the city to make a series of investments in its growth in exchange for a share of the national tax take that resulted from the investments in order to repay the loan. Development Deals in Newcastle, Sheffield and Nottingham allow them to borrow against future business rates growth to invest through Tax Increment Finance. The power to pool multiple funding streams into one single investment fund was negotiated for Greater Birmingham and Solihull, Bristol and West of England, Greater Manchester, Leeds City Region, Liverpool City Region and Sheffield City Region (HM Government, 2012).

Wave 1 cities also negotiated Deals with central government that gave them more control over their skills budgets and apprenticeships, pool business support programmes, funding for major local transport projects, and franchising and commissioning for local rail.

A second round of Deals, called 'Wave 2,' involved 20 cities including the 14 largest city regions outside of London and six small and medium cities with the highest population growth during 2001 to 2010. The Wave 2 City Deals were a significant expansion in devolution policy, because they opened the door to small- and medium-sized cities to secure more freedoms and built new relationships between these cities and central government. These cities often did not carry the same political or economic clout as the Core Cities, and the Deals process opened up a platform to bring them into the fold while providing a framework for devolution (Bolton, 2012).

But the City Deals were not a devolution programme; they were bespoke deals between cities and government that offered funding for specific policies and projects in exchange for local accountability. In the first two waves, only the Manchester Deal represented a step-change in devolution.

THE PUSH FOR DEVOLUTION IN ENGLAND AFTER THE SCOTTISH REFERENDUM

In 2014, a series of events finally shifted gear in the Devolution movement. Figure 9.1 below shows the time line of major events that led to the historic Greater Manchester devolution agreement as well as the one in Greater Sheffield and the establishment of the Northern Powerhouse and One North, a coordinated approach by large Northern cities to improve the transport infrastructure between them to build scale and rebalance the economy away from London.

The Scottish Referendum played a particularly important role in driving pressure in devolution to Wales and English cities. Collectively, the Scottish Independence Referendum and the promises from the Coalition for greater

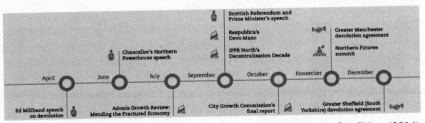

Figure 9.1 Progress Towards Devolution in 2014. *Source:* Centre for Cities. (2014). Cities Outlook 2015. London.

devolution to Scotland in the event of a 'no' vote put pressure on the Government to offer something more to cities.

Immediately following the decision of Scotland to stay in the United Kingdom, the Government set off to keep its promises of offering a new deal to Scotland. But any devolution to Scotland would also set a precedent for passing down powers to sub-national bodies, including cities.

The focus of devolution has remained on the larger cities in the United Kingdom, especially in the North. Increasingly, the focus on the Northern Powerhouse has kept ministers' attention on the large cities in the North, especially those with combined authorities. The historic deal in Manchester agreed in November 2014 and enhanced in March 2015 is unparalleled compared with any other cities. Sheffield and Leeds had more devolution, but their rejection of a metro mayor meant that their deals were much less comprehensive. So the new fire stoked by the Referendum still burns in Manchester, but many other places have been left as glowing embers seeking more fuel from government.

Desipite this progress, England's smaller and medium-sized cities have played second fiddle for the most part. They have received piecemeal projects and funding, and delivery of their City Deals has been slow, with some deals delivered in the summer of 2014. Now that devolution has subsequently been predicated on certain governance contingencies such as combined authorities and metro mayors, England's small and medium cities will face large institutional challenges in seeking out more powers (HM Treasury, 2015).

The rest of this chapter examines the devolution prospects for small- and medium-sized cities in the United Kingdom. Given the national scene and landmark deals for larger cities, many small- and medium-sized cities are still looking to Government for their devolution deals.

WHY DEVOLUTION, AND WHY TO CITIES AND CITY REGIONS?

The Power Deficit in Local Government

The root of the devolution movement lies in the power deficit in local government. If local government is meant to support economic growth, they need to have the resources and policy levers that underlie growth (Larkin, Wilcox, and Gailey, 2011). Relieving congestion on roads, providing infrastructure for new homes, giving people the skills they need for good jobs – all these rely on councils' ability to fund and respond to local business and resident needs.

The centralized governance and funding system in the United Kingdom hinders cities from making the most of their local economies (ibid). Councils lack the scale, control and financial systems to adequately respond to the needs of their local economy.

First, the scale of governance is either too large or too small. Budgets are set by Whitehall departments and allocated by local council boundaries rather than reflecting the 'real' economy of city regions. For example, most housing development decisions are made locally and are susceptible to NIMBY behaviours rather than responding to the housing need across the area people commute. Because the scale of funding and strategy are wrong, councils find it challenging to respond to the needs of the functional economy in city regions.

Second, local government also lacks adequate control over its finances and policies for the public services it delivers. Central government determines the funding for the majority of local authorities' budgets and exercises varying degrees of control over how local government spends grants. Local taxes, like Council Tax, are a small portion of local government budgets; Council Tax is less than 15 per cent of budgets on average. Councils spend most of their money on nationally set statutory services, with limited flexibility available to spend money according to local priorities (ibid).

Third, the finance system restricts councils' spending and investment behaviours and does not provide adequate incentives to support local development. Newly localized funding through business rates retention provides a small pot of funds and minimal growth incentive for local government. Also, local councils rarely benefit financially from being more efficient; cost savings or additional revenues often accrue to HM Treasury in the form of cost savings to central government departments. City Deals and Government's Community Budget programmes were important first steps, but on their own they are too limited in scope and scale to drive the economic growth the country needs.

In order to grow the UK economy, city economies need to be equipped with the tools, powers and flexibilities to drive growth. This means putting more powers and funding on the table at the city region and local levels to incentivize and enable places to act strategically when responding to local economic, social and political circumstances (McGough and Wilcox, 2014).

Why Cities Are Important to the National Economy and Policy

The case for devolution to cities has centred on a means to grow the national economy through growing local economies (HM Government, 2011). In the United Kingdom, national growth depends on cities. According to the 2015 *Cities Outlook* (Centre for Cities, 2014), cities account for 54 per cent of businesses and population in the United Kingdom but 59 per cent of jobs, 63 per cent of the Gross Value Added (GVA) and 72 per cent of high-skilled jobs.

Cities are, on the whole, more productive and hubs of increasing economic activity.

Cities represent the majority of the national economy and economic assets, but many UK city economies are performing below the national average. And economic performance has varied widely across the country. The Centre for Cities found:

> Only Bristol consistently performs better than the national average on a range of indicators, with four of the nine cities consistently underperforming the nation as a whole. This is in line with previous work that has showed that England's large cities are much smaller than large cities in other countries and tend to perform less well than their European counterparts. (ibid)

In turn, much of the City Deals initiative was predicated on the idea that Deals would help close the productivity gap for underperforming cities.

The United Kingdom's largest cities – the Core Cities – are incredibly important to the national economy in terms of both scale and trajectory of their economies. They represent some of the most successful and most challenging economies in the country, with London, Bristol, Manchester, Leeds and Newcastle adding the most net jobs nationally in the decade prior to the recession (1998–2008), while Birmingham and Nottingham had the biggest job losses over that period. While these cities are the biggest contributors to the country's economy, they also face some of the largest challenges with deprivation, skills and wages.

But the United Kingdom's small and medium cities (SMCs) are more dynamic. Examining the change rate rather than net number puts SMCs at both the top and bottom of jobs growth over that 1998–2008 period. Similarly, house price growth in Cambridge and Brighton has exceeded London's, and many SMCs are more innovative with more patents granted per capita than the larger cities in the United Kingdom (ibid).

In the devolution and City Deals process, this means that Government had the decision of pursuing scale and overall impact with the core cities or dynamism and speed of change with small and medium cities.

CITY REGIONS: GOVERNANCE AT SCALE

Having made the different cases for devolving to large cities and SMCs, Government still had to make the decision about how to define 'cities.' The Centre for Cities, Cities Growth Commission and various government departments define cities in different ways, be it the core local authority, the Primary Urban Area (which measures the built up environment) or the wider travel to work area (TTWA). It was recognized, though, that something larger than an individual local authority was needed as a basis for devolution.

City Regions: Policy and Strategy at Scale

City-region government helps fill a policy and strategy gap between the national and very local scales in England. Most businesses operate outside of their local authority – through sales, supply chains or the commuting of their employees – and rely on good transport links to support their activities. Almost half of commuters in cities live and work in different local authorities, and people conduct their daily lives across local authority boundaries for school, healthcare and shopping.[2]

But, most policies and programmes are still managed by Whitehall or by individual local authorities rather than at the scale of everyday life. The evidence suggests that urban areas perform better when administrative and economic areas match up (Cheshire and Gordon, 1998, Cheshire and Magrini, 2002). Local government increasingly recognizes that it needs to work together to be more efficient, reform services and coordinate their growth strategies. Investing in transport, skills, housing and the local economy needs to be at a scale larger than local, but smaller than national – the city region.

City Regions: Fiscal Management at Scale

Sub-national government can benefit from better fiscal management by working at the city-region level. Local authorities handle relatively small and fragmented pots of money for transport, housing, skills and economic development. This makes it harder to co-invest in major projects that span council boundaries, and it creates silos between investment areas, such as housing and transport, that are intrinsically linked.

City-region government, as a statutory body, can manage local government money differently. Because the body covers a wider geography, holds a larger sum of money and can pool resources, it can invest in projects to support their local economy more efficiently and effectively. Centre for Cities found that combined authorities can:

- Build scale: Councils have a larger pot of money which they can use to leverage additional investment from the private sector. This allows councils to undertake more activity than they could do on their own.
- Share risk: Since councils have more money to spend on a range of projects of varying risk levels, councils can develop a better portfolio of projects across the functional economic area (FEA).

- Coordinate investments: Local authorities can coordinate investment more effectively, planning strategically where and when to invest in housing, transport and regeneration schemes to maximise the effect.
- Invest efficiently: By pooling budgets, councils can achieve economies of scale in making and managing investments.
- Develop a project pipeline: The FEA should be able to better plan for and develop a pipeline of projects across the FEA. (Wilcox, Nohrova, and Williams, 2013).

PRINCIPLES FOR DEVOLVING TO SMALL AND MEDIUM CITIES

The Principles of an Effective Devolution Programme

The devolution programme that has suited the United Kingdom's largest cities will not necessarily suit its small and medium cities. The following three principles will shape devolution that suits the more dynamic SMCs:

First, government needs to offer something to every place. This means making devolution work for all sizes of cities as well as the more rural hinterlands. Within any new governance structures, urban and rural areas will need to have a better balance of powers to work through the tensions of urban development and better share the costs and benefits of growth.

Second, government must devolve to the appropriate geographic scale. The most effective devolution model would put the appropriate incentives and tools at the lowest level at which they are economically efficient. This means some powers may stay in Whitehall, some will be passed on to new city-region governments, and others may pass down direction to councils.

Lastly, good design of devolution will require strong local democratic accountability. George Osborne's requirement of a city-region mayor will help ensure that any new combined authorities or city-region structures are accountable to the public, and it will encourage that structure and the mayor to shape city-region policies around local knowledge and preferences. (McGough and Wilcox, 2014).

WHERE SHOULD DECISION MAKING AND FINANCIAL POWERS LIE?

Only those powers, responsibilities and funds that need to be more reactive to local needs should be devolved, and this may mean that some policies are designed nationally but delivered locally while others are wholly national or local (ibid).

Many powers that currently reside within Whitehall should remain within Whitehall. Fiscally, mobile taxes should be managed at the national level to avoid inefficient local tax competition. Policy areas that set the standards for the well-being and natural protections of UK citizens should stay at the national level, such as welfare or educational standards. Local government can still adapt the implementation of these programmes to local circumstances, but the outcomes and standards should remain nationally set and managed (London Finance Commission, 2013).

Local authorities and communities are still the most effective, efficient places to deliver many of the services and programmes they currently provide. Vital services, such as social care and business support, can be delivered effectively by councils, while communities should continue to develop neighbourhood plans, run youth programmes and maintain parks (ibid).

The role, therefore, of city-region government is to take on strategic policy, planning and financing of projects that should be more reactive to local needs than central government can provide, but support more coordination and scale compared to individual councils. Largely, this is reflected in the powers bestowed upon combined authorities in current legislation covering transport, housing, economic growth and skill strategies. (HM Government, 2009). But there is additional scope for bringing in public health, policing and other public services that could more effectively be planned across a city region.

WHAT WILL DEVOLUTION LOOK LIKE?

In a bottom-up, deal-based devolution system, different cities will design different solutions. Local historical and place-based factors (like existing relationships between councils and long-term economic performance) and complexity of local government system means that one size will not fit all. The boroughs in London have been working together for decades, and the GLA cemented additional powers for the capital that local government has been exercising since 1999. The Greater Manchester authorities have two decades of working together, which has built up their institutional capacity to manage additional powers.

But the two-tier system of local government in the United Kingdom means that some cities and their surrounding areas face institutional complexity. Because many small and medium cities are districts within counties or unitary authorities that border two-tier areas, the responsibilities and funding structures of those councils vary across the functional economic area. This

means that creating a London- or Greater Manchester-style combined authority where each member has equal powers is challenging.

The next section outlines a proposal for what devolution could look like
for SMCs and the implications for their scrutiny and accountability and the
corresponding role for Local Enterprise Partnerships.

PROSPECTS FOR DEVOLUTION TO MAJOR CITIES
AND SMALL AND MEDIUM-SIZED CITIES

Large, medium or small, devolution will only come about when the 'Four I's
align. But, these 'Four I's work for and against cities based on their scale and
individual characteristics. They are:

* *Incentives:* Government must put the strong and positive incentives on the
  table. Councils will not go for devolution unless there is a powerful upside
  for them, like more flexibility and funding for transport, housing and regeneration. The economic benefits of working together are often overshadowed
  by political issues.
* *Initiative:* Local government has to want to take devolution forward and
  be willing to accept the associated governance structures, responsibilities
  and risks.
* *Institutions:* Local government is institutionally complex, with different
  councils managing varying policies, programmes and services depending
  on its status as a two-tier county or district, unitary authority, metropolitan
  authority or London borough.
* *Imposition:* Central government will impose some changes on to local
  authorities, for example, George Osborne's requirement that devolution
  deals like Manchester's only go to combined authorities with a metropolitan mayor.

The closer a city is to the middle of the Venn diagram in Figure 9.2, with
the right incentives, local initiative, appropriate institutions and acceptance
of imposed rules from central government, the more likely it is to receive a
better devolution deal. Economic, political and institutional factors all affect
the prospects for devolution to UK cities. But one of the major challenges
for government is designing a form of English devolution that would work
through those factors to support cities – large and small – to adapt to more
austere ways of working and be more reactive to local economic needs.

Additionally, the Key Cities group is providing an important platform for
small and medium cities to speak to government with a collective voice. The
group of twenty-six cities has a collective population of 7.9 million and GVA

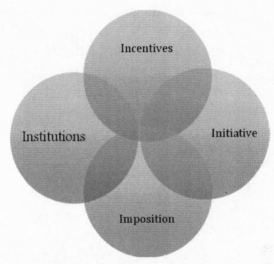

Figure 9.2   The 'Four I's of Devolution

of £164 billion, which means working with them is a more efficient political process and gives government a platform to discuss scale and impact when working with small and medium cities (Key Cities, 2015).

COMBINED AUTHORITIES IN ENGLAND'S LARGE CITIES SET THE PRECEDENT FOR DESIGNING DEVOLUTION

The seven largest English city regions outside of London represent about 25 per cent of the population, 23 per cent of jobs and just under 21 per cent of GVA (McGough and Wilcox, 2014). Five city regions have already come together to work in combined authorities: Greater Manchester, Liverpool City-region, the North East, Sheffield City-region, and West Yorkshire. Birmingham and Bristol city regions could be the next combined authorities to be established.

The combined authorities in England's largest cities set the precedent for the institutions other cities will need to receive additional powers. First, they have a statutory body status, which allows them to receive and spend money from central government (unlike LEPs). Second, the policy areas they manage – economic development, transport, regeneration and, increasingly, skills – match the key areas for city-region coordination. Third, they set in place a framework for transitioning powers to the appropriate scale, with some responsibilities passing up from constituent authorities to the combined authority. Together, this institution provides a long-term, recognized form of governance for city regions.

Table 9.1　The Size and Scale of the Core Cities and Combined Authorities

	Population (2013)	Jobs (Workplace-Based, 2013)	GVA (£m, 2012)
Combined Authority			
Greater Manchester	2,714,900	1,207,400	50,990
	5.0%	4.9%	4.3%
Liverpool City-region	1,512,600	594,800	25,320
	2.8%	2.4%	2.2%
North East	1,945,400	770,700	31,170
	3.6%	3.1%	2.7%
Sheffield City-region	1,358,200	531,900	20,640
	2.5%	2.2%	1.8%
West Yorkshire	2,252,300	993,900	42,910
	4.2%	4.0%	3.7%
Greater Birmingham (potential)	2,453,700	1,039,400	43,310
	4.6%	4.2%	3.7%
Greater Bristol (potential)	1,092,800	457,100	26,730
	2.0%	2.2%	2.3%
Combined Authority Total	13,329,900	5,685,200	241,070
	24.7%	23.2%	20.5%
	8,416,700	4,336,100	309,340
Greater London Authority	15.6%	17.7%	26.4%
	21,746,600	10,021,300	550,410
Total	40.4%	40.8%	46.9%

DESIGNING COMBINED AUTHORITIES FOR SMALL AND MEDIUM CITIES

The established combined authority structure and arrangements of the larger cities do not necessarily adapt well to the structures, politics and scale of SMCs. Thus, the system must take into account the particular needs of cities within the two-tier governance system.

SMCs also need a structure that can put cities and counties on an equal footing. Many cities are governed by district councils within a county system, meaning the city cannot plan for or invest in many of the factors that contribute to their economic growth and social well-being including education, transport and strategic planning (Figure 9.3). Thus, cities need to be empowered to work alongside their suburban and other neighbouring districts rather than competing against them for resources and attention at the county level.

For many SMCs, the creation of a combined authority-style body would be relatively straightforward. Seventeen cities outside the seven major city-region areas constitute unitary or metropolitan authorities. They could come together with their neighbouring counties in one single step to establish a combined authority.

The situation is more complex for other cities. Twelve small- and medium-sized cities are shire districts governed in two-tier systems, and another nine

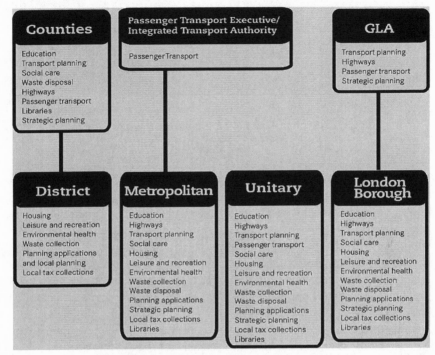

Figure 9.3 The Administrative Remit of Local Government Bodies. *Source*: Centre for Cities (2014). Economic Growth through Devolution.

Institutional Type	Number of Cities
Combined Authorities	14
PUA district	13
PUA Mets	4
PUA Unitary	15
PUA district & unitary	9
London (GLA + 13)	1

Figure 9.4 Complexity of City-Regions and Cities (Primary Urban Areas) in Small and Medium Cities. *Source*: Centre for Cities (2014). Economic Growth through Devolution.

cities are made up by some combination of shire districts and unitary or metropolitan districts. This is outlined in Figure 9.4.

The Local Democracy, Economic Development and Construction Act 2009 has provided for some cities – those represented by single metropolitan or unitary authorities – to establish a combined authority. And The Legislative Reform (Combined Authorities and Economic Prosperity Boards) (England)

Order 2015 removes burdens within the original legislation to allow councils to form combined authorities with all or part of their neighbouring counties (HM Government, 2015b). Together, the legislation now opens the doors to a wide range of different administrative and geographic combinations of councils (see Figure 9.5).

THE TWO-STEP PROCESS FOR ESTABLISHING SMC COMBINED AUTHORITIES

Ideally, a combined authority for a small or medium city would fulfil two criteria. First, it would incorporate the entirety of its associated county; else the county's strategy and budgets covering transport, planning, housing and skills would be split between its districts in the combined authority and those outside – generating institutional and financial complexity. Second, it should put the city on an equal footing with the county and remove administrative boundaries within the core urban area. This might mean that, ideally, a city would apply to the Secretary of State to become a unitary authority.

Depending on the statutory designation of a city, one of two approaches will need to be taken to establish a combined authority in that area.

If the city is a single unitary or metropolitan authority, the process is simpler. The city council has powers on an equal footing with the county, which allows it to form a strategic partnership. But if the city comprises one or more shire districts within a county, the process comprises two steps. It must first complete step one (below) to give the city equal powers with the county before coming together into a combined authority.

Step 1. Cities governed by shire districts within a county or multiple districts (shires and metropolitan or unitary bodies) could apply to the Secretary of State to become a single unitary authority. This provides a single governance structure for the core urban economy that has the management and funding powers to cover local issues. Of course, a city could forgo this step, but it would be underpowered in managing its local economy within the combined authority.

Step 2. The unitary authority (or authorities) form a statutory body with a county, forming the new combined authority. This body would manage transport, economic development, regeneration and some skills functions across the functional economic area.

The economic and political geography of city regions is complex. Even defining which areas are economically linked and best suited for these structures will be difficult in economic terms and challenging to agree politically. Often, city-regions may face resistance between the urban core and the more

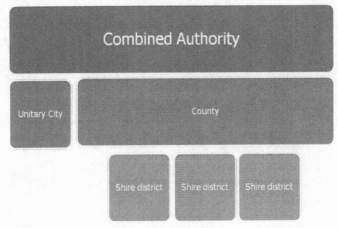

Figure 9.5   Structure of SMC Combined Authorities

rural areas of counties, which may not easily see how they are economically tied and are often of different political colours.

WHICH POWERS TO DEVOLVE

The exact powers that can be devolved to combined authorities are sufficiently vague in the legislation. Broadly, they constitute the administrative areas of local transport, economic development, regeneration and, to some extent, skills and housing (HM Government, 2009). Forthcoming legislative changes will allow combined authorities to regulate local bus services and take over the role of Police and Crime Commissioners (HM Government, 2015c).

On top of these powers, local government and public policy research groups have called for additional policy and finance powers. The City Growth Commission called for city regions to coordinate strategy through place-based budgeting and for longer term financial settlements for city regions among other powers not currently on the table (City Growth Commission, 2014). Figure 9.6 below summarizes the additional powers the Centre for Cities called for combined authorities in SMCs to gain.

GOVERNANCE, LEADERSHIP AND SCRUTINY

While the appropriate governance, leadership and scrutiny arrangements had been debated, the Conservative Government has made a clear commitment

Combined authority or city-county authority	Constituent authorities (unitary, county, metropolitan)
Strategic Planning	**Housing and planning**
Statutory strategic plan maker, control of public sector assets	Neighbourhood planning and development control
Transport	**Funding and finance**
Transport for London style body operating at city-region or city-county authority, integrated highways and rail functions, long-term funding settlements	Local taxation (rate setting and collection).
Jobs and Skills	(other functions of unitary authorities remain unchanged as a result of CA or CCA working)
Strategic co-commissioner in partnership with constituent authorities, central government and delivery bodies.	
Funding and finance	
City-region or city-county-region wide capital budgets, powers to raise local taxes or precepts, and borrow against income streams	

Figure 9.6   Additional Powers for Combined Authorities in Small and Medium Cities.
Source: Centre for Cities. (2014). Economic Growth through devolution.

to devolve to places with metro mayors. After the 2015 General Election, George Osborne made a speech in which he effectively coupled devolution with metro mayors, saying:

Here's the deal:
   We will hand power from the centre to cities to give you greater control over your local transport, housing, skills and healthcare. And we'll give the levers you need to grow your local economy and make sure local people keep the rewards.
   But it's right people have a single point of accountability: someone they elect, who takes the decisions and carries the can.
   So with these new powers for cities must come new city-wide elected mayors who work with local councils.
   I will not impose this model on anyone. But nor will I settle for less.
   London has a mayor.
   Greater Manchester has agreed to have a mayor as part of our Northern Powerhouse – and this new law will make that happen.
   My door now is open to any other major city who wants to take this bold step into the future.
   This is a revolution in the way we govern England.
   It's power to the working people of our country.

And it means a stronger democracy and greater prosperity for all. (HM Treasury and The Rt Hon George Osborne MP, 2015)

This was confirmed in the Queen's Speech and will enshrine in legislation the connection between devolution and metro mayors.

Thus, only those SMCs that come forward with a directly elected metro mayor will reap the full benefits of devolution. But small and medium cities will link in with more suburban and rural areas compared to the metropolitan combined authorities in the North. Thus, having one voice and accountable leader from a metro mayor will be both a big advantage and politically challenging.

Mayors provide the visibility, legitimacy and decision-making power to work across councils and with the private sector that no other leadership structure can offer. A mayor can help city governments to be decisive on issues of strategic economic importance, represent the city to local business and central government, coordinate strategy and investments of the public sector and collaborate with local authorities, business and other players in the wider local economy (Swinney, Smith, and Blatchford, 2011).

Direct election by residents from across a city, not just a single ward, should encourage strategic decision making that aligns the interests of the functional economy. This is because mayors should be elected to represent the interests of a city as a whole, be a figurehead for the city region and represent the urban, suburban and further-reaching interests. A single, visible leader for the city region also provides a clear point of contact and responsibility with whom central government and business can engage with the area.

Directly elected city-region mayors should be held to account by the leaders of the combined authorities. Unlike the assembly model in London, it is likely that in combined authorities the Mayor would be held to account by the combined authority. To that end, the Mayor should be required to:

- Act as a public figure and representative for the city region
- Consult on his or her draft statutory strategies and must consider doing so before exercising the general powers of the authority (similar to s. 30(1) of the GLA Act 1999)
- Set and publicize his or her strategies, produced through the combined authority
- Produce annual reports
- Hold an annual 'State of the City Debate'
- Hold public meetings, where members of the public may ask questions.[3]

Combined authorities in SMCs could opt to either have the metro mayor work with the combined authority leadership (made up of the leaders of the individual councils) or put in place a directly elected cabinet below the metro mayor, similar to the London Assembly model. While the cabinet is currently not being debated in government, this model has been discussed in the policy arena as an option to support democratic accountability for small and medium cities, (McGough and Wilcox, 2014).

A cabinet could bring together many voices – both urban and rural – to build a consensus and strategy for the area. All cabinet members would be elected to represent the combined authority area as a whole, since the constituent authority leaders in the combined authority would represent the local authorities' interests.

IMPLICATIONS OF DEVOLUTION FOR LOCAL ENTERPRISE PARTNERSHIPS

Local Enterprise Partnerships are the only comprehensive sub-national governance structure above individual councils. Their geography is complex, often overlapping one another, and LEPs can cover parts of counties. This geographic complexity has also led to political and strategic planning complexity. For example, Government took strategic decisions on how to allocate funding to LEPs in which a single council is covered by two different LEPs. And, while county councils currently manage transport for their districts, LEPs make strategic decisions over some infrastructure funding; this can cause inefficiencies and coordination challenges when a county is covered by multiple LEPs.

LEPs are currently tasked with coordinating government programmes and the business community around economic strategy for groups of local authorities. LEPs also have responsibility for developing multi-year Strategic Economic Plans for their area and receive allocations from the Growing Places Fund to tackle infrastructure investment constraints and they now have responsibility for delivering part of the EU Structural and Investment Funds for 2014–2020.

The Role of LEPs with the Emergence of Combined Authorities

The roles and responsibilities of LEPs have evolved over time, and they will need to adapt to the new powers and geography of combined authorities. LEPs are not statutory bodies; thus, they are not best situated to manage budgets or deliver services. In addition, they could duplicate work undertaken by city-region government or local government, adding additional costs.

With combined authorities taking the strategic position for city regions, and since they are a statutory body that can make investments and hold funding, they are the best suited for driving the city-region investments and strategies. But there is still an important role for LEPs.

LEPs provide a vital strategic business perspective, and they should keep combined authorities accountable to the business community. To that end, LEPs should maintain three key roles: those of advisor, promoter and co-signatory. As advisor, LEPs should provide private sector input and insight for policy and strategy. As a promoter, LEPs should promote the city-region assets for inward investment and lobby government for supporting the business environment in their city region. Finally, as co-signatory, LEPs should provide partnership and de-risk investment through commitment. They should be required to sign off strategic priorities and investment plans for transport, economic development, housing and skills for their area.

Implications for the Boundaries of LEPs

The spatial challenge with LEPs will lie in creating a coherent map that aligns with the geography of combined authorities. Because the purpose of LEPs and combined authorities is to provide a coherent strategy for city regions, their boundaries should align to ensure they are working together effectively.

Government has not expressed an interest in redrawing the LEP map, but it will become increasingly important as more combined authorities come forward and LEPs become more established in their role of bringing together local government and the private sector.

In order to make the most of combined authorities and LEPs – to ensure they are complementary and additional to one another – they should cover the same geography. One LEP could cover multiple combined authorities, but the outer boundaries should align. LEPs should not split a combined authority nor should they overlap. This could potentially reduce the number of LEPs.

CONCLUSION

The United Kingdom is only at the beginning of a long process of devolution. The Scottish devolution bill, negotiations with Wales and Northern Ireland over passing down powers, and the Northern Powerhouse are only in their infant states. There is much more work to be done, and Government will have to prioritize their attention and funding.

Given the 'Four I's necessary for devolved power, devolution will be uneven across the country in both scope and scale depending on places' ability to meet the criteria. Government has set out the incentives and imposed the rules of the game: metro mayors and combined authorities. That leaves local initiative and the right institutions for local councils and government to set out.

Manchester and London meet all the criteria and have the most powers of any city regions. In particular, their willingness to accept a mayor and form the appropriate institutions laid the foundation for a body to receive new powers. Not to mention, their size and economic importance put them at the forefront of devolving power. Other cities with combined authorities are likely to receive new devolution deals, but their acceptance of metro mayors and their own ambition and initiative will largely determine how revolutionary their deals will be.

More and more cities are bringing forward proposals for combined authorities because they recognize the importance of those institutions and of showing the initiative to getting more control from Whitehall. Those small and medium cities that bring forward the right institutions will be the most successful, but designating combined authorities in the two-tier county system can be difficult to define and messy to assign. An ideal combined authority for SMCs would ensure that cities operate on an equal footing with counties, managed by a unitary authority. Previously, there has been little political appetite to do this.

The ambition of SMCs will play an important part in how much they get from Government, reflecting the range of devolution in the Wave 2 City Deals. Now is the time for cities to think radically and make a strong economic case for how devolution will support economic growth.

It is highly unlikely that any city, large or small, will receive another Greater Manchester-style deal, but the opportunities are out there for significant devolution in England's small and medium cities to revolutionize local government and drive economic growth.

NOTES

1 This research was largely conducted by the author and colleagues at the Centre for Cities and draws heavily from the research conducted and coauthored by the author at the Centre for Cities. Accordingly, this work reflects the analysis and insights represented in works preceding its publication. However, updates to the research conducted after the Centre for Cities publications are those of the author.

2 See 2011 Census Commuting Data.

3 See London Assembly. How the Mayor of London is held to account. http://legacy.london.gov.uk/assembly/docs/how-mayor-held-to-account.pdf

REFERENCES

Bolton, T. (2012). *Wave 2 Breaks: Deals on the Table for English Cities*. London: Centre for Cities.

Centre for Cities. (2014). *Cities Outlook 2014*. London: Centre for Cities.

Cheshire, P., and Gordon, I. (1998). Territorial Competition: Some Lessons for Policy, *The Annals of Regional Science*, 32, 3: 321–46.

Cheshire, P. C., and Magrini, S. (2002). The Distinctive Determinants of European Urban Growth: Does One Size Fit All?: *LSE Research Online*, Available at http://eprints.lse.ac.uk/archive/00000569 (accessed 01/06/15).

City Growth Commission. (2014). *Unleashing Metro Growth: Final Recommendations of the City Growth Commission*. London: Royal Society for the Arts, Available at http://www.citygrowthcommission.com/wp-content/uploads/2014/10/City-Growth-Commission-Final-Report.pdf (accessed 01/06/15).

HM Government. (2009). *Local Democracy, Economic Development and Construction Act 2009*, Available at http://www.legislation.gov.uk/ukpga/2009/20/pdfs/ukpga_20090020_en.pdf (accessed 01/06/15).

HM Government. (2011). *Unlocking Growth in Cities*, Available at https://www.gov.uk/government/uploads/system/uploads/attachment_data/file/7523/CO (accessed 01/06/15).

HM Government. (2012). *Unlocking Growth in Cities: City Deals – Wave 1*, Available at https://www.gov.uk/government/uploads/system/uploads/attachment_data/file/221009/Guide-to-City-Deals-wave-1.pdf (accessed 01/06/15).

HM Government. (2015a). *2010 to 2015 Government Policy: City Deals and Growth Deals*. Policy Paper, London: Stationary Office, Available at https://www.gov.uk/government/publications/2010-to-2015-government-policy-city-deals-and-growth-deals/2010-to-2015-government-policy-city-deals-and-growth-deals.

HM Government. (2015b). *Giving Local Authorities Greater Flexibility in Forming a Combined Authority or Economic Prosperity Board, The Legislative Reform (Combined Authorities and Economic Prosperity Boards) (England) Order 2015*, Available at http://www.legislation.gov.uk/ukdsi/2015/9780111135419/pdfs/ukdsiod_9780111135419_en.pdf (accessed 01/06/15).

HM Government. (2015c). *Queen's Speech 2015*, Available at https://www.gov.uk/government/speeches/queens-speech-2015 (accessed 01/06/15).

HM Treasury and The Rt Hon George Osborne MP. (2015). Chancellor, on Building a Northern Powerhouse. Speech at Victoria Warehouse, Manchester. 14 May.

Innes, D., and Tetlow, G. (2015). *Central Cuts, Local Decision-Making: Changes in Local Government Spending and Revenues in England, 2009–2010 to 2014–2015*, London: Institute for Fiscal Studies, Available at http://www.ifs.org.uk/publications/7617 (accessed 01/06/15).

Key Cities. (2015). *About Key Cities*, Available at http://www.keycities.co.uk/about Accessed: 11 June 2015.

Larkin, K., Wilcox, Z., and Gailey, C. (2011). *Room for Improvement: Creating the Finance Incentives Needed for Economic Growth*. London: Centre for Cities.

Local Government Association. (2013). The General Power of Competence. Empowering Councils to Make a Difference. London: Local Government Association.

London Finance Commission. (2013). Raising the Capital: The Report of the London Finance Commission, London: London Finance Commission, Available at http://www.london.gov.uk/sites/default/files/Raising%20the%20capital.pdf (accessed 01/06/15).

McGough, L., and Wilcox, Z. (2014). *Economic Growth Through Devolution: Towards a Plan for Cities and Counties Across England.* London: Centre for Cities, Available at http://www.centreforcities.org/wp-content/uploads/2014/11/14-11-13-Economic-growth-through-devolution.pdf (accessed 01/06/15).

Swinney, P., Smith, R., and Blatchford, K. (2011). *Big Shot or Long Shot? How Elected Mayors Can Help Drive Economic Growth in England's Cities.* London: Centre for Cities and Institute for Government.

Wilcox, Z., Nohrova, N., and Williams, M. (2013). *Breaking Boundaries: Empowering City Growth Through Cross-Border Collaboration.* London: Centre for Cities: London.

Wilcox, Z., and Sarling, J. (2013). *Ways and Means: Money Management and Power in Local Government,* London: Centre for Cities: London.

Chapter 10

City Dealing in Wales and Scotland

Examining the Institutional Contexts and Asymmetric Arrangements for Policy Making

David Waite

INTRODUCTION

The institutional dimensions underpinning an ongoing wave of city dealing in Wales and Scotland are the core concern of this chapter. Lagging behind steps made in England – as has historically been the case for cities policy in Wales and Scotland – city dealing is firing the imagination of local leaders around the potential for metropolitan development. This chapter considers how city dealing, originally reflecting a bilateral bidding programme involving central government and local bodies in England – with long-term funding made available for infrastructure, sector and labour market programmes *inter alia* – in Scotland and Wales is being inflected by (1) austerity; (2) local entrepreneurialism; and (3) the shifting logics of localism.

Not privy to the closed-door negotiations that mark City Deals, this chapter sets out the institutional framings that are likely to be shaping deal-making in Wales and Scotland. Given the role of the administrations at Cardiff Bay, in Wales, and Holyrood, in Scotland, a complex tri-partite negotiating position is immediately presented (e.g., Glasgow and neighbouring local authorities; the Scottish Government and the UK Government). To hint at the key institutional dimensions, in what is a fast-shifting policy context, material in this chapter is compiled from an analysis of secondary data sources, including the serious media; think tank reports; and policy documentation from council and government sources.

Positioned as the empirical focus, City Deals permit a broader discussion of how urban policy is becoming entangled within logics and demands for spatially balanced economic development; parity in sub-national policy making; and a coherent state system across the United Kingdom. Additionally, as a conceptual concern, City Deals provide a rich lens for considering how cities policy takes shape at relational rather than closed territorial geographies.

The chapter proceeds with an outline of the asymmetric policy making contexts that city dealing both reflects and contributes to. Following a brief sketch of prior Welsh and Scottish approaches to cities policy, an overview is given of what City Deals encompass, including the stakeholders involved, the policy programmes embedded and their overall objectives. Three key institutional dimensions that shape dealing in Scotland and Wales are brought into focus, before some concluding thoughts are set out with reflections given on recent political developments.

ASYMMETRIC CONTEXTS

To begin to consider how and on what terms city dealing is emerging in Wales and Scotland, some sense of the fragmented institutional arrangements at play is required. Simply put, cities across the United Kingdom are starting from different positions as they seek to negotiate funding and policy arrangements. This reflects what powers and levers are in the gift of local authorities at present, and what attention such authorities receive from levels of national government, where the future distribution of public funds is partially at stake. To varying degrees, such contexts shape compulsions for and capacities to participate in deal making.

The polycentric state in the United Kingdom was set in train, most substantially, by the establishment of a parliament at Holyrood and an assembly at Cardiff Bay in 1999, as well as by the formation of the Greater London Authority (GLA) (Morgan, 2007). This placed powers over housing, planning and economic development *inter alia* with the devolved entities, though the powers are not distributed evenly. What powers the aforementioned bodies should have responsibility for have been brought into sharper focus through recent political developments.

First, the London Finance Commission has argued that the GLA warrants greater ability to raise revenues and glean appropriate rewards from the capital investments being made. Such matters are likely to come to attention once more through the upcoming mayoral vote (in 2016). Second, and more starkly, the Scottish Referendum, and the follow-up work of the Smith Commission, has shredded any sense that Scotland can be administered as it had been before, through the dominant levers held in Whitehall and Westminster. New, strengthened (though hotly contested) settlements for Scotland have in turn triggered debates in Wales about the more modest allocation of powers to Cardiff Bay to date. In this regard, policy makers in Wales – granted less powers than Scotland to start with (Morgan, 2007) – see a Westminster

Government focusing energies on attempting to appease the now embold-ened Scottish nationalists. This results, it would appear, in the challenges for Wales emerging almost as an afterthought. I will return to this fragmentation further below; however, an initial sense of the complex institutional back-cloth to city dealing can be gleaned.

Departing from the asymmetry in place now – as elucidated by the London, Scottish and Welsh contexts – asymmetric devolution has also been used to frame arguments concerning ways or, more particularly, steps, by which to fiscally equip and empower sub-national areas in England. In this sense, asymmetric devolution is a recommended path to take for further agreeing to and delivering cities policies. Arguments developed in this second, normative sense hinge on the differing perceived capacities of local bodies. IPPR North has noted, for example, that for too long, devolution has been held up by the least able or the 'slower ships in the convoy' (Cox, Henderson, and Raikes, 2014). This time, they contest, local bodies that can demonstrate capacity through accountable governance mechanisms, coherent prioritization and a willingness to manage risk should be handed the powers to drive economic development forward, and not be held back by those that do not demonstrate the requisite capacity (Cox, Henderson, and Raikes, 2014). Such logics underpin, in part, why the deal for Manchester looks different, qualitatively and quantitatively, from the deal for Birmingham.

Taking a non-proceduralist bent, perceived outcomes from devolution also sit behind rationales for pursuing devolution in a piecemeal manner. Though rarely articulated in such express terms – and resting on patchy empirical bases that concern the link between devolution and economic growth (Pike et al., 2012) – the logic here is that giving powers to drive growth in Leeds is likely to have a greater effect on the UK economy than giving powers to Car-lisle. In other words, and reflecting the vogue for metropolitan issues as held by policy makers, the appetite for devolution to cities is influenced by actual or perceived agglomeration economies. As a result, some places are simply left out of city dealing altogether,[1] while for those smaller medium-size cities such as Plymouth and Hull that have forged a city deal in Wave 2, policy and fiscal settlements appear to be far more modest.

Asymmetric devolution thus has two dimensions as concerns this chapter: one, the prevailing political structure stemming from the piecemeal handing down of powers to nations and dominant regions within the United Kingdom; and, two, the ethos of enabling those local bodies that signal that they can manage the risks and responsibilities for economic development policy and that reside in a context where dynamic economies of scale and scope can be triggered. City dealing in Wales and Scotland must be read, I argue, as a com-ing together, perhaps uneasily, of these two asymmetric patterns. While for some, asymmetry reflects the practical path to take within an incrementalist political system, the ad-hoc piecemeal approach has raised questions about equity and cohesiveness (Waite, Maclennan and O'Sullivan, 2013; Martin, Pike, Tyler and Gardiner, 2015).

POLICY MAKING FRAMEWORKS IN WALES AND SCOTLAND

Offering further context, in addition to the issues brought about by policy asymmetry in the United Kingdom, some similar and some divergent characteristics can be observed in Welsh and Scottish approaches to cities policy. In Wales, cities policy has suffered from a perceived 'anti-urban bias' as well as a lack of persistence and continuity, some have argued (Morgan, 2014). Previous attempts at fashioning urban policy have, indeed, resulted in approaches that, while giving rhetorical support, perhaps lacked bite and a commitment to delivery. Compulsive reorganization – including the winding up and internalization of the Welsh Development Agency (WDA) by the Welsh Government – may be cited as one contributing factor. Moreover, contestation between local authorities and the Welsh Government at various points, animated by 'personality clashes', have further contributed to fitful policy undertakings (Morgan, 2006a). The redevelopment of Cardiff Bay – a high-profile regeneration project – was realized, however.

Strategic planning also shapes, at a technical level, how urban places have been and are being conceived in Wales. In 2008 the Wales Spatial Plan was set out, framing spatial development in terms of nodes and corridors. This pointed to Cardiff's role in the spatial hierarchy of south-east Wales, for example. Though the spatial plan has now been cast aside, new planning legislation in the form of the Planning (Wales) Bill (2014) does seek to re-install a systems approach through the requirement for spatial development plans.[2] Taking a congruent territorial focus, some revival has also been given to city-regionalism through the recommendations of the Haywood 'task and finish group', which, in 2012, suggested that city-region Boards be established for Cardiff and Swansea. The transitory bodies take advisory roles and, at present, are involved in setting out high-level visions as well as working up suggestions for future urban governance (mindful, in Cardiff at least, of City Deal opportunities). Finally, and impacting the appetite and capacity for cities policy, the future shape of local government is under the spotlight in Wales. This followed the report of the Williams Commission, which recommended a reduction in the numbers of local authorities across Wales through consolidation (in the Cardiff city region, ten local authorities presently exist) (Commission on Public Service Governance and Delivery, 2014).

Policy approaches in Scotland have also suffered from fits and starts, though there is arguably a greater institutional capacity for place making.

With respect to cities policy set out by the Scottish Executive, a review was delivered in 2003. The review set out recommendations for governance and funding; however, this gained little traction. A concerted restatement of cities policy did not emerge from the Scottish Government until 2011, when the Scottish National Party (SNP) administration followed through on its manifesto commitment to establish the Scottish Cities Alliance (SCA). The SCA, covering seven cities, has developed investment plans, which, though set out for each city on a case-by-case basis, were commissioned in unison. Joint property promotion activities, through events such as MIPIM, have also been coordinated through the SCA. Focus has now moved on to managing and negotiating city deals (as other cities look to emulate what has been agreed for Glasgow).

As in Wales, spatial planning offers a systems lens to the economy in Scotland. The National Planning Framework (NPF), now in its third iteration, coupled with strategic development plans for the four major city regions,[3] gives some perspective on how nationally significant infrastructure frames urban development. Institutionally, Scottish Enterprise has had a role in promoting a place narrative and, at one point, sponsored significant urban regeneration activities (such as 'Glasgow East Area Renewal' and the 'Leith Project'). Capacity for financing urban infrastructure is also provided by the Scottish Futures Trust.[4] With respect to local government, finally, some local authorities have expressed frustration with the Scottish Government's decision to freeze council taxes (Glasgow City Council, 2014). Aberdeen, a prospective dealing city, has also long contested that it has been underfunded, given the Scottish Government's approach to calculating local authority grants (Urquhart, 2014; Hebditch, 2015).

One can argue that cities policy has been pursued hesitantly and sporadically in Wales and Scotland over recent decades (though this needs to be distinguished from a wider suite of policies impacting cities, such as regeneration). However, the lure of funding pots offered through city dealing is serving to galvanize metropolitan interests.

CITY DEALING

City Deals reflect a striking innovation in urban development policy in the United Kingdom. Rolled out in two waves to date – with Scotland and Wales perhaps representing Wave 3 – City Deals have bound the economic development of the United Kingdom's 'core', and a number of 'key', cities in agreements with Whitehall. City Deals, through medium to long-term funding commitments, and are seen to be critical tools in shaping the trajectory, pace and nature of local economic development.

Central to City Deals is a *quid pro quo* – demonstrable local accountability and capacity for long-term central government funding commitments. In
terms of the latter, City Deals provide resources for infrastructure development, labour market programmes and welfare delivery, amongst a wider set
of interventions. A recent note by the Centre for Cities (2014) usefully charts
the features of deals agreed to date – including the governance arrangements
put in place across the Core Cities – however, the following factors and
themes can be drawn out in the context of this chapter:

- First, City Deals are typically struck for functional geographies rather than
  for existing administrative scales. This is considered to be important, in
  that, for many of the core cities, local authorities significantly underbound
  the real urban geography (consider Manchester City Council within Greater
  Manchester, for example). A push to city-regionalism – taking the form
  of cross-LA collaborations and combined authorities – has thus been supported by city dealing.
- Second, a number of city deals contain innovative approaches to urban
  infrastructure development. In Manchester through 'earn back' and in
  Cambridge through 'gain share', local and combined authorities are incentivized to invest in infrastructure as a portion of additional growth in tax
  receipts, stemming from the investment, will return to local actors (rather
  than the UK government).[5] In Greater Manchester, this is seen to create
  the opportunity to establish a 'revolving infrastructure fund' to support
  future public investment needs (GMCA, 2012). Other cities have arrived
  at 'development deals', which are predicated on tax increment financing
  (TIF)- type arrangements (HM Government, 2012).
- Third, City Deals respond to the sectoral and economic bases of cities in
  various ways. This can involve apprenticeships and collaborations with
  education providers (Leeds) or may refer to the provision of small business
  support (Southend-on Sea), enabling firms to more effectively grasp supply
  chain opportunities (Tees Valley). In this way, City Deals may have a role
  in conditioning the 'strategic coupling' of places within global production
  networks (Mackinnon, 2012).
- Fourth, welfare issues feature in different ways and with variable emphases
  across the deals. In Glasgow, a collaboration with the Department for Work
  and Pensions (DWP), working with recipients of employment support
  allowance, takes a prominent position. In Leicester, the city deal involves
  approaches with young offenders to secure employment and training,
  while, in Hull, a 'personalised budget' has been set out for young people,
  enabling them to acquire services that lower barriers to employment.

It must be recognized, moreover, that City Deals do not exist in isolation
in England. Indeed, the establishment of local enterprise partnerships (LEPs),

a replacement for the regional development agencies (RDAs), and funding provided through Growth Deals, point to a multifaceted policy environment. City deals mesh, moreover, with a prominent narrative concerning spatial rebalancing, whereby policy makers are increasingly eager to address the differential economic performance of London and the south-east relative to the rest of the United Kingdom. A complex institutional environment that in various ways binds central and local government is therefore present.

With Greater Manchester capturing the limelight – as the push for 'Devo Manc' continues (Blond and Morrin, 2014) – cities and city regions in Scotland and Wales have been interrogating City Deal possibilities. In the summer of 2014, Glasgow became the first city region outside of England to strike a deal with the UK government (HM Government, 2014a). The Glasgow and Clyde Valley City Deal secures over £1 billion worth of investment for infrastructure and sets out cooperative arrangements for the delivery of labour market interventions as well as sector-based programmes *inter alia*. The deal document claims that 29000 jobs will be created as a result of the interventions made (HM Government, 2014a). Significantly, and reflecting the institutional differences presented in Scotland vis-à-vis England, the infrastructure commitment is premised on an equal contribution of £500 million from both Westminster and Holyrood (with the residual provided by partner city-region authorities). An inescapable politics, tied to the Scottish Independence Referendum, underpins the Glasgow deal, however, and this is outlined further below.

Whatever the drivers or rationales, Glasgow provides a precedent for City Deals in the Celtic nations. Indeed, it is now apparent that deals are being sought by Edinburgh, Aberdeen, Dundee, Inverness and Cardiff (while signals are also being made by authorities in Belfast in Northern Ireland). Edinburgh's bid, though at a nascent stage, is being prepared under the slogan 'gateway to new investment' (City of Edinburgh Council, 2014a) and, in associated policy positions, the possibility has been raised that the changing development trajectories for the Leith Docks may feature in some form (Edinburgh Council, 2014b). Longer in gestation, Aberdeen has been staking its claim for a city deal since early 2014. This has taken on a new urgency since late 2014, as a result of falling oil prices (given the reliance of the city-region economy on the natural resources sector) (Aberdeen City Council, 2015). In a less evolved state, Dundee is considering making a City Deal bid with Perth (*The Courier*, 2015), while Inverness saw City Deal plans advocated for by the now ousted Liberal Democrat MP, Danny Alexander (Ross, 2015).[6]

In Wales, a recent cabinet paper shows that jobs and output growth, along with reducing welfare dependency, are key focus points for City Deal negotiations for Cardiff (City of Cardiff Council, 2015). While project prioritization is yet to take place, advocates for the south-east Wales Metro claim that city deal funds could be usefully directed towards connectivity aims hinging on improved transport links between Cardiff and the surrounding Valleys and urban centres (Deans, 2015).

Mindful of these emergent bidding and negotiating arrangements, what are the key institutional factors that will shape how and on what terms City Deals are struck in Wales and Scotland?

INSTITUTIONAL DIMENSIONS SHAPING CITY DEALING IN SCOTLAND AND WALES

There are three logics or conditions that, though not exhaustive, reflect critical institutional dimensions for city dealing in Welsh and Scottish cities: austerity, local entrepreneurialism, and localism. These reflect different urgencies from economic rupture to long-running concerns about the cohesiveness and optimality of the state system. Varied political geographies also come into focus, from the relationally administered to the territorially validated. Each dimension is now detailed in turn.

Austerity

Following the vicissitudes of the Global Financial Crisis (GFC), public sector budgets have been in retreat. This has been variously framed, on the one hand, as necessary 'difficult decisions' to keep the house in order following a decade of largesse (HM Government, 2014), to an ideological commitment of the current Westminster administration to reduce the size and scope of the state (Harrop, 2013), on the other. Regardless of legitimating or counter narrative, local authorities have faced, and are continuing to face, stark budgetary challenges – leading some to raise the notion of 'austerity localism' (Mackinnon, Cumbers and Featherstone, 2015). This has proven to be the case in England; however, in Wales and Scotland, because of local government being a devolved area, the nature and timing of budgetary constraints have differed.

In terms of the cities with, or looking at, dealing arrangements, there is a striking realization that there is a need to do more with less. For example, Cardiff, facing a drop in grant from the Welsh Government of 2.9% (Blake, 2014), needs to make up a budget gap of £124 million over the next three years (to 2017–2018) (City of Cardiff Council, 2014). Proposed arrangements to deal with this have led to ongoing political disputes and a no confidence motion imposed on the leader (Mosalski and Silk, 2014).[7] In Scotland, Glasgow needs to make up a funding gap of £28.9 million for 2015–2016, with the council leader pointing the finger at the Scottish Government and their determination to freeze council taxes (Glasgow City Council, 2014).

Edinburgh, on the other hand, needs to save £22 million for 2015–2016 (City of Edinburgh Council, 2015), then £67 million by 2017–2018 (Audit Scotland, 2014). For some, the strains of austerity have changed the nature of local democracy by impairing service provision (Bale, 2015). This goes from hygiene factors and areas of local service delivery, to strategically significant investments. Pressure on local budgets is not exclusive to the United Kingdom, however, with Peck (2012) bringing into view the politics of urban austerity in North America.

As financial constraints on local authorities bite further, a key rationale is provided to agree to a deal with the UK government, as City Deals channel in funds to support policies and investments over the medium to long term. A number of commentators have argued, indeed, that infrastructure investment takes on heightened importance following economic shocks, given its role in stimulating economic activity (Summers, 2014; Krugman, 2014). For cities that have been hit hard by recession, such as Glasgow, this may be particularly vital (Townsend and Champion, 2014).

However, a key aspect of City Deals is risk sharing, and it is expected that local authorities – as has proven to be the case in Glasgow – will provide a financial contribution for the proposed capital investments (£130 million of the total £1.13 billion in Glasgow). This, some consider, is an essential part of having 'skin in the game', (RSA, 2015). In Cardiff, given the need for financial contributions, questions have recently been raised as to whether such a commitment can be justified given the council's fiscal challenges (Shipton, 2015; also see Martin, Gardiner and Tyler, 2014). More generally, in the ongoing negotiations taking place, careful scrutiny will need to be given to how local authority contributions mesh with the episodic release of central government funds at key programme 'gateways' and the risks around further periods of slow growth.[8]

Most hard to fathom for local authorities in Wales and Scotland, perhaps, is that, it is not at all clear when financial settlements for local authorities will begin to improve. The age of long austerity may give the impression to some that city dealing is simply central government giving with one hand while taking with the other.

In summary, austerity makes city dealing attractive, as local authorities can consider investments that would have otherwise been beyond reach. However, agreeing to and implementing deals can be challenging and local authorities must be able to find contributing funds from already stretched budgets.

Local Entrepreneurialism

While austerity reflects the reach of global and national logics impacting local finances, there remains a local political narrative that affects city dealing arrangements. In this respect, and with the aim of propelling economic growth, local entrepreneurialism reflects the eagerness of local leaders to advocate and seek resources for investment in their local economies. At the heart of local entrepreneurialism, alongside the prominent roles taken by business interests, is the positioning of cities and city regions as trailblazers for economic development (in terms of both the spatial system in focus and the policies attending to the system) in a context where, by itself, perhaps, centrally orchestrated policy is seen to lack the ability to support growth. The ubiquity of entrepreneurialist positions can be evidenced through (1) the boosterist claims of policy makers, (2) the tendency to privilege 'flag-ship' projects (Macleod, 2002); and (3) the primacy afforded to marketing and branding initiatives (McCann, 2013). Propping up entrepreneurialism, moreover, are the careers of politicians who may seek public recognition and upward mobility.

Though locally reasoned and validated, local entrepreneurialism is a prod-uct of policy transfer, with key organizations and actors promulgating the story of city empowerment (Hollis, 2015). For example, work by ResPublica (Blond and Morrin, 2015) and the RSA City Growth Commission (2014) – which, in many aspects, resembles the core narrative of the Brookings Metro-politan Policy Program in the United States (Katz and Bradley, 2013a) – form part of a wider policy lobby that sets out to arm leaders with stories of strong local leadership spurring city success. Bringing the entrepreneurial logic into sharp focus, Katz and Bradley (2013b) note with respect to the US context:

> In the face of federal gridlock, economic stagnation and fiscal turmoil, power is shifting away from Washington, and even state capitals towards our major cit-ies and metropolitan areas. These communities, and the networks of pragmatic leaders who govern them, are taking on the big issues that Washington won't, or can't, solve.

Emphasis on city leadership has inflected policy narratives in the United Kingdom for a significant period of time (Morgan, 2006b). The new mayor for powers regime – which offers greater devolution where a mayor is installed at a city-region level (as is being pioneered in Greater Manchester) – reflects the latest manifestation (Wintour, 2015; Elkes, 2015). Co-opting support from business interests critically shapes and validates local leader-ship, moreover. As an example, the city-region advisory boards in Cardiff and Swansea consist of members from the private sector alongside local authority representatives.[9]

Given the competitive nature of city dealing, local entrepreneurialism, one may argue, is perhaps necessary for local bodies to be heard by Whitehall and Westminster. Indeed, the *quid pro quo* of city dealing requires local bodies to develop, along with robust governance, a clear sense of what opportunities exist in their local area – leading to the preparation of an offer that the UK Government 'can't refuse' (Denholm-Hall, 2015). In delineating the ask and mindful of the competition for funding pots, leaders and officials may be prone to overstating the nature of economic transformation that can emerge.

While city dealing arguably gives renewed emphasis, local entrepreneurialism is not a new phenomenon. In this respect, Harvey's (1989) conjecture that local governance has pivoted from managerialism – and the effective provision and distribution of public goods and services – to entrepreneurialism, remains a seminal reflection.

Localism

Mindful of the policy contexts in Wales and Scotland set out earlier, changing governance relationships, which can be grouped under the broad rubric of localism (Clarke and Cochrane, 2013), are noteworthy. These relationships concern the actor dimensions and the related power geometries, as well as shifts in the underpinning logics for localism.

In the first instance, the relationships between local bodies and the administrations in Cardiff Bay and Holyrood are of interest. Shot through debates about council tax freezes and the retention of growth in business rates, in this respect, is a narrative, articulated by local bodies, that Holyrood and Cardiff Bay are simply centralizing power themselves (of the powers the UK Government has ceded). For example, Cllr Phil Bale, leader of Cardiff Council, recently noted:

> I believe we in Wales need a debate about further devolution. But this debate shouldn't exclusively focus on which powers should now be devolved to Wales. It must be about investing in and devolving powers to Cardiff and its metropolitan region, and how this can best be done to ensure the greatest prosperity for the greatest number of people in South Wales. (September 11, 2014; WalesOnline)

Similarly, Gordon Matheson, the leader of Glasgow City Council, suggests that greater powers need to be passed down to local authorities from Holyrood:

> It will be an historic missed opportunity if the [Smith] Commission leads only to the transfer of powers from one centralising parliament to another. Devolution cannot just be about empowering Edinburgh's parliament; the Scottish ministers should view further devolution not as a power grab, but as 'pass the parcel.' Big cities like Glasgow are the country's over-achievers and the powerhouses of the economy. Glasgow is certainly Scotland's success story and we have the

capacity to do much more to stimulate growth and tackle poverty, but we must
be given the freedom to do so. (December 2, 2014; *Daily Record*)

Such quotes are striking, as concerns for devolution in Scotland and Wales
have principally focused on the relationships that Holyrood and Cardiff Bay
negotiate with Westminster. City Deals, as an artefact of a new metropolitan
policy fervour, provide, however, a tool for leaders of city authorities to
effectively by-pass and cajole national administrations into new funding and
policy arrangements. In essence, City Deals have the effect of flanking intra-
nation ties. Because of the independence referendum and the vying political
affiliations at play, this was starkly enacted in Glasgow. It remains to be
seen how tripartite agreements will take shape in other cities in Scotland and
Wales, as negotiations progress.

Shifting from localism as conceived between different sets of actors, to the
principles on which localism is being legitimized, one might be prompted to
question whether – following the Scottish independence referendum (and the
debates leading up to it) – the arguments for devolution have taken on a new
character. Prior to the referendum, with large city regions positioned as priority sites, City Deals built upon a devolution narrative that suggested local
areas need greater powers to stimulate economic growth. Devolution was thus
rationalized as a key driver of economic development, with arguments made
that policies and investments need to be tailored to distinct local contexts and,
therefore, designed and administered locally. The Centre for Cities and IPPR
North have long advocated, indeed, that the economic development of city
regions outside of London will hinge on what powers and tools local leaders
can draw on. In an early note, for example, Finch (2007)[10] made the claim:
'To grow further, [England's largest city regions] need more powers. Greater
devolution to city regions over economic development would improve their
performance, and their leadership'.[11]

While economic arguments were by no means trivial to the Scottish referendum – indeed, currency and oil revenue issues were debated at length
– this was a process animated, it can be argued, by broader concerns around
the London-centric nature of the state system. As a consequence, it would
appear that calls for devolution across the United Kingdom are increasingly
connecting to claims for local legitimacy alongside rationales for sub-national
economic development. The geographic dimension of such a devolutionary
logic relates, therefore, to all regional or sub-national contexts in the United
Kingdom, not simply large metropolitan areas.

Though not as yet halting the metropolitan revolution being proclaimed,
some evidence of a shift in narrative can be observed. For example, Growth
Deal arrangements set in place by the previous coalition government, offers
funding to all thirty-nine local enterprise partnerships (LEPs) across England

(HM Government, 2014c; HM Government, 2015). Additionally, the Labour Party's pre-election policy statement on devolution – drawing its focus from the Adonis review (Adonis, 2014) – suggested that cities and counties in England should be treated even-handedly (Labour Party, 2015). In Wales and Scotland – perhaps because the links to Westminster have drawn the bulk of attention over recent years – questions about devolution from the national level to non-metropolitan areas have not penetrated policy discourse to the same extent.[12]

City dealing rests, in summary, on treating metropolitan areas in a privileged manner, predicated on the perception that such areas are ripe for further investment. A shift in logic to provide devolutionary packages to a wider set of regional areas – as one can begin to observe in England – poses questions about the sufficiency of city dealing as a mode of regional policy. Indeed, it may be interesting to consider the possibility of Ceredigion County Council or a coalition of local authorities in Ayrshire negotiating with Westminster, and their respective national administration, for a local Growth Deal.

CHANGING SHAPE OF THE UK STATE SYSTEM AND THE FUTURE FOR CITY DEALS

The Scottish Referendum and the consequent moves to resolve a devolutionary settlement, raises questions, not only about the cohesiveness of the UK state system, but also about the incentives and logics for deal negotiations. With talk of a quasi-federalist future for the United Kingdom (Torrance, 2015), how and on what basis cities bid for powers and funding could conceivably take on new complexities.

Much of this new drive for city dealing in the Celtic nations follows the Glasgow experience. A brief reprise is necessary, however, to lay bare the unique context – ahead of the Scottish independence referendum in September 2014 – in which this deal was struck. Indeed, the Glasgow and Clyde Valley City Deal emerged through an initial engagement involving local councils in the Glasgow city region, led by Glasgow City Council, and the UK Government (McGuire, 2014; Nicoll, 2014a). With the city council run by a Labour administration and the Scottish Government headed by a SNP majority, a clear political tension concerning the delivery of economic development policy was engendered. With broad deal outlines agreed to with local partners, the Prime Minister called for a Scottish Government commitment (HM Government, 2014d). While some have intimated that the deal essentially amounted to a bribe by unionist politicians (Malcolm, 2014), the Scottish Government, regardless, would likely have found it politically difficult to not make an equal contribution, given the significant investment commitments at stake (Nicoll, 2014b).[13] The deal was finalized, trilaterally, in July 2014.

With the recommendations of the Smith Commission being debated under the auspices of the Scotland Bill in parliament, it remains to be seen how a new devolved settlement for Scotland may affect the tripartite basis of ongoing city dealing for Scottish cities (consider the possibilities for devolving aspects of welfare and corporation tax, for example). Moreover, the Glasgow City Deal should be seen, to some extent, as a product of political opportunism, set in conditions and motives that are not likely to be replicated in the short term. Equivalency, or at least a close resemblance to the Glasgow deal, will be sought by those negotiating deals at present, such is the nature of precedent. However, different opportunities and constraints, presented in the post-referendum context, will now confront deal makers in Edinburgh, Dundee, Aberdeen and Inverness.

At the UK level, the recent Conservative majority, stemming from the general election in May 2015, would appear to offer continuity to a policy programme based around city dealing. While the Liberal Democrats would contest that they were the principal advocates for localism in the previous coalition administration, the Chancellor has personally championed the narrative of spatial rebalancing and appears eager, *prima facie*, to pursue commitments concerning the 'Northern Powerhouse' (which is based on infrastructure investments linking cities in the north of England) (HM Government, 2014e).[14] The appointment of a Minister for the Northern Powerhouse, along with Jim O'Neill's recent peerage,[15] offers some reflection of this commitment (Forsyth, 2015).[16]

In Wales, with Welsh Assembly elections looming in 2016, there will be an eagerness, from all parties, to agree to a City Deal for Cardiff (and the first such deal for Wales). The intricacies of the devolved settlement in Wales, including the complexities of transport policy, may be brought into sharp relief through the negotiation process. Furthermore, it will be interesting to observe if city dealing may align with or act as a trigger for an enhanced devolutionary settlement across Wales.

Given the discussion above, the following table captures the key elements of the varied institutional conditions shaping city dealing across the United Kingdom (Table 10.1).

CONCLUSION

Changing institutional contexts are having a bearing on City Deal negotiations that are taking place across Scotland and Wales. Logics and conditions relating to austerity, local entrepreneurialism and localism appear to reflect critical institutional dimensions for city dealing; yet, relative to England, these dimensions may exhibit somewhat different characteristics in Scotland

Table 10.1 Institutional Conditions for City Dealing in the United Kingdom

	Wales	Scotland	England
Policy Interest	• Haywood task and finish group has revived interest in cities policies as an economic development concern. • City-region advisory boards established for Cardiff and Swansea (since 2013).	• SCA was formed in 2011 by the SNP administration. Focus is now on City Deals • A cities review in 2003 failed to gain traction.	• Cities Unit within Whitehall takes responsibility for negotiating deals. • Office of the Deputy Prime Minister (ODPM) built capacity on city issues.
Framing the Cities Problem	• Systems thinking has been expressed in the Wales Spatial Plan (2008) and has scope to emerge through the Wales (Planning) Bill (2014).	• The National Planning Framework and Strategic Development Plans reflect some heritage of systems thinking. • Individual deals emerging; individual investment plans for all cities set out (commissioned in tandem).	• Individual bidding arrangements dominate; no spatial plan as such. • "Powerhouses" have been suggested by the RSA City Growth Commission to introduce scale and coupling benefits.
Devolution Problematic (and implications for cities)	• Seeking parity with Scotland on devolution settlement. • Debate about inequities in the devolutionary settlement vis-à-vis Scotland, and ongoing consideration of Silk Commission recommendations. • Argument made by local leaders that Cardiff Bay needs to devolve to local bodies.	• Referendum evoked strong sentiments about the over-centralized nature of the UK, resulting in vows for 'home rule'. • Smith Commission set up to recommend on advancing devolution to Holyrood. • Argument made by local leaders that Holyrood needs to devolve to local bodies.	• Sub-national areas have suffered from repeated re-organization of economic development approaches and vehicles (e.g. RDAs to LEPs). • UK Government remains centralized despite waves of localizing deals. Calls, made by think tanks, for devolution to be granted to those places that can demonstrate governance capacity. • Scottish Referendum has sharpened the focus on equipping English city-regions with greater powers.
Institutional Capacity	• Emergent capacity within Welsh Government, supported by city-region advisory boards. • WDA scrapped in 2006 through quangos 'bonfire'. • Local authorities under extreme budgetary pressure.	• Arguably greater capacity, reflecting, in part, institutional certainty and support by SCA. • Previous 2003 cities review left little residual capacity. • Local authorities under extreme budgetary pressure.	• Capacity in Whitehall, supported by urban think tanks. • Combined authorities taking shape (following Greater Manchester). • Local authorities under extreme budgetary pressure.
Financing Urban Development	• More limited, despite some earlier discussion of TIF and other tools depending on the development context.	• Experimentation in financing urban infrastructure. Glasgow TIF advanced through Scottish Futures Trust, for example. • Infrastructure fund within Glasgow city deal.	• Advanced; including 'earn back' and 'gain share' and wider development deals (with TIF characteristics).
City Deals Experience	• None to date – though discussions taking place for Cardiff.	• Initial City Deal for Glasgow city-region. • Discussions taking place for Aberdeen, Edinburgh, Dundee and Inverness.	• Wave 1 and Wave 2 for the core and key cities respectively.

and Wales. This is because dealing in the Celtic nations takes place within more complex governance architectures, involving an additional layer of government as well as different heritages of spatial policy. How such issues play out in the context of a changing and somewhat unstable UK state system – with other places in the United Kingdom also forming cases for funding commitments – will shape the nature and scope of the City Deals to emerge.

NOTES

1. Though they may benefit from a growth deal, through their local enterprise partnership (LEP).

2. One will be required for south-east Wales in some form.

3. Aberdeen, Dundee, Glasgow and Edinburgh.

4. Such as tax increment financing.

5. The details underpinning such additionality calculations are yet to be revealed.

6. Inverness indicates, perhaps, the more flexible definition of what constitutes a city in Scotland vis-à-vis the rest of the United Kingdom.

7. Who eventually held his leadership position.

8. Where jobs growth and gains in tax receipts may fall short of what is expected, as a result of broader economic conditions.

9. In England, private sector interests are starkly apparent in terms of LEP governance, which, party to a number of city deals, require private sector leadership and representation.

10. The then chief executive of the Centre for Cities.

11. As noted previously, the evidence to support a devolution to growth link, however, is patchy.

12. With the exception, in Scotland, of some claims made by councils from the Shetland, Orkney and Western Isles (Orkney Islands Council, 2013).

13. The Scottish Government response, in part, was that prior funding for and investments in Glasgow, by the Holyrood administration, far outweighed what the City Deal is proposing (Scottish Government, 2014).

14. Including Leeds and Manchester.

15. Lord O'Neill previously chaired the RSA City Growth Commission.

16. Note, however, the recent decision to reduce the priority of rail investment in the North, leading some to proclaim that it was the 'great northern power cut' (*The Guardian*, 2015).

REFERENCES

Aberdeen City Council and Aberdeenshire Council. (2015). Aberdeen City Region Deal: Powering Tomorrow's World. Interim Proposals. Available at http://www. aberdeencity.gov.uk/nmsruntime/saveasdialog.asp?lID=63430&sID=26262.

Adonis, A. (2014). Mending the Fractured Economy. Independent Review for the Labour Party, July. Available at http://www.yourbritain.org.uk/uploads/editor/files/Adonis_Review.pdf.

Audit Scotland. (2014). Some Progress at Edinburgh but Budget Shortfall Increases. News Release. Available at http://www.audit-scotland.gov.uk/docs/best_value/2014/bv2_141204_edinburgh_pr.pdf.

Bale, P. (2015). 2015: A Critical Year for Public Services. Blog Post. Available at https://cardiffleadersblog.wordpress.com/page/2/.

Blake, A. (2014). Councils in Wales Will Be Worse Off by More Than 3% Under New Budget Settlement Announced by Welsh Government. Walesonline, 8 October. Available at http://www.walesonline.co.uk/news/wales-news/councils-wales-worse-more-3-7905139.

Blond, P., and Morrin, M. (2014). Devo Max-Devo Manc: Place-Based Public Services. ResPublica, September.

Blond, P., and Morrin, M. (2015). Restoring Britain's City States: Devolution, Public Service Reform and Local Economic Growth. ResPublica, February.

Centre for Cities. (2014). Cities Policy Briefing: Setting Out Coalition Government Policies Across a Common Framework. September. Available at http://www.centreforcities.org/wp-content/uploads/2014/10/14-09-22-Cities-Policy-Briefing.pdf.

The Courier. (2015). 'City Deal' Could be £400m Winner for Tayside and Fife. Available at http://www.thecourier.co.uk/news/local/angus-the-mearns/city-deal-could-be-400m-winner-for-tayside-and-fife-1.847994.

City of Cardiff Council. (2014). Budget Strategy for 2015/2016 and the Medium Term. Cabinet Proposal, 24 July. Available at https://www.cardiff.gov.uk/ENG/Your-Council/Council-finance/Council-Budget/2015-16/Documents/Councl_F_14_07_24_A_Rep_D.pdf.

City of Cardiff Council. (2015b). City Deal Implications and Next Steps Report of Director of Economic Development. Report to Cabinet Meeting, 2 April. Available at https://formerly.cardiff.gov.uk/objview.asp?object_id=30020.

City of Edinburgh Council. (2014a). City Growth and Infrastructure Investment. Report to Economy Committee, 18 December.

City of Edinburgh Council. (2014b). Leith Study Report. Public Consultation Report. 18 December. Available at https://consultationhub.edinburgh.gov.uk/cd/leith-economic-framework/user_uploads/leith-study-report.pdf-5.

City of Edinburgh Council. (2015). Council Budget 2015/2016. Available at http://www.edinburgh.gov.uk/info/20200/budget_and_finance/1128/council_budget_201516.

Clarke, N., and Cochrane, A. (2013). Geographies and Politics of Localisms: The Localism of the United Kingdom's Coalition Government. *Political Geography*, 34: 10–23.

Commission on Public Service Governance and Delivery. (2014). Full Report. Available at http://gov.wales/docs/dpsp/publications/psgd/140120-psgd-full-report-env2.pdf.

Cox, E., Henderson, G., and Raikes, L. (2014). Decentralisation Decade: A Plan for Economic Prosperity, Public Service Transformation and Democratic Renewal in England. IPPR North, September.

Deans, D. (2015). South Wales Metro Project Could Become a Reality Under Cardiff's Regional City Deal, Says Welsh Secretary Stephen Crabb. Walesonline, 11 June. Available at http://www.walesonline.co.uk/news/wales-news/south-wales-metro-project-could-9438450.

Denholm-Hall, R. (2015). Make the Government an Offer It Can't Refuse, Minister Tells Business Leaders Hoping to Bag a City Deal for Cardiff. Walesonline, 27 March. Available at http://www.walesonline.co.uk/business/business-news/make-government-offer-cant-refuse-8933510.

Elkes, N. (2015). George Osborne Says Only Elected Mayor Will Guarantee Full Funding and Powers for West Midlands. *Birmingham Mail*, 1 June. Available at http://www.birminghammail.co.uk/news/midlands-news/george-osborne-says-only-elected-9369854.

Finch, D. (2007). Giving Cities More Power Over Their Economic Destinies. Centre for Cities, May. Available at http://www.centreforcities.org/publication/giving-cities-more-power-over-their-economic-destinies/.

Forsyth, J. (2015). The Final Flourishes Have Been Made to the New Government. *Spectator*, 14 May. Available at http://blogs.spectator.co.uk/coffeehouse/2015/05/the-final-flourishes-have-been-made-to-the-new-government/.

Glasgow City Council. (2014). Glasgow City Council to Find Nearly £30 Million of Savings Next Year. Press Release, October. Available at https://www.glasgow.gov.uk/index.aspx?articleid=14241.

GMCA. (2012). Greater Manchester City Deal. Available at https://www.gov.uk/government/uploads/system/uploads/attachment_data/file/406275/Greater-Manchester-City-Deal-final_0.pdf.

The Guardian. (2015). The Guardian View on Network Rail: The Great Northern Power cut. 25 June. Available at http://www.theguardian.com/commentisfree/2015/jun/25/the-guardian-view-on-network-rail-the-great-northern-power-cut.

Harrop, A. (2013). Osborne's Plan to Permanently Shrink the State Is Not Necessary. *New Statesman*, 6 December. Available at http://www.newstatesman.com/politics/2013/12/osbornes-plan-permanently-shrink-state-not-necessary.

Harvey, D. (1989). From Managerialism to Entrepreneurialism: The Transformation in Urban Governance in Late Capitalism. *Geografiska Annaler. Series B, Human Geography*, 71, 1: 3–17.

Hebditch, J. (2015). Aberdeen Council Warn of Cuts Over Funding Deficit. *The Scotsman*, 5 January. Available at http://www.scotsman.com/news/politics/top-stories/aberdeen-council-warn-of-cuts-over-funding-deficit-1-3651182.

Hollis, L. (2015). George Osborne's 'Northern Powerhouse' Project will Devastate Whole Cities. *The Guardian*, 18 May. Available at http://www.theguardian.com/commentisfree/2015/may/18/northern-powerhouse-cities-devolution-england-manchester-george-osborne.

HM Government. (2012). *Unlocking Growth in Cities: City Deals - Wave 1*. London: Stationary Office.

HM Government. (2014a). Glasgow and Clyde Valley City Deal. Policy Paper. Available at https://www.gov.uk/government/publications/city-deal-glasgow-and-clyde-valley.

HM Government. (2014b). Chancellor George Osborne's Budget 2014 Speech. Available at https://www.gov.uk/government/speeches/chancellor-george-osbornes-budget-2014-speech.

HM Government. (2014c). Local Growth Deals. Website. Available at https://www.gov.uk/government/collections/local-growth-deals.

HM Government. (2014d). Glasgow City Deal: Article by David Cameron and Danny Alexander. News Story, 4 July. Available at https://www.gov.uk/government/news/glasgow-city-deal-article-by-david-cameron-and-danny-alexander.

HM Government. (2014e). Chancellor: We Need a Northern Powerhouse. Speech, June 23. Available at https://www.gov.uk/government/speeches/chancellor-we-need-a-northern-powerhouse.

HM Government. (2015). Growth Deals Gain Momentum: Firing Up Local Economies. Website. Available at https://www.gov.uk/government/news/growth-deals-gain-momentum-firing-up-local-economies.

Katz, B., and Bradley, J. (2013a). *The Metropolitan Revolution: How Cities and Metros Are Fixing Our Broken Politics and Fragile Economy.* Brookings Institution Press: Washington, D.C.

Katz, B., and Bradley, J. (2013b). What Can the UK Learn from the US Metropolitan Revolution? *The Guardian*, Public Leaders Network, 18 November. Available at http://www.theguardian.com/local-government-network/2013/nov/18/uk-cities-metropolitan-revolution-us-bruce-katz.

Krugman, P. (2014). Ideology and Investment. *New York Times*, 26 October. Available at http://www.nytimes.com/2014/10/27/opinion/paul-krugman-ideology-and-investment.html.

Labour Party. (2015). Labour's Proposals to Devolve Economic Power and Funding. February. Available at http://www.yourbritain.org.uk/uploads/editor/files/Devolution_paper.pdf.

London Finance Commission. (2013). Raising the Capital. March. Available at https://www.london.gov.uk/sites/default/files/Raising%20the%20capital_0.pdf.

McCann, E. (2013). Policy Boosterism, Policy Mobilities, and the Extrospective City. *Urban Geography*, 34, 1: 5–29.

McGuire, J. (2014). Glasgow's Billion-Pound-Plus City Deal Slammed for Lack of Vision Over Infrastructure Choices. *Daily Record*, 9 July. Available at http://www.dailyrecord.co.uk/news/local-news/glasgows-billion-pound-plus-city-deal-slammed-3834340.

Mackinnon, D. (2012). Beyond Strategic Coupling: Reassessing the Firm-Region Nexus in Global Production Networks. *Journal of Economic Geography*, 12, 1: 227–45.

Mackinnon, D., Cumbers, A., and Featherstone, D. (2015). Local and Regional Economic Development in Britain, in J. Green, C. Hay, and P. Taylor-Gooby, (Eds.), *The British Growth Crisis*. Palgrave Macmillan: Basingstoke, 201–20.

Macleod, G. (2002). From Urban Entrepreneurialism to a "Revanchist City"? On the Spatial Injustices of Glasgow's Renaissance. *Antipode*, 34, 3: 602–24.

Malcolm, E. (2014). Cameron Exposes SNP's Blind Spot. *The Scotsman*, 6 July. Available at http://www.scotsman.com/news/euan-mccolm-cameron-exposes-snp-s-blind-spot-1-3467667

Martin, R., Pike, A., Tyler, P., and Gardiner, B. (2015). Spatially Rebalancing the UK Economy: The Need for a New Policy Model. Regional Studies Pamphlet, March. Available at http://www.regionalstudies.org/uploads/documents/SRTUKE_v16_PRINT.pdf.

Martin, R., Gardiner, B., and Tyler, P. (2014). The Evolving Economic Performance of UK Cities: City Growth Patterns 1981–2011. Report Commissioned for the UK Government's Foresight Future of Cities Project.

Morgan, K. J. (2006a). The Challenge of Polycentric Planning: Cardiff as a Capital City Region? Papers in Planning Research, 185. Cardiff University.

Morgan, K. J. (2006b). Governing Cardiff: Politics, Power and Personalities, in A. Hooper, and J. Punter, (Eds.), *Capital Cardiff 1975–2020*. University of Wales Press: Cardiff, 31–46.

Morgan, K. J. (2007). The Polycentric State: New Spaces of Empowerment and Engagement? *Regional Studies*, 41, 9: 1237–51.

Morgan, K. J. (2014). The Rise of MetroPolitics: Urban Governance in the Age of the City-Region, in N. Bradford, and A. Bramwell, (Eds.), *Governing Urban Economies: Innovation and Inclusion in Canadian City-Regions*. Toronto: University of Toronto Press, 297–318.

Mosalski, R., and Silk, H. (2014). Cardiff Council Leader Phil Bale Defends His Position and Blames Opposition Groups for a 'Petty' No Confidence Motion. Walesonline, 27 February. Available at http://www.walesonline.co.uk/news/wales-news/cardiff-council-leader-phil-bale-8739776.

Nicoll, V. (2014a). PM Announces £500m Cash Boost for Glasgow, Challenges SNP to Match It. *Scotland Herald*, July 3. Available at http://www.heraldscotland.com/politics/referendum-news/pm-announces-500m-cash-boost-for-glasgow-challenges-snp-to-match-it.1404383732.

Nicoll, V. (2014b). Real Deal: SNP Match Cash as Scotland Hails . . . £ Billion City Prize. *Evening Times*, July 4. Available at http://www.eveningtimes.co.uk/news/glasgow-set-for-1-billion-cash-injection-169867n.24666063.

Orkney Islands Council. (2013). Our Islands – Our Future. Orkney Islands Council, Joint Position Statement. Available at http://www.orkney.gov.uk/Files/Council/Consultations/Our-Islands-Our-Future/Joint_Position_Statement.pdf.

Peck, J. (2012). Austerity Urbanism. *City: Analysis of Urban Trends, Culture, Theory, Policy, Action*, 16, 6: 626–55.

Pike, A., Rodríguez-Pose, A., Tomaney, J., Torrisi, G., Tselios, V. (2012). In Search of the 'Economic Dividend' of Devolution: Spatial Disparities, Spatial Economic Policy, and Decentralisation in the UK. *Environment and Planning C: Government and Policy*, 30, 1: 10–28.

RSA. (2015). Devo Met: Charting a Path Ahead. March. Available at https://www.thersa.org/discover/publications-and-articles/reports/devo-met-charting-a-path-ahead/.

RSA City Growth Commission. (2014). Unleashing Metro Growth: Final Recommendations of the City Growth Commission. October. Available at http://www.citygrowthcommission.com/publication/final-report-unleashing-metro-growth/.

Ross, C. (2015). Breakthrough in £300million Inverness City Deal Plan. *The Press and Journal*, 16 March. Available at https://www.pressandjournal.co.uk/fp/news/

inverness/521749/breakthrough-300million-inverness-city-deal-plan/ rough in £300million Inverness City Deal Plan.

Scottish Government. (2014). £1 Billion Fund for Glasgow and Clyde Valley. News Release, 20 August. Available at http://news.scotland.gov.uk/News/-1-billion-fund-for-Glasgow-and-Clyde-Valley-101c.aspx.

Shipton, M. (2015). City Deal for Cardiff Could Be in Jeopardy If City Council Cannot Afford a Contribution, May 18. Available at www.walesonline.co.uk/news/wales-news/city-deal-cardiff-could-jeopardy-9282540.

Summers, L. (2014). Why Public Investment Really Is a Free Lunch. *Financial Times*, 6 October. Available at http://www.ft.com/cms/s/2/9b591f98-4997-11e4-8d68-00144feab7de.html#axzz3dPEsnz1y.

Torrance, D. (2015). Scotland Talks: Is Federalism the Answer? *Prospect Magazine*, May 15. Available at http://www.prospectmagazine.co.uk/politics/scotland-talks-is-federalism-the-answer.

Townsend, A., and Champion, T. (2014). The Impact of Recession on City Regions: The British Experience, 2008–2013. Local Economy, 29, 1–2: 38–51.

Urquhart, F. (2014). Aberdeen City Council to Break Away from COSLA. *The Scotsman*, 7 February. Available at http://www.scotsman.com/news/politics/top-stories/aberdeen-city-council-to-break-away-from-cosla-1-3298084.

Waite, D., Maclennan, D., and O'Sullivan, T. (2013). Emerging City Policies: Devolution, Deals and Disorder. Local Economy, 28, 7–8: 770–85.

Wintour, P. (2015). George Osborne: City Mayors Could Get Power Over Business Rates. *The Guardian*, 26 April. Available at http://www.theguardian.com/politics/2015/apr/26/george-osborne-city-mayors-power-business-rates-northern-powerhouse-election.

Index

Notes on Contributors

David Bailey is Professor of Industrial Strategy at the Aston Business School.

David Bell is Professor of Economics at the University of Stirling.

Leslie Budd is Reader in Social Enterprise at the Open University Business School.

Linda Christie is a PhD student at the Adam Smith Business School, University of Glasgow.

Lisa De Propris is Professor of Regional Economic Development at the Birmingham Business School.

Jim Gallagher is Visiting Professor, University of Glasgow, and Nuffield Associate Member at the University of Oxford.

Ken Gibb is Professor of Housing Economics at the University of Glasgow.

Paul Hidreth is Visiting Policy Fellow at the Centre for Sustainable Urban and Regional Futures (SURF), University of Salford, Manchester.

Mathew Jackson is Deputy Chief Executive, Centre for Local Economic Strategies.

Neil McInroy is Executive, Centre for Local Economic Strategies.

Gerry Mooney is Staff Tutor (Scotland) and Senior Lecturer in the Department of Criminology and Social Policy, Open University.

Rebecca Rumbul is Head of Research at mySociety, and a Lecturer in Politics at Cardiff University.

David Waite is Research Associate, Cardiff Capital Region.

Zach Wilcox is Senior Consultant, Arup.